THE FIRST YEAR®

Autism Spectrum Disorders

NANCY D. WISEMAN is founder and president of First Signs, Inc., a national nonprofit organization whose mission is to educate parents and professionals about the early signs of autism and other related disorders.

Before devoting herself to First Signs, Nancy worked for more than twenty years in corporate communications. Now she is dedicating her life to improving the lives of children and families affected by autism. She has made a significant contribution to changing policy, improving awareness, and changing pediatric practice in how we screen, refer, and detect developmental delays in young children today.

Nancy counsels parents nationwide, and she has appeared in interviews with *USA Today*, *Parents* magazine, NBC's *Today Show*, and CNN's *Larry King Live*. She is the author of *Could It Be Autism? A Parent's Guide to the First Signs and Next Steps* (Broadway Books). And she is the 2006 recipient of the American Academy of Pediatrics' Dale Richmond/Justin Coleman Award for her outstanding achievement in the field of child development.

Nancy is the mother of Sarah, who was diagnosed with autism at the age of two. Today—at age thirteen—Sarah stands as a powerful example of the impact that early identification and intensive intervention can have on young children with autism and other related disorders.

THE FIRST YEAR®

Autism Spectrum Disorders

An Essential Guide for the Newly Diagnosed Child

Nancy D. Wiseman
with Robert L. Rich

Foreword by Kenneth Bock, MD, FAAP, FACN, CNS

Da Capo
LIFE
LONG

"The Early Indicators of Autism" ASD Video Glossary text copyright © 2007 Florida State University and First Signs, Inc. All rights reserved. Used by permission.
"Is Your Baby Meeting These Important Milestones? Key Social, Emotional, and Communication Milestones for Your Baby's Healthy Development." © 2001 First Signs, Inc. All rights reserved. Used by permission.
"Functional View of the Autism Spectrum" illustration © 2008 First Signs, Inc. and Florida State University. All rights reserved. Used by permission.
Excerpts from *Educating Children with Autism* reprinted with permission from the National Academies Press, © 2001 National Academy of Sciences.
Excerpts from *Healing the New Childhood Epidemics* reprinted with permission from Kenneth Bock, M.D., © 2007 Kenneth Bock, MD and Cameron Stauth.
Excerpts from *Could It Be Autism? A Parent's Guide to the First Signs and Next Steps* reprinted with permission from Nancy D. Wiseman, © 2006 First Signs, Inc.

Set in 11 point Adobe Garamond by the Perseus Books Group

Library of Congress Cataloging-in-Publication Data

Wiseman, Nancy D.
     The first year : autism spectrum disorders : an essential guide for the newly diagnosed child : a parent-expert walks you through everything you need to learn and do / Nancy D. Wiseman with Robert L. Rich ; foreword by Kenneth Bock. — 1st ed.
        p.   cm.
     Includes bibliographical references and index.
     ISBN 978-1-60094-065-1 (alk. paper)
     1. Autism in children—Popular works. I. Rich, Robert L. II. Title.
RJ506.A9W57 2009
618.92'85882—dc22   2008048673

First Da Capo Press edition 2009

Published by Da Capo Press
An imprint of Perseus Books, LLC, a subsidiary of Hachette Book Group, Inc.
www.dacapopress.com

Note: The information in this book is true and complete to the best of our knowledge. This book is intended only as an informative guide for those wishing to know more about health issues. In no way is this book intended to replace, countermand, or conflict with the advice given to you by your own physician. The ultimate decision concerning care should be made between you and your doctor. We strongly recommend you follow his or her advice. Information in this book is general and is offered with no guarantees on the part of the authors or Da Capo Press. The authors and publisher disclaim all liability in connection with the use of this book. The names and identifying details of people associated with events described in this book have been changed. Any similarity to actual persons is coincidental.

Da Capo Press books are available at special discounts for bulk purchases in the U.S. by corporations, institutions, and other organizations. For more information, please contact the Special Markets Department at Perseus Books, 53 State Street, 9th floor, Boston, MA 02109, or call (800) 810-4145, ext. 5000, or e-mail special.markets@hbgusa.com.

For my mom and stepdad,
Beverly and Peter Eagleson, who have
been there for me every step of
the journey, helping me to face so many
daunting challenges and offering their
unwavering love and support.

And for Sarah,
who has shown me the true meaning of
acceptance and unconditional love.

Contents

Contents

MONTH 8

MONTH 9

MONTH 10

MONTH 11

MONTH 12

Foreword

THE LANDSCAPE OF autism is changing. Thankfully, the dark, destructive images of Bruno Bettelheim's "refrigerator mother" (the theory that autism is caused by bad parenting) have long since become a thing of the past. However, autism is still viewed by many as a purely psychiatric disorder, and it is still coded as such in the DSM-IV, the psychiatrist's coding bible. Newer perspectives view autism as a medical disorder, defined by its behavioral symptoms, impairments in communication and social interaction, and restricted interests and repetitive behaviors. Further shifts in this landscape include movement of autism from a purely neurological disorder to a disorder affecting the entire body, including the brain, gut, and immune and metabolic systems.

This shifting perspective has huge implications, both in the understanding of autism spectrum disorders and in their evaluation and treatment. Medical problems call for medical solutions. My practice has seen nearly two thousand patients with autism spectrum disorders. Many come from countries around the world, including Hong Kong, Australia, New Zealand, England,

Scotland, Italy, Spain, South Africa, India, and the Middle East. The vast majority of our patients are children, but we also see some teens, young adults, and even some older adults. They all have very real medical problems—diarrhea and constipation, abdominal pain and bloating, skin rashes, allergies, asthma, recurrent infections, metabolic imbalances, and sleep disorders. We can no longer simply write off these patients' physical symptoms to their autism. The understanding of underlying and/or associated medical problems is essential to their care. In fact, there are times when "autistic" behaviors are actually pain-based. And lo and behold, when you treat the underlying medical problems, such as inflammation in the gut, not only do the physical symptoms, including pain, improve, but frequently so do behaviors as well as the levels of functioning.

We are in the midst of an epidemic of autism spectrum disorders (ASD) with an increase of at least 1,500 percent (conservatively, from 1 in 2,500 children to 1 in 150 children) in the past two decades. I have dedicated my professional life to helping these children, but it is not only my practice that is exploding with these affected children. Pediatric practices and family practices across the country and the world are seeing more and more children affected with autism spectrum disorders. In fact, it's hard to travel these days without meeting someone who doesn't know at least one child affected with ASD—whether in his or her own family or a friend's child. This meteoric increase cannot be explained away simply by a loosening or expansion of diagnostic criteria (i.e., including higher-functioning children on the spectrum). Nor can genetics alone account for the increased incidence of autism, as there is no such thing as a genetic epidemic.

A more current point of view, which is gaining more momentum and research support, acknowledges the contribution of genetic vulnerabilities or susceptibilities and emphasizes the importance of environmental triggers in the causation of autism. This perspective not only helps to better explain the epidemic of autism, but also offers the possibility of real hope and solutions. Environmental factors are more amenable to treatment than genetics. These environmental factors include toxins, such as common chemicals and heavy metals, which can contribute to increased oxidative stress (extremely reactive molecules that damage cells and tissue) and chronic inflammation. It is believed that these increases in tissue damage and inflammation may not only underlie autism but also contribute to many other childhood disorders, which have also experienced significant increases in the past few decades.

These include asthma, allergies, and ADHD: the other "4-A" disorders, as I have coined them. But many of our chronic adult disorders, such as Alzheimer's disease and other neurodegenerative problems, as well as heart disease and arthritis, are being attributed to these same underlying factors: increased oxidative stress and inflammation. In many ways, autism may be the childhood equivalent of some of these adult chronic inflammatory neurological disorders.

Applying these newer perspectives to the treatment of ASD mandates an integrative and individualized approach. This is a group of diverse and complex disorders with multiple contributing causative factors. This perspective dictates the focus of the clinical work that many of us are doing, and in addition to some of the newer research initiatives, it encourages us to differentiate subgroups of autism, such as gut-brain, immunological, metabolic, infectious, toxin-related, and inflammatory. These subgroups are frequently interwoven, but discovering biomarkers that can help us recognize the relative importance of one or several subgroups in each affected child can lead us to more individualized and more effective treatments.

As a parent, having your child receive a diagnosis of autism is a jolting experience, evoking a whole range of emotions—from denial, fear, and anger to abject despair, among others. These emotions are certainly worsened by the frequently misapplied "doom and gloom" prognosis that accompanies a diagnosis of ASD. Once you've come to grips with this diagnosis, your understanding and expectations for your child at that time will change with the acceptance of your child's situation. Acceptance must not lead to despair, but rather to a determination to do whatever is possible within your reach, to help your child improve. Present treatment approaches offer real hope and real improvement, and even the possibility of recovery, as autism is treatable. This treatment must always take a comprehensive integrative approach, consisting of biomedical treatments coupled with appropriate clinical and educational interventions.

Thankfully, as a new parent presented with this diagnosis in your child, you do not have to take this journey alone. Nancy Wiseman's book presents all of these necessary approaches in a masterful and integrated way, providing an invaluable guide to parents of children with a newly diagnosed autism spectrum disorder, giving them practical directions and replacing the old "doom and gloom" veil with possibilities of realistic hope, improvement, and even, in some cases, recovery. I reiterate, you are not alone, and although this can be a long and difficult journey, it is important to rely on the support of physicians, clinicians, therapists, educators, family, friends, and other parents with affected children. With their help and this book as your companion and guide, you can help your child to live the happy, healthy, full life that all children deserve.

Kenneth A. Bock, MD, FAAFP, FACN, CNS, is board-certified in family medicine, a clinical instructor in the Department of Family Medicine at Albany Medical College, cofounder and codirector of the Rhinebeck Health Center, and the immediate past president of the American College for Advancement in Medicine. For more than twenty-five years, he has dealt with complex medical problems by integrating alternative treatments with conventional medicine into a comprehensive integrative medicine practice, and for the last nine years he has focused that approach on children with autism spectrum disorders and ADD/ADHD. He is coauthor of four books, the most recent being *Healing the New Childhood Epidemics: Autism, ADHD, Asthma and Allergies,* and he lectures nationally and internationally on immune system health and integrative approaches to autism spectrum disorders. He lives in upstate New York with his wife and two children.

Introduction

THE FIRST YEAR: *Autism Spectrum Disorders* is essential for every parent of a child diagnosed with autism. It will provide you with a step-by-step road map for helping you get the care, treatments, therapies, and services your child needs, as quickly as possible. Whether you are beginning this book within days of receiving the diagnosis, or weeks, months, or even years later—no matter where you are in your journey—it will be a valuable guide for you. And even if you have not yet had your child formally diagnosed, this book can help.

Using This Book

As you may have noticed, the chapters in this book are laid out according to a calendar—day-by-day for the first week, week-by-week for the first month, and month-by-month for the year—from the point of first finding out your child has autism. Please do not be daunted by how much I am suggesting should be done in the first year, or in any given day, week, or month. To some degree, these chapter titles are really metaphors for the process of discovering what you need to know about autism and prioritizing your actions, no matter how long it takes. Some parents may be able to accomplish everything given here within the first year, while others will need a lot more time. This is okay, and I cannot emphasize this enough. Every parent travels at a different pace—what works for you won't necessarily work for another parent. Travel at your own speed, and try not to compare.

Naturally, the sequence of need and path of the journey will be different for every family, since some children will already be receiving early intervention services or be enrolled in grade school long before the official diagnosis. Other children will be diagnosed at a very young age and not even nearly ready for school services. And still other children will have received their diagnosis long ago, but perhaps you are looking for a new direction.

Each chapter is divided into two sections: Learning and Living. The Learning sections present a great deal of the technical "how-to's," nomenclature, lists of options, forms to fill out, and other knowledge that you should find valuable. The Living sections tend to focus more on actions to take and perspectives on the journey. I sincerely hope that this format works for you.

Life in the autism world can get a little technical at times, so I have tried to be thorough in defining any terms that may be new to you. (See page 313 for a glossary.)

As you know (or will soon find out), autism is not a single disorder. It is a wide assortment of disorders that vary in intensity from person to person. So any time you see the term "autism" or "ASD" in this book, it is referring to all autism spectrum disorders in general, and not to any particular disorder.

Dealing with the Diagnosis

Please remember, only bite off what you can comfortably chew. If your emotions are just too raw right now and all this information is too overwhelming, then put the book down until you are ready to read it. Or read only one chapter per week—whatever it takes to get you going. Because doing *something* is better than doing nothing!

I know this is a traumatic time in your life and just getting out of bed may be too overwhelming for you. I know because I have been there. The healing process is so different for everyone, and I cannot predict how you or any parent will react, or what supports you will need to get through this early stage, or how long it will take. So much depends upon your emotional well-being prior to receiving the diagnosis, your resilience, the relationships you have with family members and friends, and the supports already in place. A few books can help you deal with the emotional aspects of this disorder; I list them later on (see page 21). However, this is not one of those books. This book is about getting down to business and giving you the tools, structure, information, and steps you need to take to get you and your family through the first year and beyond. If this sounds a bit clinical, I apologize, but time is of the essence, and my job is to help you get going.

Consider that you have just crash-landed somewhere in the mountains of Chile—in the wintertime. You are almost certainly not prepared for what is to come. I am your guide; I know these mountains well, and there is a good chance I can steer you out of them. But if I am to do this, I will have to be very direct and not mince my words. Consider this book one of your basic survival manuals when it comes to navigating the wilds of autism. There are other books you may need, and I'll refer you to them as we go along.

What I Cannot Tell You

I am not a physician nor a clinician, and so I cannot tell you what would be best for your child, particularly since prescribing a course of treatments for any child with autism via a book is, of course, completely impossible and even dangerous. Without a qualified team of specialists to properly evaluate, diagnose, prescribe, and monitor treatments, you will most likely feel as though you are walking in quicksand. But not to worry: I will spend a lot of time showing you how to go about finding specialists and getting this done.

While Month 3, "Living: Getting to Know the Treatments Available," introduces you to many of the treatments and therapies for autism, it is not an exhaustive list of options. There are so many wonderful treatments available, and I would encourage you to check them out. Those mentioned in this book are merely the therapies commonly in use at this time.

Keep on Learning

Throughout the book, I offer a number of ideas for suggested reading and other steps you can take to continue your autism education. I hope you will take these suggestions to heart; there is a great deal to learn about getting started and probably just as much to absorb as your child grows older.

As you start down this path and become more knowledgeable about autism and how it affects your child, never forget:

YOU ARE NOT ALONE. Approximately 1 in 150 children are diagnosed with autism; 67 children are diagnosed every day. Even in your local community, you will find many parents facing similar challenges.

There is *much* you can do to help your child reach his or her greatest potential as long as you are willing to educate yourself and take charge of your professional team.

My Journey

I first had concerns about my daughter, Sarah, when she was twelve months old. Little by little, her babbling faded away, her eye contact became fleeting, and she stopped responding to her name. By eighteen months she had only a few words, but they were not meaningful words. She flapped her hands when she was excited, and she paced back and forth in her crib obsessively. Cow's milk made her sick, and soy milk caused a bright red rash on her face. I mentioned these concerns over and over again to our pediatrician, but I received the same responses: "Don't worry—she'll outgrow it." "Let's wait and see."

There were other signs, more heartbreaking and difficult to accept: she stopped sharing affections, and she became increasingly disconnected from her dad and me, increasingly more remote and unaware of what was going on around her. She no longer climbed onto my lap for hugs and snuggles the way she used to. These signs were impossible to ignore yet too frightening to fully acknowledge. I felt as if I were losing my daughter a little each day.

I remember the denial. For every concern, I found a justification. But my mother, a former school psychologist, suspected autism all along. My mother came with us to Sarah's eighteen-month well visit, and while I was dressing Sarah, my mother followed the doctor into her office and told her flat out that Sarah had autism. Her concerns were completely dismissed by the pediatrician.

At my mother's urging, I brought Sarah at age twenty-one months to have her hearing tested. The tests indicated that her hearing was within normal range, so the clinician suggested a language evaluation. I called our local Early Intervention Program, and within three weeks Sarah's development was assessed. The results were devastating. Sarah was several months behind in her cognition, self-care, and motor skills, but her language skills were those of an eight-month-old and social skills were those of a seven-month-old.

We went through agonizing weeks of tests, some of which were quite invasive, as the doctors ruled out different disorders. When I later learned that she did have autism, it actually came as a relief, since not knowing was far worse. Now, at least, I could begin to do something about it.

Sarah began intensive intervention almost immediately, and after just a few days, she spoke her first truly communicative word: "Help." Slowly, she became more and more connected. By day, I had a house full of therapists and a schedule full of appointments, assessments, and medical tests; by night, I searched the Internet and read articles, books, and research studies.

Almost overnight, I became driven by my love for my child. I learned how to move mountains, draw on the skills I already had, and uncover other skills I never knew existed. I will share with you what I learned through my journey, but you have to remember, everyone's journey is deeply personal and very different.

I quit my job as director of marketing communications for a high-tech company so I could be with my daughter full-time to manage her treatment program, interact with her throughout the day, and advocate for her the way I knew no one else could.

At the same time, I put my marketing skills to work to try to change the way doctors were educated about early childhood development and screening. I felt strongly that no child should ever have to "wait and see," losing month by month the gains that early intervention could bring. I created First Signs, a national nonprofit organization dedicated to educating parents and professionals through public awareness and training about the early warning signs of autism and other related disorders.

Just like the organization she inspired ten years ago, Sarah made steady, amazing progress through the early years. Though her progress has been met with many obstacles, plateaus, and difficult times during the past few years, she stands as a powerful and positive example of the impact that early and intensive intervention can have on children with autism. We still have our daily struggles, but Sarah is warm and funny, and a nonstop talker. She is an avid reader, loves school, and has friends. In her free time, she is a competitive figure skater, and she is working hard to achieve her goal of becoming an accomplished equestrian. I never dreamed this would be possible back in 1998.

Sadly, my marriage could not weather the toll this journey took on us as a couple. We were too many worlds apart and unable to stand together as a team with the same goals in mind. Financially, it nearly destroyed everything we built up. But if given the choice all over again, I would walk the same path and go live in a hut if I had to, just so I could have my daughter back again.

If I look back on the past ten years of my journey, I can tell you it's been challenging, stressful, exhausting, and sometimes turbulent. At times I have felt like a warrior, occasionally bruised and even knocked down, but never defeated. In spite of this, the journey has been rewarding, exhilarating, and life changing. I have arrived at the lowest points in my life and at other times found highs that were truly the most defining times of my life.

All of us find our own way, travel at our own speed, and sort through our bumps, roadblocks, and tears along the way. But one thing is certain: it is a journey unique to every parent. I wish you success in yours.

learning

What Are Autism Spectrum Disorders?

Starting at the Beginning: What Do the Words Mean?

For most parents and professionals, autism can be a puzzling and complex disorder. This is not surprising since, until quite recently, very little about it has been understood. Though a great deal of its mystery has yet to be uncovered, we definitely know much more about it than we did a decade ago. Just as our understanding has evolved over the years, so has the way we define, diagnose, and treat it. Let's begin with how we now define autism and other key terms used in its description.

Autism is an umbrella term for a wide spectrum of disorders considered neurological in nature. The disorders affect how a child communicates and interacts with others, how he learns, how he plays, and even how he imagines. Originally, autism was classified as a developmental and behavioral disorder; however, more recent investigations suggest that the spectrum of disorders we call "autism" not only affects the brain and nervous systems but also appears to be related to the immune, gastrointestinal, and metabolic dysfunctions.[1]

When we speak of a "**disorder**," we are talking about a disturbance to what is considered the normal functioning of the body or mind. The meaning of the word "normal" itself is a bit of a booby trap, causing a great deal of disagreement and confusion in the field of human behavior. In general usage, it can mean any of the following:

1. Conforming to some cultural standard or expectation; the result of averaging together what the majority of people in a group or a culture would expect at any particular time
2. What is proven by correct scientific method to be most probable to occur under specified circumstances (statistically what most people being studied would do in some situation)
3. What some appointed authority declares to be "typical" or "usual"

The trick, of course, lies in knowing which definition of "normal" is being used at any given time.

Another word you are going to hear repeatedly is "**developmental**." In this usage the word refers to the stages of physical and behavioral growth a child is expected to pass through from infancy to full maturity. This term is commonly applied to skills and activities in the areas of:

Social—interacting with and engaging other people
Emotional regulation—control of one's emotions, responses, etc.
Communication—nonverbal and verbal behavior to share ideas, exchange information, and regulate interactions
Motor—movement produced by large and small muscles
Sensory—sight, sound, taste, smell, touch, balance, etc.

"**Behavioral**" refers to how a person is expected to act in various situations, as judged against some specific set of cultural standards—against what is normal.

Now we can put the words together: A "**developmental and behavioral disorder**" is considered by professionals to be a cluster of delays, regressions, or outright failure in one or more areas of development. These delays would cause a child to acquire skills at a slower rate and impair her ability to function and behave like most children her age.

Autism spectrum disorders have a certain set of features or characteristics that are used in diagnosis. I will cover them in more depth later on (detailed in Appendix 1, page 303, but in summary they are:

1. Impairment in social interaction
2. Impairment in communication
3. Repetitive behaviors and restricted patterns of interests
4. Impairment in regulatory and sensory systems[2]

Additionally, there is a very wide range of intensity, symptoms and behaviors, types of specific disorders, and other individual variations. The autism spectrum can be characterized as a range (from mild to severe) of impairments in the above areas. To further complicate the picture, a large number of factors in the child's personal biology (medical conditions, etc.) and environment (family life, etc.) can strongly affect the manner in which autism is manifested.[3]

At one end of the spectrum are people who have a limited interest or ability to interact and communicate, and show repetitive behaviors and distress in response to changes in their routines or environment. Persons with these conditions were commonly identified as having "classic autism."

On the other end of the spectrum are persons who function well in terms of language and thinking skills but have very restricted interests, marked lack of social skills, and repetitive behaviors, as with **Asperger syndrome**.[4]

A Functional View of the Autism Spectrum

From the practical perspective of how a professional might look at a child's behavior to detect and diagnose a disorder on the autism spectrum, the four categories of impairments can be broken down further, making a total of sixteen subcategories:

Social Interaction
1. Nonverbal Behaviors
2. Engaging in Interaction
3. Sharing Attention
4. Social Reciprocity

Communication
5. Expressive and Receptive Language
6. Conversation
7. Repetitive Language
8. Socially Imitative Play

Repetitive Behaviors and Restricted Interests
9. Restricted Patterns of Interest
10. Insistence on Sameness
11. Repetitive Motor Mannerisms
12. Preoccupation with Parts of Objects

Regulatory and Sensory Systems
13. Over Reactivity
14. Under Reactivity
15. Unusual Sensory Interests
16. Emotional Regulation[5]

See Appendix 1 (page 303) for a detailed explanation of each subcategory. A child can be examined by each subcategory, on a scale from **neurotypical** to severely impaired. "Neurotypical" means consistent with what most people would perceive as a normal ability to process language and social cues. The term was coined by the autism community and has since come into general usage.[6]

For example, here is a graphic representation of an extremely simplified scale of just one of the sixteen characteristics: the sharing of attention, enjoyment, interests, or achievements with others applied to a child of sixteen months.

Scale of Shared Attention

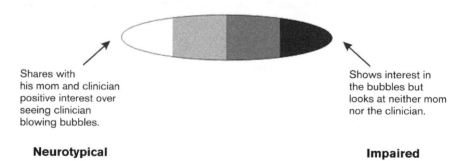

Shares with his mom and clinician positive interest over seeing clinician blowing bubbles.

Shows interest in the bubbles but looks at neither mom nor the clinician.

Neurotypical　　　　　　　　　　　　　　　　　**Impaired**

Evaluating all sixteen characteristics as overlapping scales of behavior, neurotypical to impaired, one can get an estimation of where a child falls on the autism spectrum.

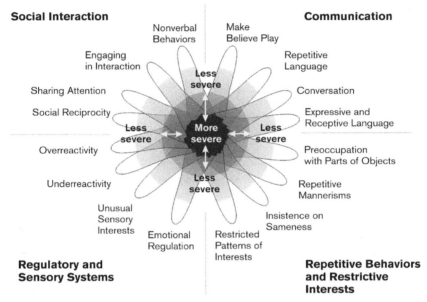

Functional View of the Autism Spectrum

Causes

The causes of autism spectrum disorders are unknown and may, in fact, be different for each of the disorders. Research has improved over recent years, so we hope to understand it even better as time goes on.

Initially, it was claimed by psychiatrist Leo Kanner around 1950 that autism was caused by bad parenting, specifically coldness of the mother toward the child. Though this theory has absolutely no scientific merit, it was long held to be true by many professionals. In fact, despite overwhelming evidence to the contrary, some practitioners still hold on to this discredited belief.

Later, scientific research provided strong evidence that autism is a genetic neurological disorder of the brain and nervous system that causes delays in communication, social, and motor skills.

Subsequent research revealed that autism has **neurobiological** causes—that is to say, it is an illness of the nervous system caused by genetic, metabolic, or other biological factors.

Current research is looking at autism as a behavioral condition provoked by biological factors, such as dysfunction of the gastrointestinal tract, the immune system, etc., in addition to the individual's genetics.[7]

In fact, some experts are now exploring the idea that autism may be a purely biological disorder caused by the interaction of:

○ genetic factors
○ exposure to toxins commonly found in water, air, food, and vaccines
○ failures (large and small) in the functioning of various bodily systems: immunological, gastrointestinal, and metabolic

Accompanying improvements in analysis, ASD has gone from being considered completely untreatable to being highly responsive to therapeutic, educational, and biomedical treatments in a significant number of cases.

Psychiatric Classification of Autism

The Diagnostic and Statistical Manual of Mental Disorders (DSM) is a handbook produced by the American Psychiatric Association that establishes the official categories of mental disorders. It is used widely by clinicians, researchers, insurance companies, pharmaceutical companies, and policymakers. Its most recent (fourth) revision was in 1994 and was thus dubbed "DSM IV." (A later "Text Revision" in 2000 had relatively minor changes but led to the current version being known as "DSM IV-TR.")

The assessment and evaluation of your child against the DSM definition of autism is very important, because ultimately it determines whether the child is eligible for services and insurance coverage.

All ASD professionals must be fully conversant with it.

The DSM IV-TR refers to autism as Pervasive Development Disorders (PDD), but more recent literature uses Autism Spectrum Disorders (ASD). The terms "PDD" and "ASD" are used interchangeably. According to the current version of the manual, PDD/ASD have five subclassifications:

Outside of the United States, the corresponding manual is the World Health Organization's publication, the *International Statistical Classification of Diseases and Related Health Problems*, Tenth Revision, Clinical Modification (ICD-10-CM). According to DSM IV-TR, "The codes and terms provided in DSM-IV are fully compatible with both ICD-9-CM and ICD-10. The clinical and research drafts of ICD-10 were thoroughly reviewed by the DSM-IV Work Groups."[8]

1. AUTISTIC DISORDER OR CLASSIC AUTISM

This is considered the most severe form of autism. People with classic autism have problems communicating and relating to people. They can be hypersensitive to their environment. Certain sounds, colors, and textures can upset them. They cling compulsively to rituals, such as eating the same foods or watching the same TV show every day at the same time. Changes in routine can upset them.

2. RETT'S DISORDER OR RETT SYNDROME

This affects mostly girls and is a rare genetic disorder that occurs in normal development during the first six to eighteen months of life, followed first by a period of stagnation and then by rapid regression in motor and language skills. Marked by severe impairments in thinking, learning, social, and communication skills, as well as the loss of purposeful hand use, stereotyped hand-wringing, often screaming fits, and other behavioral problems. (It does occur in a small percentage of boys; those who have it are usually stillborn or die shortly after birth.)[9]

3. CHILDHOOD DISINTEGRATIVE DISORDER

This is a rare disorder in which the child shows typical development for at least the first two to four years of life followed by a marked regression in at least two of the following areas: expressive or receptive language, social skills or adaptive behavior, bowel or bladder control, or play or motor skills.[10]

4. ASPERGER'S DISORDER OR ASPERGER SYNDROME

Children with Asperger's have near normal language acquisition accompanied by marked delays in social skills and have normal to above-normal intelligence but tend to have restricted areas of interests. They are often precocious in speaking and reading and may use sophisticated language. The condition is also marked by a lack of empathy with others and a reduced ability to engage in two-way communication. They often have uncoordinated motor skills and odd body postures. Persons with Asperger's typically have a hard time understanding other people's nonverbal expressions and tend to interpret verbal statements literally.

5. PERVASIVE DEVELOPMENT DISORDER— NOT OTHERWISE SPECIFIED (PDD-NOS)

Children with PDD-NOS have some but not all characteristics of autism or one of the other defined Pervasive Development Disorders. Their behavior is marked by impairment of social interaction, communication, and/or stereotyped behavior patterns or interests. Typically they have difficulty relating to their peers as well as unusual sensitivities to noises, colors, textures, etc. However, their social skills are often better than those found in classic autism. PDD-NOS is called a "subthreshold" category; that is, there are no specific guidelines given, and it has become a catchall for disorders that have the appearance of autism but don't quite qualify for one reason or another.

Autism Is a Complex Disorder

One of the most remarkable characteristics of Autism Spectrum Disorders is that no two cases are alike. You can have ten children in a room, each with ASD, and each child will manifest it differently—in terms of how he or she relates socially, behaves, communicates, etc.

Additionally, children with ASD may be diagnosed with other **comorbid** disorders (disorders or conditions that accompany ASD)—such as intellectual disabilities, seizures, allergies, gastrointestinal disorders, immune dysfunction, hyperactivity, obsessive behaviors, anxiety, or depression. Thus, each child will require different treatments, and the outcomes will vary. This makes treatment and research particularly complex compared with other disorders or diseases.

BUT DETECTION IS NOT DIFFICULT

The early signs of autism (detailed in Appendix 1, page 303) are often subtle and, to the untrained eye, easily missed. But despite what is sometimes believed, detection of autism in young children is no longer as difficult for parents and professionals who have received proper training. The availability of validated screening and diagnostic tools enables clinicians to make early identification much more likely.

Up to this point, clinicians have had too few opportunities in medical school and elsewhere to learn enough about autism and accurate early detection. Hopefully, this is beginning to change.

By eighteen months, a child should be using a variety of communicative gestures with words, be imitating others as part of a playful, ongoing interaction, and be able to orchestrate more complex chains of interactions to show you what he needs.[11] Without sufficient training, health care providers (and, indeed, parents) are unlikely to notice the absence of these characteristics, which are so fundamental to social reciprocity and considered to be the cornerstone of healthy development.

PAY CLOSE ATTENTION TO KEY DEVELOPMENTAL MILESTONES

Parents and physicians together need to monitor a baby's learning, behavior, and development on an ongoing basis, paying particular attention to the presence or absence of key developmental milestones.

"While each child develops differently, some differences may indicate a slight delay and others may be a cause for greater concern. The following milestones provide important guidelines for tracking healthy development from four months to three years of age.

These milestones should not be used in place of a screening, but should be used as discussion points between parents and physicians at each well visit. If a child does not have the skills listed—or if there is a loss of any skill at any age—be sure to let your physician know.

At 4 Months, does your child:

- Follow and react to bright colors, movement, and objects?
- Turn toward sounds?
- Show interest in watching people's faces?
- Smile back when you smile?

At 6 Months, does s/he:

- Relate to you with real joy?
- Smile often while playing with you?
- Coo or babble when happy?
- Cry when unhappy?

At 9 Months, does s/he:

- Smile and laugh while looking at you?
- Exchange back-and-forth smiles, loving faces, and other expressions with you?
- Exchange back-and-forth sounds with you?
- Exchange back-and-forth gestures with you, such as giving, taking, and reaching?

At 12 Months, does s/he:

- Use a few gestures, one after another, to get needs met, like giving, showing, reaching, waving, and pointing?
- Play peek-a-boo, patty cake, or other social games?
- Make sounds, like "ma," "ba," "na," "da," and "ga"?
- Turn to the person speaking when his/her name is called?

At 15 Months, does s/he:

- Exchange with you many back-and-forth smiles, sounds, and gestures in a row?
- Use pointing or other "showing" gestures to draw attention to something of interest?

- Use different sounds to get needs met and draw attention to something of interest?
- Use and understand at least three words, such as "mama," "dada," "bottle," or "bye-bye"?

At 18 Months does s/he:

- Use lots of gestures with words to get needs met, like pointing or taking you by the hand and saying, "want juice"?
- Use at least four different consonants (for instance, "m," "n," "p," "b," "t," and "d") in babbling or words?
- Use and understand at least 10 words?
- Show that he or she knows the names of familiar people or body parts by pointing to them or looking at them when they are named?
- Do simple pretend play, like feeding a doll or stuffed animal, and attracting your attention by looking up at you?

At 24 Months, does s/he:

- Do pretend play with you with more than one action, like feeding the doll and then putting the doll to sleep?
- Use and understand at least 50 words?
- Use at least two words together (without imitating or repeating) and in a way that makes sense, like "Want juice"?
- Enjoy being next to children of the same age and show interest in playing with them, perhaps giving a toy to another child?
- Look for familiar objects out of sight when asked?

At 36 Months, does s/he:

- Enjoy pretending to play different characters with you or talking "for" dolls or action figures?
- Enjoy playing with children of the same age, perhaps showing and telling another child about a favorite toy?
- Use thoughts and actions together in speech and in play in a way that makes sense, like "Sleepy, go take nap" and "Baby hungry, feed bottle"?
- Answer "what," "where," and "who" questions easily?
- Talk about interests and feelings about the past and the future?"[12]

The Importance of Screening

In the world of medicine, screening refers to conducting examinations or tests to detect diseases before symptoms are present. Screening is not diagnosis. It is a quick, simple series of steps designed to identify which children may be at risk for developmental delays or disorders, such as ASD. For that reason, it would ideally be done on all children, whether or not they show obvious signs of delays.[13]

If screening reveals evidence of developmental delays or regressions, the next step would be diagnosis, that is, a comprehensive evaluation of the signs and symptoms examining the nature and causes of the symptoms.

While there are several diagnostic tools used by developmental professionals today, the **Autism Diagnostic Observation Schedule (ADOS)** is the instrument considered to be the current gold standard for diagnosing ASD and, along with information from parents, should be incorporated into a child's evaluation. Although a diagnosis of ASD is not necessary to get state-funded services, in some states the differences in the services provided to children with and without a diagnosis of ASD can be huge. Once a child has had a diagnostic evaluation and is determined eligible for services, additional assessments may be completed to better understand the child's strengths and needs in order to plan intervention goals and strategies.

Autism Myths

There are many, many myths and false ideas associated with autism spectrum disorders. A few common ones are:

"IF SOMEONE HAS AN ASD SYMPTOM, THAT MEANS THEY HAVE AUTISM."

The presence of a few spectrum symptoms does not mean a person has an autism spectrum disorder. A full and searching evaluation must be performed to grasp the full picture of a child's condition before any diagnosis can be determined.

"PEOPLE WITH AUTISM ARE UNABLE TO FEEL EMOTIONS OR DEVELOP PERSONAL ATTACHMENTS."

Quite to the contrary, most people with autism are highly capable of feeling emotions and love. They can be very empathetic, though they may express their understanding in uncommon ways.

"EVERYONE WHO HAS AUTISM IS MENTALLY RETARDED."

About 75 percent of individuals with ASD are diagnosed with intellectual disabilities; however, it has been found that this is attributable to the types of tests being used to measure intelligence. We now understand that the validity of the results is heavily influenced by the communication and perception deficits associated with ASD.[14]

"PEOPLE WITH AUTISM ARE ALL ALIKE."

In fact, persons with autism are as different from one another as people can possibly be. The only thing they really have in common is difficulty with social communication and repetitive behaviors and/or restricted interests.

"NO ONE CAN BE CURED OF AUTISM."

While it's true that there is no known cure just yet, many children who have received early and intensive intervention no longer meet the current diagnostic criteria for ASD. And all children, no matter how severe their disorder, can benefit significantly from intensive intervention. Early and intensive intervention can improve the quality of life for all children and families affected.

Autism in the United States: Some Facts and Statistics

Autism is more widespread than most people realize.

- ❍ CDC's Autism and Developmental Disabilities Monitoring (ADDM) Network released data in 2007 that found about 1 in 150 eight-year-old children in multiple areas of the United States had an ASD.[15]

○ Between 1 and 1.5 million Americans have it.[16]

○ Autism spectrum disorders cut across all lines of race, class, and ethnicity. Boys have a significantly higher incidence of autism than girls, ranging from more than three to more than six boys for every girl with ASD.[17]

○ Because of the genetic link, siblings of a child with autism have a greater chance of being diagnosed with an autism spectrum disorder.

○ ASD is more common than pediatric cancer, juvenile diabetes, and Down syndrome combined in the U.S.[18]

IN A SENTENCE

Autism is a complex disorder; no two children are affected in the same way.

living

Affirming the Diagnosis

PERHAPS AS A consequence of the steady stream of news stories, interviews, documentaries, and public service announcements about autism, parents often have two general types of responses to autism concerns:

○ those who have dismissed out of hand their child may have autism, having told themselves that it won't happen to them
○ those who worry about it constantly and are fretting that their child might have it

But those extremes aside, researchers know that many of the warning signs are the very ones that often trouble parents months or years before the child is formally diagnosed. They are the very phenomena parents worry about when a baby seems distant or unresponsive, when an eighteen-month-old is not talking, or when a three-year-old is not playing with other children.

The rule you should count on is this:

If you think something is not quite right with your child, trust your instincts, and check it out. You know your child best.

Commonly, parents hear from physicians that they should just "wait and see." But in the case of a young child showing possible developmental delays or difficulties, waiting is definitely the *wrong* thing to do. A few months in the developmental life of a very young child can make a huge difference. If the child does turn out to have autism or another developmental problem, each month of delay for a child under the age of three is so many missed opportunities to speed recovery. Of course improvements can be made after age six or even as an adult; however, it is so much easier if treatment is begun before the age of three.

The Earlier the Intervention, the Better the Outcome

Often family members and even doctors with insufficient training and experience with child developmental disorders will tell parents things like:

"Wait and see."
"Watch and wait."
"All kids do that."
"She'll grow out of it."
"Boys talk later than girls."
"She's just going through a shy phase."
"He's just quirky."
"Einstein was a late talker." (Which he was, but he was also known to have
    Asperger syndrome.)

The trouble with this kind of misplaced reassurance is that it can push parents into denial. All parents want to believe their child is developing typically. No one wants to hear that there may be problems arising in their child. But it is this denial that is pushing the parents further and further from exploring the possibility that their child has fallen off a healthy developmental trajectory.

If you just "wait and see," your child may go undiagnosed until grade school or even years later, which can dramatically impair the outcome.

Most health care providers don't have the tools to detect developmental problems early on. You would like to believe that your doctor has the expertise to spot autism in a young child, but the fact of the matter is that most don't.

Fewer than 30 percent of pediatric doctors are able to diagnose developmental disabilities before the child is of grade school age.[19]

By that time, you will have lost out on all opportunity for early intervention. Furthermore, without a diagnosis it is difficult, if not impossible, to get proper services. Better to know and get the help your child needs than to wait and wonder needlessly. Why extend the angst? When in doubt, check it out.

The Original Diagnosis

If you don't have a formal diagnosis, an important early step is to get one. However, if you are having to deal with a long wait to see a specialist, it is important that you get started right away with intervention, regardless of whether or not you have a diagnosis.

If you do have a diagnosis, you'll need to consider: Who gave you the diagnosis?

- ○ Was it a school educator or an Early Intervention professional (neither of whom can formally diagnose)?
- ○ Was it your pediatrician?
- ○ Was the child diagnosed accurately? Did the professional who gave the first diagnosis have the expertise, and did he or she check for *overlapping disorders*?

> To receive an accurate diagnosis for autism, your child should be evaluated by an experienced developmental specialist (a developmental pediatrician or a pediatric neurologist, psychologist, psychiatrist, or other qualified professional).

Who you really want giving the diagnosis is a developmental specialist *who has specific and extensive expertise in diagnosing and treating autism spectrum disorders.* Ideally, you should find an experienced developmental pediatrician to see your child. Often they specialize in developmental or behavioral disorders and thus are quite likely to have experience with autism spectrum disorders. Unfortunately, there are fewer than six hundred developmental pediatricians in the United States, so trying to see one without having a long wait to get in may prove difficult.

Some people believe most neurologists understand all there is to know about autism, but that is just not true. Many neurologists specialize in particular nerve or brain disorders and may actually know little about specific autism spectrum disorders. Ask your doctor about his or her experience with autism spectrum disorders.

If you cannot get a quick appointment with an autism expert, getting a diagnosis from any licensed professional is a much better bet than just waiting.

The reason for this is simple: Providing your child with special services *now* rather than waiting is vital if she does have autism. If you later find out she does not, there is no harm done.

> In some states, you need a diagnosis to receive specialized ASD services from your school or local Early Intervention Program. It is better to receive a "false positive" diagnosis and begin your child on services immediately than suffer the denial, anxiety, and potentially harmful delays of treatment.

Where should you go to find someone to diagnose autism? Try getting referrals from:

- your local Early Intervention or Child Find Program
- a local or state autism organization
- a local university that has an autism program (often the professors in these programs can connect you to the community providers)
- parents who have kids with autism and have been down this path already

But read on; there is additional, specific information about this up ahead.

IN A SENTENCE

If you suspect something is wrong with your child, trust your instincts, and don't delay seeking an experienced professional.

DAY **2**

learning

Are You Doubting the Diagnosis or Denying It?

RECEIVING THE INITIAL diagnosis that your child has autism may come as a devastating blow. You may experience a wide range of emotions in response to this revelation; it is important that you acknowledge these feelings. Are you doubting or denying that it is so? Or have you been searching long and hard for answers? If the latter, then perhaps the diagnosis came as somewhat of a relief.

Typically a parent will disbelieve ("the diagnosis must be incorrect") or will see some developmental progress and doubt things are as serious as the doctor says. This may be followed by a host of other reactions (listed in the chart on the following page) in no particular order and often experienced more than once.

Know this: the diagnosis was not your fault, and there is hope. If you do not allow yourself to pass through these intense feelings, no matter how much you may wish to avoid them, you will find that repressing or avoiding them may lead to even more severe reactions, even illnesses.

All spiritual, religious, and self-improvement practices offer some approach to recovering from emotional traumas. I encourage you to avail yourself of such help.

Fear	What it could mean for your child's and family's future
Anger	At the doctor for giving you the diagnosis; at yourself for "being responsible" for it
Guilt	You feel you did something to your child through your genetics, during the pregnancy, or because of vaccines, diet, etc. You feel you waited too long to get a diagnosis.
Frustration	You are not sure how to work the system, who to see, or where to go. You experience long waiting lists to see professionals.
Isolation	You feel it's happening only to you and that you can't talk to anyone about it. If there are severe behavioral problems, you feel you cannot take your child out in public.
Paralysis	You feel you cannot move, that you are stuck. You know you should be doing something but you don't know how to help your child and you just want to put your head under the covers and plead "why me."
Overwhelming grief	Your hopes for your child's future feel shattered.
Hopelessness	You feel the condition is not treatable; you feel you have nowhere to go.
Helplessness	You feel you have no supports and you're going to have to deal with this all alone.
Being obsessed	You go into "mission mode"; all you think about is autism and allow no time for your family, your spouse, or yourself.

Recovering from the shock by fully experiencing it is an essential step in preparing yourself for the tasks ahead.

Your Reason for Denial

In one sense, feeling in denial about a diagnosis can actually play a beneficial role. It can protect you from an initial shock that might otherwise render you incapable of action. It can give you time to find the strength to cope with an unbearable situation or problem.

It is time to be honest with yourself. Do you doubt the diagnosis because:

❍ you don't agree with your child's assessment or you have doubts about the expertise of the clinician?

○ you don't fully understand what autism is and how it can affect children differently?

○ you simply do not want to acknowledge what the clinician is observing?

○ you cannot accept the fact that your child may be "different" and that this will profoundly affect your future?

○ all emotion aside, you have *real, legitimate reasons to doubt* the quality of the diagnosis?

Suggested reading to help you deal with the emotional impact of receiving the diagnosis:

• Robert A. Naseef, *Special Children, Challenged Parents: The Struggles and Rewards of Raising a Child with a Disability,* revised edition (Baltimore: Brookes Publishing, 2001)
• Barry Neil Kaufman, *Happiness Is a Choice* (New York: Ballantine Books, 1994)
• Martin Seligman, PhD, *Optimism: How to Change Your Mind and Your Life* (New York: Free Press, 1998)

Make a Conscious Effort to Replace Denial with Doubt

Unfortunately, staying in denial will, for the most part, only prevent you from getting the help your child needs. But let's assume you simply cannot yet shake the overwhelming sense of disbelief you may feel. There is still something you can do.

Just for the moment, substitute *doubt* in place of your feelings of *denial.* You know there is *something* amiss with your child, and you've already received one diagnosis. You don't have to assume the worst is true, but you *do* have to jump in with both feet and take additional steps to really find out— by getting a second opinion.

It has long been understood that the early years in a child's development are critical. As Dr. Stanley Greenspan, a child psychiatrist, says, "The mind and brain are growing very rapidly in the first three years of life and our most important human abilities are being mastered during that time. Children are learning complex social, emotional, intellectual, and language skills. If we allow a child to be off on the wrong pathway for a long period of time, we're doubling or tripling the ultimate challenges for that child."[1] Doubt it all you want, but do something about it right away. If you know your child has missed developmental milestones, red flags are waving in your face. It is very unlikely these signs will go away on their own; they are likely to get worse if you do nothing.

Whatever the truth may be, it is a lot healthier for you and your child to get a second opinion and find out without delay.

Getting the Real Answer Now Will Contribute to Your Peace of Mind

Every parent must find the right balance of hope and reality. Do you really want to live in a continuous state of angst caused by uncertainty? Getting the proper diagnosis and intervention as soon as possible will lead to your child's best chance for recovery.

Many parents simply do not understand the most important reason for getting answers early: *When it comes to autism, you are in a race against the calendar.* By waiting, you slow down the treatment process and greatly reduce your child's chances for recovery.

One parent contacted me on and off for about three years, beginning when her child was two. Every time she called, it was "to disprove" that her child had autism; she gave me every reason why her child couldn't possibly have autism—and yet here she was, calling me again. I gave her names and phone numbers of experts to contact, but she did nothing. By the time she dropped out of touch three years later, her child had missed out on opportunities for early intervention.

If you knew your child had painful swelling under his arm or possibly a blood infection, would you wait to get it checked out? Of course not. You know that not treating a serious medical problem right away could lead to a more serious condition down the road.

Autism is no different. Early warning signs can be spotted in the first two years of life, provided one knows what to look for.

Early Detection: The Red Flags of Autism Spectrum Disorders in the Second Year of Life

Impairment in social interaction:

- ○ lack of appropriate eye gaze
- ○ lack of warm, joyful expressions

○ lack of sharing interest or enjoyment

○ lack of response to name

Impairment in communication:

○ lack of showing gestures

○ lack of coordination of nonverbal communication

○ unusual prosody (little variation in pitch, odd intonation, irregular rhythm, unusual voice quality)

Repetitive behavior and restricted interest:

○ repetitive movements with objects

○ repetitive movements or posturing of body[2]

These early signs may be easy to miss if you are in denial or you do not know what to look for. If left untreated, they will undoubtedly progress into a full-blown autism spectrum disorder. On the other hand, if you intervene early enough with the appropriate treatment, you may be able to divert the disorder and get your child back on a healthy developmental path. Intensive, well-designed, and timely intervention may profoundly improve the quality of life for your child and family. To see what these signs may look like in a child under three years of age, I encourage you to check out the ASD Video Glossary at www.firstsigns.org. There you will see side-by-side comparisons of children with ASD and typically developing children.

IN A SENTENCE

> *Denial is the road to delay and difficulty; doubt can be the road to certainty and help.*

living

Getting a Quick Start and a Second Opinion

TO GET THE proper help for your child, you need to pursue two critical pathways *simultaneously*. Begin by making arrangements to have your child assessed by your local Early Intervention Program or school district, depending upon the age of your child, and one or more independent developmental specialists who have specific expertise in the diagnosis and treatment of autism spectrum disorders.

The **Early Intervention Program** (EIP or just EI) is a statewide, federally funded program, available locally, that provides early intervention services for infants and toddlers with disabilities and their families. They are charged with assessing children from birth to age three (and through age five in some states) for developmental delays at no cost to families. Contacting EI immediately is essential.

To find the contact information and eligibility criteria for EI in your state, visit the National Early Childhood Technical Assistance Center website: http://www.nectac.org/. For more in-depth information about Early Intervention, see Week 4 (page 110).

Even if your child does not yet have a formal diagnosis, if she shows any signs of developmental delay, it is critical that you begin intervention immediately. Because of how the human brain develops, children learn best when they are young. It is *so* much easier (and, in the long run, less expensive) to bring about a positive outcome if treatment is begun as soon as the first signs emerge.

If your child is too old for Early Intervention, your local school district is responsible for identifying, assessing, and making recommendations for services based upon that assessment at no cost to families. For more information about your local school district, see Month 6 (page 214).

Whether performed by EI or by your school district, this assessment is essential if you are to receive public (state) assistance for your child and will add strength to any other evaluations you obtain from other independent sources.

The Second Opinion

Everyone should consider getting a second opinion, whether you doubt the first diagnosis or not.

Why? Because:

- ❍ no matter how much you like or trust the clinician, it's natural to wonder if something was missed
- ❍ getting a second opinion is a very common and accepted practice
- ❍ missed diagnoses and misdiagnoses are extremely common among young children with complex learning, developmental, and behavioral disorders
- ❍ it's your right as a parent!

The previous section gave you a list of questions to help clarify why you had doubt about the diagnosis. If you do doubt a clinician's assessment or his or her ability to assess, or if you are searching for a new clinician, get answers to the following questions:

- ❍ What is the specialty of the clinician who first diagnosed your child?
- ❍ What are his or her credentials?

○ What percentage of children within his or her practice is diagnosed with autism?

○ How often does he or she diagnose children with autism? Daily? Monthly?

○ What is the clinician's reputation with parents? Within the medical community?

○ Has the clinician published any articles, books, or research studies?

Although the last bullet is not essential to choosing a qualified clinician, this information may reveal the clinician's specific area of interest and expertise. It is essential that your child be evaluated by a professional who has the training and expertise to diagnose and treat children on the entire autism spectrum, and not just the more severe end of the spectrum.

At this point, start looking for a developmental specialist—or better yet, a multi-or interdisciplinary team of specialists—with the expertise to diagnose and treat autism spectrum disorders.

Both terms, "multidisciplinary team" and "interdisciplinary team," refer to a group of key health care professionals from different disciplines who come together to provide comprehensive assessment and consultation for patients. In common use, a "multidisciplinary team" usually refers to a group of professionals who are employed by one institution (hospital, health care clinic, etc.). The term "interdisciplinary team" is often used when the team members are assembled from different institutions and/or private practices.

The team approach to diagnosis and treatment is vital. Autism spectrum disorders manifest themselves in the child's life in a wide variety of ways (behavior, speech, ability to learn and relate, pathology, allergies, etc.); thus a variety of integrated treatments is also required.

Depending upon the qualifications of the first person who diagnosed your child, you may want to incorporate that professional into the multi- or interdisciplinary team evaluation.

When you begin your search for developmental specialists or a team, good places to start are:

○ large medical centers
○ children's hospitals
○ large university hospitals
○ children's developmental clinics
○ autism centers

Usually these facilities are found in major metropolitan cities. Even if you live far from such an area, traveling the distance may be well worth the time and trouble. Just remember to check credentials before you schedule an appointment.

Some large medical centers and children's hospitals have autism clinics and should be able to perform multidisciplinary evaluations. However, many health care facilities do not offer extensive cross-disciplinary services; when they do, they rarely have top experts on staff. In many cases, you will have to take charge of assembling your own team. Of course, you can integrate members of your EI team if you feel they are qualified and understand your child's needs.

Begin this process by seeking help from your local autism organizations or your local Early Intervention Program. If cost is a factor, check to see if there is a university in your state recruiting young children into an autism research study. If your child meets the criteria, you might be able to get your child accepted into the study and evaluated without cost to you.

Ideally, a multi-or interdisciplinary evaluation team would consist minimally of a:

○ developmental pediatrician, pediatric neurologist, or child psychiatrist
○ biomedical specialist
○ child psychologist
○ speech and language pathologist
○ occupational therapist or physical therapist
○ social worker
○ educational specialist

What is key is that these professionals have the training and expertise to diagnose and treat children with ASD. A full discussion of how to assemble your team is presented in Day 6, "Living: Begin to Assemble Your 'A' Team."

If you cannot arrange for a full multi- or interdisciplinary team to evaluate your child, Early Intervention may be able to provide you with parts of the assessment team—perhaps a speech and language pathologist, an occupational/physical therapist, a special educator, and/or a social worker. While they cannot diagnose autism, many of these professionals are experienced and do know what autism looks like. But keep in mind that not all Early Intervention Programs are created equal and they are only as good as their clinicians. You must determine if the clinicians at your EIP are experienced enough to participate in your multi- or interdisciplinary team evaluation.

Evaluations and Assessments

EIP and your assembled multi- or interdisciplinary team will independently assess or evaluate your child in a variety of developmental domains: social/emotional, communication, motor, cognitive, and self-help. Generally speaking, the EIP assessment will be much briefer—often completed in one or two hours. A multi- or interdisciplinary evaluation should be much more extensive, often lasting several hours and requiring more than one visit even if the specialists are colocated.

During an assessment or evaluation, clinicians should be interacting with your child, who is asked to do a variety of tasks. In various ways the evaluators should be trying to observe how well your child engages with the parent(s) and with the evaluator as a stranger. You should also be asked to fill out a number of questionnaires covering your child's health and development, your concerns and priorities, and your family's lifestyle and support system. If this does not happen, it may be a sign that they do not value parent feedback and involvement.

A multidisciplinary or interdisciplinary team should include one or more autism specialists who perform autism-specific evaluations, including the Autism Diagnostic Observation Schedule (ADOS) mentioned in Day 1. These are often designed to cause a certain amount of anxiety in order to provoke autism-specific behaviors so that they can be observed. While some of the evaluations involve fun activities, others may not be so enjoyable for the child. Because the process itself can be stressful, it may be better to stretch it over two or three days. Another reason for doing this is to give the evaluators a more accurate and complete picture of your child on more than one sitting. Either way, remember to pack a few comforts for the child (a favorite stuffed animal or toy, snacks, blanket, books).

Your child should also get a full physical examination and blood work. If the possibility of seizures or other neurological problems is a concern, a specialist may request an electroencephalogram (EEG), a test involving the monitoring of the natural electrical activity of the brain. This involves placing small recording electrodes on the scalp and is completely painless and harmless, but it can be a very traumatic experience for both the child and the parents, particularly if the child has sensory issues. Based on the outcome of the EEG, a Magnetic Resonance Imaging (MRI) may be recommended. The MRI is a noninvasive, non-x-ray diagnostic technique based on the use of magnetic fields. This test is also painless and harmless, but many children are frightened by the equipment or the procedure. Your physician may request additional tests.

RULING OUT BEFORE RULING IN

From the point of view of arranging effective treatment, it is as important to know what disorders your child does not have as it is to know what she does have. Thus certain possibilities must be ruled out before an autism diagnosis can be confirmed.

Following is a list of disorders that share common features with ASD and should be considered when making a diagnosis. Some of these disorders can be confused with ASD. Conversely, a child may have ASD plus one or more of these comorbid disorders. If your child presents with ASD, then all of these disorders should be considered. Well-experienced practitioners will be able to rule these disorders in or out—an essential step if the ultimate treatment plan is to be effective.

- Angelman syndrome
- developmental language disorders
- early-onset childhood bipolar disorder
- Fragile X syndrome
- generalized anxiety disorder
- hearing impairment
- intellectual disabilities
- Landau-Kleffner syndrome (LKS)
- metabolic disorders
- obsessive-compulsive disorder (OCD)
- oppositional defiant disorder (ODD)
- pediatric autoimmune neuropsychiatric disorders associated with streptococcal infections (PANDAS)
- phenylketonuria (PKU)

○ Prader-Willi syndrome
○ reactive attachment disorder
○ schizoid personality disorders
○ schizophrenia
○ selective mutism
○ tuberous sclerosis
○ Williams syndrome
  (See glossary for definitions.)

THE IMPORTANCE OF A BIOMEDICAL ASSESSMENT

At this time, autism is classified strictly as a psychiatric disorder. However, recent research is providing evidence that it is a neurological disorder and more specifically, a systemic disorder that affects the brain.[3] It is suspected to be caused by the presence of various antagonistic factors that injure the brain, central nervous system, and other critical functions of the body. Such factors include:

○ toxic chemicals
○ viruses
○ inflammation
○ immune cells attacking the brain[4]

For this reason, biomedical testing is essential. It is also best done in "tiers" or layers. For example, a clinician may call for full blood work, urinalysis, lipid analysis, and thyroid tests. Based upon these results, additional levels of testing may be ordered to confirm (for example) the presence of a specific metabolic disorder that can then be accurately treated.

In general, I believe some of the clinicians best equipped to diagnose and treat the medical/biological aspects of autism are those who participate in the Autism Research Institute's Defeat Autism Now! project. According to its mission statement, "Defeat Autism Now! is dedicated to the exploration, evaluation, and dissemination of scientifically documented biomedical interventions for individuals within the autism spectrum, through the collaborative efforts of clinicians, researchers, and parents."[5] While the actual experience of the Defeat Autism Now! practitioners can vary widely, the organization promotes:

- ○ an integrated approach to medical treatment, including both traditional and alternative methods
- ○ an extensive diagnostic protocol that opens the door to comprehensive treatment of the biological aspects of the disorder

Defeat Autism Now! also sponsors conferences that are some of the best venues for parents to educate themselves on the state of the art in treating the biological aspects of autism.

When Choosing a Specialist

When choosing a specialist, in addition to checking his or her qualifications as described earlier, you will need to find out what insurance he or she accepts (if this is an issue for you). If the specialist is part of an HMO, you will have to get a referral from your primary care provider, usually a pediatrician or family physician.

If your primary care provider is reluctant to make such a referral, you have a potential problem on your hands. So what can you do? When confronted with this, you can sit in your pediatrician's waiting room until he or she gives you a referral, find a new pediatrician, change your insurance policy to one that does not require referrals to specialists, or if all else fails and you are in a financial position to do so, pay privately.

You can reasonably expect your child's doctor to:

- ○ listen to you
- ○ keep an open mind
- ○ ask questions
- ○ give you an opinion
- ○ be willing to explore other options
- ○ not be territorial (that is, be willing to share information or decision making with others about the case)
- ○ be willing to work with other team members
- ○ make referrals when there is reasonable cause
- ○ provide you with the reports you will need to obtain services

As you can see, there is a lot to do when you first receive the diagnosis, and all of it is vital. Review the material in this chapter once more, and start to work at it methodically.

IN A SENTENCE

Jump in now—start researching a team to help you, and start seeking answers to all your questions.

learning

The Top Ten Most Essential Actions

ONCE YOU OFFICIALLY receive your child's diagnosis, you are most likely going to feel:

- ○ overwhelmed
- ○ paralyzed
- ○ unable to get your feet unglued
- ○ uncertain how to start
- ○ not sure where to turn for help

Who could *possibly* blame you? Who could criticize you for nearly any reaction you may go through when it seems as though the bottom has fallen out of your universe?

We all go through it; we all get through it, one way or another. And if you stay with me through this book, you'll get through it too.

Even while you are trying to grapple with this new reality, even before the shock has worn off (before it has even fully sunk in), I'm going to urge you to shift into action. Make your first response as active and as intelligent as possible. This will help prevent the shock of the news from dominating your life or cementing you into bad patterns. *It will also ensure your child has the highest probability of recovery.*

Below is a rapid summary of the most essential steps that will lift you out of the confusion. Each is a big job in itself, but don't worry; this is just a summary. The later chapters of this book will methodically walk you through all the details of how to do each of them. At this point, consider this a preview of the "medicine" that is to come.

1. UNDERSTAND AND ACCEPT THE DIAGNOSIS.

You will need to arrive at a deep understanding of the complexities of the disorder and how it may be affecting your child specifically. It is more than a matter of reading about it.

"Accepting the diagnosis" means moving from the denial stage to acknowledging that "yes, my child has autism. But I can do something about it." For some, acceptance comes quickly, while for others, it takes weeks, months, or even years.

2. DOCUMENT EVERYTHING; BECOME INFORMED AND WELL-CONNECTED.

With all the accumulating paperwork—reports, invoices, notes, test results, letters, insurance forms, and educational plans—you will soon begin to feel as if a few good-sized trees have moved into your home. Every one of these documents should be at your fingertips when you need them, so learn to document and organize everything, either electronically or into three-ring binders or expandable files. *Being methodical and organized is key to maintaining your sanity during this journey.*

3. ESTABLISH YOUR "A" TEAM.

You *must* assemble a top-notch team of medical, therapeutic, and educational specialists to ensure you have the breadth and depth of expertise you need (see page 64). There is no way you can do this all on your own. You should draw on the expertise of all these specialists to form the most accurate assessment of your child and to identify the treatments that will best meet his or her needs. Members of the team will change over time, but the team will be crucial to your success.

4. TAKE THE DRIVER'S SEAT: MANAGE THE BUSINESS OF RECOVERY.

You are the team leader and the ultimate decision maker. So while you will be relying on specialists, you still need to question everything to be sure the steps taken make sense for your child. Do not automatically assume anyone is an all-knowing expert. You may find during this process that you become more expert than some professionals if for no other reason than the fact that you know your child better than anyone.

You have to manage the recovery of your child. You will have competent professionals on your team, but you and only you can manage that team.

5. KNOW YOUR CHILD—HIS LIKES, DISLIKES, STRENGTHS, AND CHALLENGES.

Get a complete developmental profile of your child from a skilled developmental specialist. This is critical if you and everyone else on the team are to understand the depths of your child's strengths and challenges. Typically this profile will come from a developmental pediatrician or a pediatric psychiatrist or psychologist.

6. PUT THE PROPER SUPPORTS IN PLACE.

This will be a very long and often exhausting journey. You will be of infinitely greater value to your children and family if you are not falling apart. To maintain your health and your sanity, you are going to need help from a support system of family members, friends, community members, and professionals. There are many parents in the same situation who can be a great resource and assistance at this time.

It really does "take a village" to raise and support a child with autism.

7. KNOW AND EXERCISE YOUR LEGAL RIGHTS.

Federal laws—chiefly the American Disabilities Act (ADA)—and supporting state laws govern the supports and treatments you can get. If you don't know and exercise your legal rights, you will probably not get what you need (reimbursement, proper services, schooling, etc.). The more legal knowledge you have, the further you will get. You will read more about this in Month 2, "Learning: Know Your Rights" (page 123).

8. OBTAIN KEY EVALUATIONS AND REPORTS TO GET THE SERVICES YOU NEED, AND KEEP THEM UP-TO-DATE.

To get the intervention your child needs, your greatest tool will be comprehensive, detailed reports from top specialists in the field. These reports should clearly spell out the diagnosis and specifics about the educational program, therapies, and support services that best meet your child's needs.

9. LEARN WHICH TREATMENTS AND PROGRAMS ARE MOST APPROPRIATE FOR YOUR CHILD.

Many different treatment and educational options are available. So you can intelligently select what is most appropriate for your child, you and your team must:

○ have a thorough understanding of your child
○ have a thorough understanding of the treatments

10. ADVOCATE!

When it comes to obtaining treatment and educational services, you are always going to be your child's best advocate. Don't be afraid to be assertive and keep asking questions—no one can speak up for her the way you can. It is important that you learn how to advocate and how to do it well.

IN A SENTENCE

These ten essential actions will help restore hope to your life.

living

Living with Autism, an Olympic Challenge

SO MANY PARENTS (including me) become hyper-focused and obsessed with wanting to recover their child quickly. Quite rightly, much emphasis is placed on not waiting, "the sooner, the better," doing all that can be done before the child reaches the age of three.

But too often this fast action can result in fast burnout—sometimes for one parent, sometimes for both. Often enough, one parent ends up quitting his or her job because it becomes impossible to manage the child's treatment program *and* be the team leader *and* do everything to care for the child and the rest of the home *and* work a full-time job. If you are a single parent, then everything falls to you.

I tried to "do it all" for about six months before finally giving up my long commute and career in advertising and marketing. At least in my case, this had huge financial and lifestyle ramifications, reducing our household income by more than 50 percent and forcing us to downsize our home.

I must tell you, I've held several jobs in the professional world, but they all pale compared to the demands of this job.

This is the hardest job you will ever know. You can't just shut it off the way you can your computer. It will be there 24/7; you have no outs. But it is also the most important and rewarding job you will ever have.

You're going to need the other parent there helping you out, letting you take a break, doing some of the therapies with you; otherwise, the burden can become nearly unbearable. Both parents need to share the responsibilities of this unexpected situation, determine what their new roles will be, and work together as a team. Failure to do this often results in divorce and all kinds of additional hardships on the other children in the family.

For those who are single parents, you may have to rely more heavily on extended family members and friends to pitch in and help so you don't end up in burnout before the first year is up.

If you have other children in your family without autism, you may have a tendency to give most of your time to the one child with autism. Other siblings may feel left out, and they will probably get tired of hearing about autism all the time. You will have to try to devote some special time to all your children.

You should also be aware that if your first child has autism and you have been planning to have additional children, there is a greater probability that they too will have autism. According to the Yale Developmental Disabilities Clinic, "Current data suggest that the likelihood of having a child with autism if the biological parents already have one child with autism is at least 1 in 20. This rate may be an underestimate, given that many families with one autistic child will stop having children due to stress or the fear of having another child with the disorder."[1]

Early on, you may lose some friends. You may find that all you talk about is autism and that some people grow tired of hearing about it. But you will also discover that some of your best support is going to come from other parents of children with autism or similar disabilities. In such families, you will probably find siblings without disabilities who will become peer models and playmates for your child.

So what can you do? The first step is to pace yourself by setting realistic, attainable goals. Regardless of what you might want to do, the truth is that you need to divide up this mountain into a series of small hills and get good at tackling them. The second step is to get help—*you cannot do it all yourself.*

Putting the proper supports in place will be critical to your well-being, especially now. It is essential that you take care of yourself if for no reason other than if you burn out now, you won't be able to help your child. If you need to, go ahead and jump to Month 9 ("Learning: Feeling Isolated, Staying Positive" and "Living: Finding Resources and Building Your Support System").

There will be wins. And if you keep the small wins coming, there will be big wins as well. But this is not just one race—it is a monumental decathlon, and you must learn to pace yourself.

IN A SENTENCE

Do what an Olympian would do: pace yourself, get the support you need, and try to avoid burnout.

DAY **4**

learning

Is Recovery Possible?

EVERY PARENT INEVITABLY agonizes over the answer to this question: "Will my child ever recover and lead a normal life?" I can remember wanting to ask this question when my daughter was diagnosed ten years ago, but I was too afraid to say it out loud—for fear of what the answer might be.

In a very large number of cases today, recovery is unquestionably possible. But just as the word "normal" has been burdened with many meanings, "recovery" also has been given many interpretations. So let's find out exactly what this question is really asking.

The most common English-language meaning of the word is "to bring back to a normal position or condition; to return to an original state; the act of regaining or saving something lost (or in danger of becoming lost)." Recalling that the current diagnostic criteria for an autism spectrum disorder are:

- ○ impairment in social interaction
- ○ impairment in communication
- ○ repetitive behaviors and restricted areas of interests

we could consider an individual is *recovering* as he or she experiences less frequent and lower intensity manifestations of these characteristics. Just as there is a spectrum of autism disorders, we could say there is a spectrum or continuum of recovery from autism.

Thus, based on today's definition of the diagnostic criteria for ASD, we might say a child has recovered when he or she manifests no clinically significant amount of impairments or restrictions in these characteristic areas. In other words, *the individual no longer meets the diagnostic criteria for the disorder*; he or she is judged to no longer be on the autism spectrum. This is how many professionals currently define "recovery."

Other perspectives on recovery:

1. "You cannot recover from autism, but you can improve."
Some professionals believe that once a child is diagnosed as being on the spectrum, he or she will always be on the spectrum—that there is no way to fully recover from the disorder. They are not saying that a person cannot improve, just that ASD is a lifelong diagnosis.

2. "Autism is neurological diversity, not a disorder from which you can recover or be cured."
There is a growing movement within the autism community of individuals with ASD who view themselves as having neurological differences and not a disease or disorder. "We believe that the autism spectrum and those on it are important and necessary parts of the wide diversity present in human genetics," says the website of the Autistic Self Advocacy Network (ASAN). "ASAN supports Autism Acceptance through measures to promote success for each person on the spectrum. By abandoning old and inaccurate models of pathology and adopting a new approach focusing on both the unique challenges and strengths of autistics, we believe that we can improve outcomes and promote a new paradigm of inclusion and respect."[1]

This movement is new and just now gaining a voice in the autism world. While many professionals and parents strongly disagree with their view (or parts of it), it is important that we fully understand what they are saying and give them every chance to express their beliefs even if it runs contrary to what most believe about autism. By doing so, at the very least we may learn something new about the true meaning of the word "acceptance."

In my view, however, this is not the end of the story, and while there is no doubt that the diagnostic criteria for ASD must be reclassified and redefined, until this happens (the fifth edition of the DSM is expected to be published in 2012), the definition for recovery is open to interpretation.

Many children are technically no longer on the spectrum (as defined by today's definition of the diagnostic criteria) but need to continue special education services or treatments in order to remain off the spectrum or to eliminate any remaining difficulties. However, if they lose their official autism diagnosis, they could potentially become ineligible for services in their school district and become vulnerable to a serious setback. So parents are, in essence, being forced to represent their children as being in a worse condition than they actually are, in order to remain eligible for assistance.

These children may no longer meet the current diagnostic criteria for ASD but might very well have "residual issues"—subclinical symptoms. With special supports and services in place—classroom modifications and/or accommodations, therapies, medication, and/or restricted diet and supplements—they appear very typical. But this is not full recovery. Many of these children are extremely vulnerable. Without these supports, they could be right back on the spectrum to a greater or lesser degree.

This continuing need for services is not an absolute either. Perhaps over time, with further treatment or services, the individual may require fewer and less frequent special supports. Should we not be able to claim that this person is continuing to recover?

Then suppose one day the individual no longer needs any special services, supports, modifications, accommodations, or treatments at all (not even medication); he can live a stable life acceptable to himself and places no special burden on others *as judged in the light of the diagnostic criteria for ASD*. I suggest that this would be a reasonable definition for full recovery as far as autism spectrum disorders are concerned.

"Necessary and Sufficient Conditions" for Recovery

In order for recovery to be possible someday, there are many necessary steps to take. And even though we may take all the necessary steps, the conditions around us still may not be sufficient for recovery. For example, let's say you want to go shopping at the mall many miles away. There are some conditions that have to be satisfied in order for this to occur.

Probably you'd have to:

○ get into your car
○ make sure your car had enough gas to make the round trip
○ drive to the mall
○ have some kind of way to pay for what you want at the mall

Each of these conditions is necessary for you to shop at the mall, but by themselves or even collectively, they are not *sufficient* for the trip to be a success. The mall would have to be open; the stores would have to have the things you want to buy, etc.

In the world of treating autism, we do know some of the conditions necessary for successful treatment, but unfortunately we do not know them all. We do not know what would be *sufficient* conditions to guarantee success.

The following are some of the conditions found to be *necessary* for significant improvement and even recovery:

○ getting a team of experts in place who
  • conduct the proper in-depth evaluations
  • can identify the underlying problems
  • know the best possible treatments for your child's particular condition
○ committing the time and resources necessary to work toward recovery
○ dedicating yourself to achieving it
○ ensuring your child receives a full range of carefully integrated therapies, supports, and programming—each of which addresses the causal factors underlying each aspect of the child's particular set of characteristics

The children who have improved the most have at least these elements in common.

However, as pointed out earlier, autism is a *spectrum* of related disorders. The spectrum is very wide, and the disorders are often very different from one another. The exact causes of the disorders are still not known with certainty.

Some children have very complex medical situations, and these can be exceedingly difficult to treat. The so-called "comorbid disorders" are currently considered separately classed disorders that are not technically part of ASD according to the DSM but demonstrably influence the severity of the ASD condition.

Additionally, many children regress after making initial progress. This can happen because unknown causes make the treatment imprecise or because comorbid disorders make treatment more complex. Thus, while the list above gives some of the conditions known to be necessary for reaching recovery, at this point no one knows all the conditions that must be satisfied to make a full recovery possible. For this reason, it's not possible to say with certainty that any particular child can recover.

Treatments: "Evidence-Based" and Otherwise

For well-understood diseases or pathologies, treatments are often very clearcut: an antibiotic for a throat infection, an antifungal agent for a skin rash, antivenom for snakebite. But when the actual causes of a disease or unwanted condition are unknown, the practitioner, to some degree, is forced to treat symptoms. Unfortunately, this is the current state of affairs with regard to autism and some of the comorbid disorders often associated with ASD: the causes and cures are not obvious.

For this reason, professionals often compare notes with their colleagues, polling one another for what seems to work well for which particular cases. Lacking a fully workable, comprehensive treatment plan, parents often try methods that have no rigorous proof of efficacy but for which there may be **anecdotal evidence** of workability.

Anecdotal evidence is informal evidence that tends to support some particular theory. Often anecdotal evidence is obtained under noncontrolled conditions or without rigorous application of the scientific method.

Parents will often hear professionals insisting on only administering "**evidence-based treatments.**"

The trouble arises when some professionals do not realize that the "evidence-based" approach in itself is a *spectrum of certainties*, with every treatment being somewhere along this scale, from an educated guess to completely proven.

When they are speaking of "evidence-based treatments" (EBT), professionals are generally referring to practices that represent the highest level of certainty of results attained—as applied to both the treatment and its method of implementation.

The concept of evidence-based treatments refers to what clinicians must do to come up with approaches to treatment when there simply isn't any clear-cut cure available. Often in these cases:

1. The treatment starts with an educated guess and some evidence of workability from an individual case report.
2. Perhaps a small, informal study will follow.
3. As more controlled experimentation is done, the evidence grows stronger.
4. More random trials are done to further prove or disprove the usefulness of the approach or to better define the limitations of the approach or in which cases it will work.
5. Ultimately, the aim is to validate the approach using large, well-designed, randomized testing by multiple researchers with systematic reviews.

Unfortunately, the term "EBT" gets misused in two directions.

Some practitioners and treatment organizations operating in the field of ASD claim their methods are evidence-based when in fact they may be economically successful because of good marketing; other researchers using the same methods may be unable to replicate the claimed results.

The EBT label also gets misused when professionals object to a treatment proposed by parents, claiming it is not evidence-based when in fact they won't even look at the evidence. The professional's judgment is based upon a personal bias or ignorance of methodologies outside their zones of immediate familiarity.

The fact is that in the world of ASD treatments, there are *no* treatment methods that are proven to work consistently and in the same way for all children. In fact there are no treatment methods that have been proven to work (per number 5 above) *at all!*

The ASD Recovery Process: The Missing Framework for Treatments

You are going to be talking with a lot of parents, some of whom have been on this journey for a long time. You will hear; "Oh, we tried X, and it worked beautifully." Another parent will tell you something else. While gathering the experiences of others is very valuable—and is often the basis for important discoveries—just jumping in and experimenting on your child with what *appeared* to work for someone else is unwise.

Why? Well, first of all, inasmuch as parents try to do everything possible for their children, often they may try numerous treatments at once. If they did not use a controlled, methodical process, they did not know what really worked—it could have been something else they were doing at the same time that caused (or added to) the improvements seen.

Second, since each child can have a wholly different configuration of contributing disorders, what works for one child may not necessarily work for another.

Parents must have a thorough understanding of their child's unique profile so they don't end up chasing treatments based on hearsay, not knowing if it is truly appropriate for their child.

Additionally, when you do find a treatment that works, it may work for a few weeks or months and then cease working altogether. Treatments that work at one point must be modified or changed as they cease to show results, and new treatments may be added as they are developed and recommended by practitioners or discovered by the parents.

A lot of this confusion may be due to the fact that, at the present time, there is no standardized, globally accepted process for the creation and operation of comprehensive treatment plans that also treat the immunological, gastrointestinal, and metabolic problems that so many children with ASD experience. Such a process would provide a kind of framework or context for the selection, operation, monitoring, evaluation, and refinement for all ASD treatment methods.

Perhaps such a process will be forthcoming in the near future, once there is a better definition of ASD and we have a better understanding of the root causes. Until then, we must depend upon the initiative and genius of researchers, practitioners, and each parent, as the team leader who assumes the many roles outlined in this book.

IN A SENTENCE

At this time, recovery is a long and uncertain road; however, there are many children who no longer meet the current diagnostic criteria for ASD and many more who have made vast improvements.

living

Understanding, Accepting, and Embracing the Diagnosis

COMING TO TERMS with your child's developmental disability or disorder, particularly autism, can be a lengthy process. While every parent responds differently, most parents instinctively educate themselves on what to do to take immediate action. Understanding in great detail what autism is about is what makes acceptance possible. This book and the materials referenced in these pages will help you considerably in that regard.

You don't need a degree in psychology or medicine to help your child. But you will come out of this process feeling as if you have earned that degree! And certainly, you will become the top expert on your child.

Acceptance is the second step. This is an emotional leap from a detached, rational understanding of the information to internalizing it into your life and your future. This can be very difficult for some parents.

Acceptance means fully internalizing the reality of the diagnosis and that it is what it is. Having reached this point, you will be able to move onto the third and final step.

I highly recommend that you read *Voices from the Spectrum: Parents, Grandparents, Siblings, People with Autism, and Professionals Share Their Wisdom*, edited by Cindy N. Ariel and Robert A. Naseef (Philadelphia: Jessica Kingsley Publishers, 2006). It is a must-read for any parent struggling to accept the diagnosis.

Embracing the Diagnosis

Understanding and acceptance are necessary steps, but they won't take you to your final destination. The point you really want to reach is embracing the diagnosis.

This is where you will experience a sense of inner strength. Embracing it means: *"I'm not going to live in denial. I am going to climb that mountain."* It is that unbending determination; it is diving into the situation headfirst. You bring yourself to the point where you can say, *"This is my world; this is what I live in; I'm not going to fight it. I'm going to welcome whatever help I can get, whatever understanding, whatever support."*

Your mission becomes your primary focus. You accept the fact that the dreams you once had for your child may be different—they won't be over. She may not go on to college; she may not have the same kinds of experiences you once thought she would. Your family life is going to be different; your daily life will be different; your future will be different. That doesn't make it better or worse; it's just going to be different.

In fact, in many respects my life has changed for the better. I've learned to prioritize things in my life, the good things are more meaningful to me, and I have learned to let go of the bad things more quickly. I've learned to roll with the punches better. I've learned to figure out what really matters in life and go after what I know and want. It becomes a new way of life.

I do *not* accept the claim that ASD is not treatable. I accept that my daughter may have limitations and that her life will be different, but I don't accept that my daughter won't reach her goals.

It is educating yourself, accepting the diagnosis, and ultimately embracing the diagnosis that will make you a stronger person, a better advocate, a better parent for your child.

The only magic formula is:

- ❍ Be a very active, involved parent.
- ❍ Get educated—more educated than your doctors if necessary.
- ❍ Look at your child's various difficulties from new perspectives; look for possibilities that have never been tried; challenge even the well-meaning preconceptions of others.
- ❍ Use the child's strengths as opportunities to circumvent challenges.

IN A SENTENCE

> *Understanding and accepting your child's diagnosis are necessary; however, embracing it is what will see you through the difficulties of the journey.*

DAY **5**

Getting Organized, Informed, and Connected

UP TO THIS point, the focus has been on getting started in your education on autism and moving beyond the initial shock of the diagnosis.

From this point forward, we will move you into action, specifically *effective* and *efficient* action. You will find that to the degree you become effectively active and begin to see results, your morale will begin to return and propel you to even higher achievements.

Achieving effective action begins with four important steps:

- O getting organized
- O getting (and staying) informed
- O getting connected to resources and
- O managing the process of recovery

Getting Organized

This is the moment when you need to look at all the organizational skills you have developed in your life. Whether you developed these skills while working in an office, a restaurant, or a school, or while planning your wedding and organizing a new home, the point is that, somewhere within, *you have these skills.* Now is the time to take stock of your organizational skills, because you are about to put them to important use in a whole new area. You may surprise yourself by discovering skills you never thought you had.

To obtain the services and supports you need and to guide your child through her recovery program, these skills will be invaluable. There will be endless forms to fill out, a variety of evaluations and assessments to schedule and attend, lengthy reports to review and distribute, educational plans to scrutinize, and lab results to be filed and found when needed. There will be invoices and insurance forms to be matched and submitted. There will be notes from interviews and phone conversations to be appended and filed, and endless emails to send out to team members.

All this work needs to be organized into a binder that you can easily take with you to meetings with other team members so they are kept up-to-date on evaluations, assessments, test results, and discussions with other team members.

To prevent duplication of efforts and to keep everyone on the same page, you will need to take recent copies of reports with you. By doing this, you will help each team member understand the different perspectives of the other members: how they view your child, his progress, his successes, and any regressions. This will also ensure that the recommendations from each team member are shared with the others.

Today, go out and get the organizational tools you need. Whether you organize yourself electronically or with paper, whether it is with three-ring binders or expanding files, find a system that works for you. Because my experience was in marketing and advertising, I used an artist's portfolio case that zipped all around and had handles, making it easier to carry from appointment to appointment without losing anything important.

In hindsight, I wish I had kept everything electronically by scanning documents into my computer and setting up an electronic filing system. They would have been much easier to find than by rummaging through binders. But if you do this, make at least two full backups of all these records, and store them safely in different places. Hard drives often crash, and this information you must never lose.

If you prefer to store your files electronically, you can do an internet search using the terms "personal electronic health records" to find what is available commercially. Some software programs offer a free thirty-day trial.

While you may decide to arrange your records differently, here is how I organized mine:

Section 1: Journals	
Daily journal	Track what foods your child eats daily, supplements and medications, changes in behavior, notations of illness or injury, daily routines, skills mastered, etc. (This is useful in correlating patterns of reaction to any changes in supplements, medications, and nutrition.)
Developmental journal	Document the dates your child reaches important developmental milestones (see Day 1 Learning for list of hallmark developmental milestones), and also include growth and vaccination charts, first words spoken, favorite activities and toys, likes and dislikes, etc.
Video journal	This is invaluable for visually documenting the developmental domains and showing behaviors at different stages of your child's development. (Check out the ASD Video Glossary at www.firstsigns.org to see examples of what to look for.)

Section 2: Reports	
Medical, clinical, and therapeutic	Keep reports in order of date, and include all medical, neurological, psychological, neuropsychological, and therapeutic reports, as well as lab reports. Be sure reports are signed and dated.
School reports and plans, daily notes, report cards, progress reports, and samples of your child's work	You may need to keep a separate set of binders just for this section, since it will grow exponentially over the years. You should save key samples of your child's work and relevant notes from your child's teachers, aides, and other staff members.

Section 3: Correspondence	
Correspondence (written and received)	Organize your letters so they are easy to find when you need them. If you need to append a note to the letters, use sticky notes rather than writing directly on the letter, in case you ever need to use it in court. That way, it will not be altered.

Section 4: Record of Conversations	
Record of conversations	Keep a record of all conversations, visits, and information you have gathered with regards to your child's treatments, educational program, supports, and services, especially when it comes to your child's school and insurance provider. Be sure you document the date and time of conversation, names and titles of professionals you spoke with, what was said by whom, and any follow-up action items.

Section 5: Insurance	
Insurance: Claim forms and statements	Organize statements by date. (Eventually this section became so packed that I created a binder just for insurance claims.) Always make copies of the claims you send in along with attached copies of invoices. I always indicate in the top right corner of the claim form the date it was mailed, in case anything is misplaced.

Section 6: Contact and Medication Information	
Team contact sheet	Create a contact list that contains the name, role, address, telephone number, fax number, pager number, and email address for each team member, including doctors, clinicians, therapists, and key members of your Early Intervention and school team. Always keep this contact sheet updated.
Medications and supplements list	List the names of all medications and supplements, reason for taking them, dosage and schedule, what to watch out for (side effects).
Letter of medical necessity	This is a document to use in case of emergency. If my daughter is left with a sitter, relative, or neighbor, I give the adult caring for her a letter of medical necessity, which lists all of her specialists, explains her diagnoses, gives whoever is in charge permission to treat her in case of emergency, what numbers to contact me, who to call second and third, etc.

There are many different types of organizational systems available, some less expensive than others. While the pre-designed systems may not be exactly what you want, check to see if you can modify them to accommodate your needs.

The forms you will be asked to complete by doctors and other clinicians can be very long, taking you anywhere from fifteen minutes to two hours apiece. The questions asked are often similar: when milestones were met, when she spoke her first words or first started walking, whether he points to indicate interest in something, etc.

Instead of guessing, refer to your child's baby books and journals, as this will be a time saver and provide a more accurate picture of your child. Take your time and think about each response, because the better the information you provide, the better the help you will get from each team member. I find it easier and a real time saver to complete these forms electronically, so I can edit them as much as I want and cut and paste similar responses from other forms.

It is hard to overstate the value of these organized records. When I'm being a detective, trying to determine when a particular problem began, I use these journals to trace back to the onset of specific behaviors and can sometimes relate them to changes in medication or diet or an illness. For example, by referring back to my journals, I was able to isolate *the exact week* when my daughter developed a staph infection, which may have been related to the sudden onset of her hyperactivity, tantrums, tics, and obsessive behavior beginning at the age of three and a half.

Early on, I always felt that getting organized was therapeutic. I felt I was actively taking responsibility for the situation rather than just "waiting for things to happen."

Managing your child's treatment program and recovery becomes a full-time job—and then some. It is what you will have to do in addition to your other jobs as a parent and spouse, plus any work you do outside the home. The only real way to survive this is to get organized.

Getting Informed and Connected

Now get to know all the resources that are available to you:

- who's who, what they do, who might be able to help you
- who are the top experts in your state or area
- whom you should consider going to
- whom you should stay away from
- what organizations you could tap into
- what kind of funding is available

You should also stay informed about

❍ insurance coverage
❍ your school district and what it offers
❍ your child's needs
❍ what is going on in the community that might be available to you

Here are some resources to start building your list:

❍ Wrightslaw.com: http//:www.wrightslaw.com

Peter and Pam Wright have compiled a large body of useful material on all aspects of individuals with disabilities. Look for the link to the page entitled "Yellow Pages for Kids with Disabilities" (or go to http://www.yellowpages forkids.com). From there you can select the state in which you live to see a list of resources available in your area.

❍ The ARC: http://www.thearc.org/NetCommunity/Page.aspx?&pid=207 &srcid=183

Formerly known as the Association of Retarded Citizens and now called "The ARC," this group has chapters in every state and provides access to a wide variety of assistance and services, including those specific to ASD. Many of their chapters have Autism Support Centers, which offer support groups, resource libraries, and workshops.

❍ *Schafer Autism Report:* http://www.sarnet.org

This is a newsletter sent by email in digest form (two hundred issues per year for $35 or free with a scholarship subscription) that provides a wealth of invaluable information for you as a parent.

❍ Local Support Groups

These are always great resources because of the experiences of parent-members in knowing the local "who's who"—whom to go to, whom to avoid. For more information on how to find local support groups, see Month 9.

○ Autism Speaks Family Services Resource Guide: http://www.autismspeaks
.org/community/fsdb/state.php?sid=45

This website provides an extensive listing of services available in most states.

○ Autism Speaks Family Services 100 Day Kit: http://www.autismspeaks
.org/community/family_services/100_day_kit.php

As the website explains, "The Autism Speaks 100 Day Kit is created specifically for newly diagnosed families, to make the best possible use of the 100 days following the diagnosis of autism. The kit contains information and advice collected from trusted and respected experts on autism as well as from parents of children with autism. There is a week-by-week plan for the next 100 days, as well organizational suggestions and forms that parents/caregivers can use to help with the paperwork and phone calls, as they begin to find services for their child."

It is important to stay on top of who is doing research on the etiology, biology, diagnosis, and treatments for ASD. If you cannot afford to have your child evaluated, it is valuable to know who in your area is recruiting for a research study, since often you can participate and get evaluations or services that you otherwise could not afford. Usually you can find out about these resources by contacting autism research programs operated by local universities. Autism Speaks and First Signs offer an extensive listing of scientific resources and programs on their website: http://www.autismspeaks.org/science/programs/index
.php and http://www.firstsigns.org/research/studies.htm.

Your own team members can be your most valuable source for referrals and resources. For example, if you have found a good attorney who specializes in autism, he or she may know a top-notch neurologist or neuropsychologist in your area.

As with all aspects of caring for a child with ASD, the amount of information you will have to pore over will seem overwhelming at first. Just remember that right now you are just in "first gear." As you gain experience, you will find a way to maintain a steadier pace without feeling so overloaded.

IN A SENTENCE

Take the time to get organized—knowledge is power, but knowledge and connections combined create even greater power.

living

Managing the Business of Recovery

AS YOU GET better and better organized, informed, and connected, you will find it increasingly easy to assume the mantle of Team Leader. Right now you are new to all this, and you don't necessarily know what to do, but at this point you should at least believe that you will be able to figure it out and gain the confidence you need.

At one point, near the beginning of my journey, I found myself in tears after an unfriendly meeting with school district officials, because they refused to acknowledge that the program my daughter was in was not meeting her needs. I realized I had to find a way to deal with these types of situations without letting the battles affect me so personally. The approach I took, which became very successful, was to look at this recovery program as if it were just another business project.

Even though it was not easy to think of my child as "just another business project," by viewing it this way, I found I could begin to operate much more effectively, undistorted by emotion or personal bias. By putting on my business hat, I began to fight as if I were undertaking just another necessary business encounter. I began to prepare for and participate in these team meetings as I would for any project I had run in my business career. As hard as it may be, many other parents have discovered the same trick. It is fair to say that a large percentage of those who succeed at operating their child's recovery program do look at the task as a business, putting them squarely in charge of their child's destiny.

The more you make this an objective task, rather than a subjective or personal one, the easier it is going to be. The advantages of taking this "management" approach are that you will:

- ○ feel more empowered
- ○ stay in a much more positive frame of mind
- ○ keep from being drawn down into the minutia
- ○ keep the goals in mind more easily and stay on task
- ○ stay out of the depressive quagmire—that big black emotional hole you don't really want to spend a lot of time in

Developing Your Recovery Management Plan

I'm going to explain the core approach that I found successful. There are also a lot of good books and courses on management techniques, which I encourage you to take advantage of if you feel so inclined.

Developing your management plan can be simplified by using the form that follows. The meaning of each line item is detailed in the instructions that follow the form.

Recovery Management Plan

1	Mission:	

2	Domains:	Social Interaction	Communication	Behaviors and Interests	Regulatory and Sensory
3	Long term goals:	1. 2. 3.	1. 2. 3.	1. 2. 3.	1. 2. 3.
4	Short term goals:	1. 2. 3.	1. 2. 3.	1. 2. 3.	1. 2. 3.

5	Financial condition:	
6	Insurance coverage:	
7	Other available options:	

8	a) What treatments, services, and pro-gramming does my child need in order to reach these goals?	b) What treatments, services, and pro-gramming are being offered, and are of acceptable quality?	c) Are there other options available that will bridge the gap between (a) and (b)?	d) Plan of action, considering what is attainable at this time
9	1. 2. 3. 4.	1. 2. 3. 4.	1. 2. 3. 4.	1. 2. 3. 4.

Line #	Title	Explanation
1	Mission	Identify your mission: what is the mountain you wish to climb? Mine was to recover my child as fully as possible. Some parents accept the diagnosis and whatever services they can get. They consider their mission to learn how to deal with the diagnosis. One has to decide how deep or high one's mission is and how far one is willing to go. Missions can run the gamut, from learning to accept your child just the way she is all the way to leaving no stone unturned. There are, of course, all shades in between. When you meet with other parents you will see the spectrum from one end to the other. You have to find out what your mission is.
2	Domains	The "domains" are four areas of development that are affected by autism. See Appendix 1 for full descriptions.
3	Long term goals	What you want to achieve overall before your child is __ years old.
4	Short term goals	What you want to achieve this month, within six months, within twelve months.
5	Financial condition	Overall financial picture of your current situation, including a listing of assets and liabilities.
6	Insurance coverage	Specifically which treatments and services are covered by your health insurance, and which are not? Which treatments and services are more likely to be covered if appealed? What is your co-payment and annual deductible per individual and for the entire family? (For more information on insurance coverage, see Month 2.)
7	Other available financial options	This is where you need to get creative and think outside the box. Can you get supplemental insurance, obtain grants, negotiate the fee, or borrow from relatives? Can you barter for services or use a flexible spending account? (For more information on other financial options, see Month 2.)
8a	What treatments, services, and programming does my child need in order to reach these goals?	This should be based on recommendations from your team members. Be specific in terms of the actual treatments and number of days per week needed. Begin to prioritize the treatments, beginning with the most important and ending with the least important. This will help you to eliminate a treatment or minimize the number of days per week if money should become a determining factor.
8b	What treatments, services, and programming are being offered and are of acceptable quality?	List the names of the treatments, services, programs, or providers. You may need to visit them to determine if the quality is acceptable. It's one thing to hear about them; it's another to see them in action. If you are not certain what to look for, take a trusted clinician with you to observe and make recommendations.

Line #	Title	Explanation
8c	Are there other options available that will bridge the gap between (a) and (b)?	When your child needs a particular service, program, or treatment and you cannot find one that is acceptable in quality, there are other options if you are willing to look outside your immediate area or come up with a creative solution. You may need to design a home-based program or work with other parents in the same situation to develop some alternative solutions. You can find a research study in which you can participate at a nearby university or get trained in the methodology yourself.
8d	Plan of action, considering what is attainable at this time	What action needs to be taken in order to acquire the treatment, service, program, or provider? You may need prior approval from your insurance provider or get your school district to buy into some of your options.
9	Notes about specific actions to be taken	Be sure to consider any potential roadblocks or preemptive measures you may need to take in order to get final approval or buy-in on your preferred options.

IN A SENTENCE

Taking a formal management approach to your child's recovery can remove a lot of the emotional reaction and help you feel more empowered and focused.

DAY **6**

Navigating Long Waiting Lists

IN MANY AREAS of the country there are six-, twelve-, or eighteen-month waits to see an expert. Unfortunately, this happens all too frequently, because there are a limited number of qualified autism experts and the number of children being diagnosed has increased dramatically over the past few years.

Here are some helpful tips for parents who are anguishing over long waits:

1. Always work from your prioritized choice list, from the first choices on downward. Your top choice professionals will probably have long waiting lists, but don't let that discourage you. Get on both their waiting and their cancellation lists, which are different.

   Not every practice has a cancellation list, but ask if they have one, and, if they do, let them know how much advance notice you need. If you can be available for the doctor with one day's notice or less, you stand a much better chance of getting in to see him or her quickly.

   I have heard from a few parents who tried this technique with clinicians who were in great demand and had year-long waiting lists. The parents told them they could be there with only two hours' notice, and, sure enough, they got in to see the specialists within two to three weeks (one even got in the next day), all because of last-minute cancellations. Now, that doesn't always happen—sometimes it just boils down to being in the right place at the right time.

2. You should not hang up without making an appointment with the expert you really want to see, even if it's a year away. Chances are, a year from now, you will still want that appointment. You can always cancel it down the road. Many parents end up spinning their wheels and losing a lot of time trying to get in to see different professionals. They second-guess whom they will be able to see and opt not to secure any appointments until they get the one they want. The problem with this method is they may not get to see anyone at all for over a year, and a lot of precious time will be lost.

3. Call back regularly (without making a nuisance of yourself) to check for openings. Get friendly with the office staff if possible.

4. Do not hesitate to stress the age of your child and your child's situation if it is critical. Many clinics are taking children under age three for diagnosis right away, so the children can benefit from Early Intervention services.

5. If appropriate, stress key factors that will heighten the attention of the office staff and persuade the doctor to accept the child sooner rather than later. This may be severe behavioral or medical problems or something relative to what you know the doctor is researching or especially interested in. Don't go on and on about it, however. Learn what key words to use and plead your case succinctly—in sixty seconds or less.

6. Ask your primary care provider or other specialist to place a call on your behalf in case he has some influence.

7. If your choice top specialist can't see your child right away, ask her to recommend someone who can see your child while you are waiting, so you can get the services you need. Some of the best referrals will come from these A-list people.

8. Lastly, make your follow-up appointment before you leave the office. For some clinicians who are in great demand, you have to plan as far as twelve to eighteen months in advance.

IN A SENTENCE

Do not despair over long waiting lists; your persistence will ultimately pay off.

living

Begin to Assemble
Your "A" Team

ASSEMBLING A TOP-NOTCH team of medical, therapeutic, and educational specialists will be one of the most important steps you can take to ensure accurate ongoing assessments of your child and to help you identify the treatments, program, supports, and services that will best meet his or her needs over the years. While the makeup of your team may change over time and some members may be more actively involved than others at different points, your team should play a key role in helping you map out short- and long-term plans and help you with the important decisions. As I describe in Day 2, "Living: Getting a Quick Start and a Second Opinion," the team approach is vital. Do not do this all on your own! With autism spectrum disorders as complex as they are, your team of specialists will be crucial to the success of your child.

Building a good team will take time and should be done methodically. Take the time to build your list of prospective team members, research your candidates, prioritize your choices, and learn everything you can about your candidates. In this chapter I will provide you with the tools you need to help with this process.

Primary care providers routinely refer children to specialists because the nature or severity of a condition requires special expertise. This is particularly important for children with such complex disorders as ASD, in which so many of their biological systems are affected. In fact, it is because so many systems are affected that a team of specialists is required—with members working collaboratively, along with parents or caregivers. This approach, also known as a multi- or interdisciplinary approach, is built on the concept that each participant, whether parent, physician, or other clinician, adds a new dimension of understanding and expertise.

In the case of children with autism spectrum disorders, the guidelines produced by the American Academy of Pediatrics in 2007 specifically recommend a "comprehensive multidisciplinary approach."[1]

Potential team members can be divided into four basic categories: health care professionals, therapeutic professionals, educational professionals, and other professionals.

1. Health care professionals

- **developmental pediatricians:** Medical doctors who are board-certified by the American Academy of Pediatrics, they have subspecialty training in developmental-behavioral pediatrics and specialize in the evaluation, diagnosis, and treatment of children with developmental, behavioral, or learning problems, as well as those problems that further complicate chronic illnesses and disabling conditions, such as epilepsy, diabetes, asthma, cancer, and genetic disorders. Though this subspecialty is still relatively new and there are fewer than six hundred developmental pediatricians in the United States, they are accustomed to working closely with other specialists, and they are most likely to be familiar with the neurological problems, medications, and current research related to ASD. An experienced developmental pediatrician may be your best choice for conducting your child's individual profiling.

- **pediatric neurologists:** Medical doctors who are board-certified by the American Academy of Pediatrics and the American Board of Psychiatry and Neurology, they diagnose, treat, and manage children with brain injuries, illnesses, or disorders, such as epilepsy, cerebral palsy, hydrocephalus, ADHD, autism, etc.

- **neurodevelopmental pediatricians:** Medical doctors who are board-certified by the American Academy of Pediatrics and who have specialized and received additional certification in the field of neurodevelopmental pediatrics, they are skilled in the evaluation and treatment of children with developmental delays.

- ○ **pediatric psychiatrists:** Medical doctors who are board-certified by the American Board of Psychiatry and Neurology, they specialize in the diagnosis, treatment, and prevention of mental illnesses and are trained to assess and diagnose medical, psychological, and social aspects of mental, emotional, and behavioral disorders. They order diagnostic tests, prescribe medication, and practice psychotherapy.

- ○ **child psychologists:** Pediatric professionals specializing in diagnosing and treating developmental and learning disorders, as well as emotional and behavioral problems, they are licensed by their state and board-certified from the American Board of Professional Psychology. They must have a doctorate (PhD) in psychology if they wish to practice privately. They may provide talk- or play-based therapy, offer advice on resolving life and education-related situations, provide behavior management, and help to design a school- or home-based program.

- ○ **pediatric neuropsychologists:** These are licensed child psychologists who have specialized in the relationship of the central nervous system to human skills and behavior. In clinical applications, brain functions are evaluated by various objective means (memory and thinking tests, etc.), and this information is then used for diagnosis and treatment planning. Neuropsychologists may also provide various forms of treatment, including cognitive rehabilitation, behavior management, or psychotherapy methods.

Other medical specialists relevant to your child's unique physical circumstances might include:

- ○ **pediatric gastroenterologists:** Pediatricians with additional training in pediatric gastroenterology, hepatology, and nutrition, they are certified by the American Academy of Pediatrics and are valuable in the diagnosis and treatment of childhood disorders of the gastrointestinal tract, including the intestines, stomach, liver, and other organs.

- ○ **nutritionists:** Licensed health care practitioners trained in the field of nutrition, some specialize in particular disorders or conditions.

○ **complementary and alternative medicine (CAM) practitioners:** Complementary and alternative medicine is a general classification of approaches, diagnostic, and treatment techniques that are not commonly employed by conventional medical practitioners. In many cases, this is due to the fact that there are insufficient modern, scientific test results that support their safety and/or efficacy. Naturally, it can be argued that (for example) a remedy with a two-thousand-year history of anecdotal successes shouldn't be lightly dismissed just because modern science hasn't gotten around to figuring out if or how it works. Whether or not to use CAM is a personal decision and requires, as with any treatment method, a willingness to investigate, ask questions, and fully understand before any action is taken.

Sometimes, when a technique or treatment has achieved a sufficient level of modern scientific study to validate its efficacy and safety over a long enough period of time, it becomes accepted as conventional medicine.

There is no licensing body for CAM or CAM practitioners as a whole; however, within the various disciplines that make up this general classification, there are training colleges and certifying organizations. Therefore, when researching CAM practitioners, you should check their credentials within the context of their specific discipline and any training and certifying bodies recognized within their field.

○ **integrative medicine practitioners**: The term "integrated medicine" was coined by Dr. Andrew Weil, the founder and program director of the Arizona Center for Integrative Medicine (formerly the Program in Integrative Medicine), which he started in 1994 at the University of Arizona.

Integrative medicine practitioners seek to intelligently combine what are perceived as best practices in both conventional and alternative medicine. They are oriented toward encouraging natural "wellness" and prevention rather disease and disease treatment—promoting approaches or methods that assist the body in healing itself. Integrative medicine practitioners seek to treat the whole person—body, mind, spirit, and emotions—not just the part or parts of the body in which symptoms occur. Ideally, practitioners will select therapies they believe to be the most appropriate for the patient, choosing from the wide assortment of tools available through state-of-the-art, conventional medicine as well as a multitude of other less conventional therapies found to be safe and effective, including chiropractic, massage, yoga, acupuncture, meditation, qigong, tai chi, herbal therapies, and many others.

Integrative medicine also differs from conventional medicine in that it holds that the patient's many social, personal, spiritual, and environmental relationships play critical roles in maintaining and restoring health.[2]

Integrative medicine practitioners are frequently specialized in several disciplines. As mentioned in the section on complementary and alternative medicine, education, accreditation requirements, and professional regulation vary widely for each field.

○ **medical geneticists**: These are medical doctors who have specialized and been certified in the diagnosis and treatment of human genetic diseases and disorders. Within this field there are subspecialties in the areas of inherited metabolism disorders and genetic pathology. A medical geneticist can be very helpful in ruling in or out treatment pathways when it is suspected that there may be genetic causes or vulnerabilities that contribute to the child's disorder.

2. *Therapeutic professionals*

○ **speech and language pathologists (SLPs)**: These licensed professionals evaluate, diagnose, and treat individuals with speech, language, voice, and swallowing disorders. Many specialize in children. They are credentialed by the American Speech-Language-Hearing Association (ASHA). Often a child with obvious speech delays can begin speech therapy before the formal diagnosis process is completed.

○ **occupational therapists (OTs)**: These are licensed professionals who help individuals with disabilities improve their fine motor and self-help skills (such as writing, drawing, dressing, handling tools, etc.), so they can live more productive lives. Many OTs specialize in children; some specialize in sensory integration therapy, a specialty that helps individuals with over- or under-sensitivity to touch, sound, smell, or taste. They are credentialed by the National Board for Certification in Occupational Therapy.

○ **physical therapists (PTs)**: Licensed professionals who evaluate, diagnose, and treat individuals with disabilities or impairments to improve their gross motor skills (such as walking, balancing, running, and climbing), PTs are licensed and regulated by each state; many specialize in children. PTs use a variety of treatments to help individuals build strength, improve movement, and strengthen skills needed for daily activities.

○ **social workers:** Licensed professionals who help individuals and families cope with social issues, relationships, and problems in everyday life, many specialize in marriage and family therapy, case management, individual and group therapy, and child-focused play therapy. They are licensed by the National Association of Social Workers.

○ **play therapists:** Trained professionals who help children with emotional or communication problems through group or individualized play sessions, they may also be licensed as psychologists, social workers, or speech-language pathologists or in other child specialties.

○ **behavior therapists:** These are trained professionals from a variety of disciplines, including psychology and special education, who use basic learning techniques to modify inappropriate behavior patterns by substituting new responses to given stimuli for undesirable ones. Their work is called "behavioral therapy" or "behavior modification."

3. Educational professionals

The school, for its part, should provide a team of key professionals that may include a special education teacher or specialist, lead teacher, school psychologist, speech-language pathologist and/or occupational therapist, and special education coordinator. Every school district varies, as do programs, services, and budgets.

○ **special education teacher or specialists:** Special education teachers or specialists work with children and youths who have a variety of developmental and learning disabilities. Some work with students with severe cases of intellectual disabilities or autism, primarily teaching them life skills and basic literacy, while others work with children with mild to moderate disabilities, using or modifying the general education curriculum to meet the child's individual needs. Most special education teachers instruct students at the elementary, middle, and secondary school level, although some work with infants and toddlers.

   All states require teachers to be licensed; traditional licensing requires the completion of a special education teacher-training program and at least a bachelor's degree, though many states require a master's degree.

○ **lead teachers:** These are either regular education teachers or special education teachers who are responsible for the supervision and management of a child's classroom.

○ **paraprofessionals / aides**: These are teaching assistants assigned to special education classrooms or to students in regular education classrooms who need individual support.

○ **school psychologists**: Licensed by the state and trained to collaborate with educators, parents, and other professionals to help create healthy, supportive learning environments for all students, school psychologists are not required to have a PhD, and their levels of training may vary. Typically, their training is in both psychology and education, and they provide intellectual and emotional assessments and frequently act as a liaison between parents and the school for matters related to the specific needs of children.

○ **special education coordinators / directors**: Trained professionals with experience in special education who are responsible for coordinating or managing school districts' special education programs, they are responsible for the implementation and effectiveness of children's educational programs and the services that support them.

○ **educational consultants**: These are independent professionals outside the school who provide knowledge, expertise, and objectivity to assist children and their families with educational planning by focusing on each student's strengths, weaknesses, interests, talents, needs, and objectives, and by identifying the most appropriate environment, program, or school to best meet the child's needs. Families must retain and pay for educational consultants themselves, unless they get prior approval from the school district.

4. Other professionals

○ **legal advocates and/or educational attorneys**: These professionals can help you obtain services in the face of obstacles. Their functions and this subject will be covered in detail in Month 7.

○ **assistive technology (AT) specialists**: These professionals help find devices and technologies that can extend a person's physical abilities, such as "talking" computers. They can come from a variety of different educational backgrounds, so ask about training and expertise. Many are also occupational or speech therapists.

There are four key steps to take when building your team. They are:

Step 1: Prospect for team members.

When you are searching for prospective members of your team, the cardinal rule is:

Get referrals from your other team members and from experienced parents you trust and respect. They are the most likely to already have contact or knowledge of some of the best people in the various disciplines.

Step 2: Research your candidates.

Research your candidates by:

- ○ searching their names on the Internet
- ○ checking their credentials with their profession's official organization
- ○ checking with health care providers, clinicians, educators, or legal professionals you know
- ○ reading any research papers they may have written
- ○ reading books they may have written
- ○ talking to other parents in the community
- ○ talking to their clientele—parents or family

Your initial research might take you a week or longer; however, you can expect to continue to add to your findings over time.

Step 3: Prioritize your choices.

From your research, make up a list of the professionals you want to see by discipline. Within each discipline, list your possibilities in three categories:

First choices: Top experts you most want to see

Second choices: Professionals you could be happy with

Third choices: Professionals who may not be your first choice but whom you can get in to see quickly and get a diagnosis so you can begin services right away

Create a table to help you organize your team-making efforts. It may look something like this:

Sample Team Establishment

Professional discipline	Choice level	Name	Contact information	Referred by / Endorsements	Fees	Specific area of expertise	Focus of research	Insurance accepted?	Availability
Developmental pediatrician	1st								
Developmental pediatrician	2nd								
Developmental pediatrician	3rd								
Neurologist	1st								
Neurologist	2nd								
Neurologist	3rd								
Psychiatrist	1st								
Psychiatrist	2nd								
Psychiatrist	3rd								
Psychologist	1st								
Psychologist	2nd								
Psychologist	3rd								

	1st	2nd	3rd	1st	2nd	3rd	1st	2nd	3rd	1st	2nd	3rd	1st	2nd	3rd
Neuropsychologist															
Neuropsychologist															
Neuropsychologist															
Integrative medicine practitioner															
Integrative medicine practitioner															
Integrative medicine practitioner															
SLP															
SLP															
SLP															
OT															
OT															
OT															
PT															
PT															
PT															

> **Important note for those who simply cannot afford a team no matter what:** if there is only one professional you can afford to see, make it an experienced professional who can give you the time you need and who has a broad perspective, someone who can look at the child and family dynamics and transcend all disciplines.

Step 4: Get to know your candidates.

Here are some guidelines to follow:

1. Are they accepting new clients?
2. Whenever possible, schedule a brief "meet and greet" appointment with your candidates so you can get to know them. Some professionals will give you fifteen minutes without charging you, but ask in advance what their policy is. Arrange to come without your child so you can speak one-on-one with the clinician first.
3. Come prepared as if you were a journalist. Make a list of questions or topics you would like to discuss in the interview. Start with a five-minute preprepared bio of your child and his or her issues. Be efficient and to the point.
4. Ask if the clinician has a specific approach in working with children on the autism spectrum. What is it? Determine if it is a cookie-cutter approach or tailored to meet the individual needs of each child.
5. How and when will treatment goals be set? Will any other team member be involved in setting goals?
6. How should family members be involved in your child's treatment?
7. Find out his range of services. How can he help you? What are his strengths? Does he have any limitations? Is he willing to observe or work with your child at home, school, or in the community? Will he attend team meetings, if needed?
8. Find out what particular topics or research within her field she is most interested in. (Consider if her areas of interest match what your child needs.)
9. Is his style compatible with yours? Do you like his demeanor, and do you think he will connect with your child? Look for practitioners who will treat you as a partner. They should exhibit a willingness to learn from you

and your other team members. They should be open-minded and flexible, people who will really listen to you.

10. Does she see your child as an individual or just another child with autism? (Is she seemingly going to treat the disorder and not the child and family?)

11. Ask him if he does anything in his practice that is different for children on the autism spectrum. For example, one physician eliminated the wait for children on the spectrum so they would be seen immediately.

12. Ask how she sees her role. You want to find out what she can bring to the table, but you need to hear it said from her perspective. Ask her to describe the ideal relationship between parent and practitioner, and then follow up with questions based on what she tells you.

13. Look for red flags that pop up in the conversation. For example, if a professional suggests he can "handle all your needs" and doesn't need other team members, then that tells you he may not welcome your input or be a team player.

14. Find out how she would handle various situations that might come up during the course of treatment for your child. For example, if you need to speak with her on the phone, how quickly will she call back? Or if there were an emergency team meeting at your child's school, would she be available? If not, what would she recommend you do?

15. Ask him which other team members (health care providers, therapists, educational personnel) he would recommend adding to your team. Ask him for specific names.

16. With respect to financial matters:
    - Check her fees, and find out if she accepts your primary or supplemental insurance.
    - Does she offer an affordable rate for out-of-pocket payment?
    - Does she have a sliding scale for rates based on the financial needs of the family?
    - Check for the type of help office staff can give you with insurance, pre-approvals, billing, and referrals.

17. Spend a little time in the waiting room observing the flow within a practice. How long is the average wait per family? Is it calm or overwhelming? Do they accommodate children on the autism spectrum who are having difficulty waiting? Are there toys or activities to keep them busy? Do parents seem frustrated or content? Strike up a conversation with a few parents. How long have they been with the practice? Are they happy with the practice? What do they like and dislike about the practice?

Establishing a team doesn't happen overnight—it can take years (it took me a few years to get a great team established). You will tweak it over time, since what you need in the first month will be different from what you will need in a year or in five years.

From a financial perspective, you may not be able to support having all these appointments at once, so you may have to prioritize and space them out.

Establishing Communication Among Team Members

The ideal team would be physically housed within the same facility and meet on a regular basis to collaborate on their cases. However, it is rare that you will find top experts who meet all your criteria under the same roof.

With a team whose members are at separate locations, it will be your responsibility to ensure that they consult with one another. *You cannot rely on them to speak with one another without your facilitation. Do not expect it to occur unless you specifically arrange for it.*

Here are guidelines to make sure this does occur:

1. Provide each team member with a copy of your contact sheet (see Day 5).
2. Find out how each one prefers to work with other team members. Does he have a preferred method of communicating (e.g., telephone, email, etc.)?
3. Mail reports in advance, and come prepared with copies just in case they did not receive them or the reports are not readily available. You might find the envelope unopened when you arrive, and the practitioner will read it on the spot. In this case, depending upon the length and complexity of the report, you might say, "Those are for your file; let me tell you the salient points and recommendations."
4. Email is a great way to communicate if your team members are willing to give you their addresses. Some won't use it; some will permit it but will charge for answering. I always find it valuable. It can be an easy way to initiate a conversation and obtain a prompt response to something you need to know quickly, but be respectful of their time.
5. If the practitioner is going to write a letter or email about the office visit, assessment, or consultation, see if you can get her to "cc" the other team members. Alternately, you can forward a copy to the other team members.

Maintaining the Team

Your team members are going to be a big part of your life, perhaps for years to come. Learn how to get the most out of them. The more they understand you, your child, and your needs, the more help they will be to you.

Your team needs to be nurtured! Make sure they know you appreciate what they are doing for your child. Try to make it easy for them to work with you; be thoughtful.

Obtaining Key Reports and Evaluations; Keeping Them Up-to-Date

One important part of what your team must do is to generate reports based upon continuing professional evaluations of your child. These reports should come from each team member and should include (in accordance with their specialty):

○ detailed diagnosis and any insurance codes that might apply
○ detailed information on the child's strengths and challenges
○ recommended treatment programs and specific strategies for those treatments
○ recommended individualized educational programming, including, for example, answers to these questions:
  • Should the child be placed in a classroom with typically developing children, in a self-contained classroom with other children on the autism spectrum, or in a classroom with children of varying special needs? Or should the child have a home-based program or residential placement?
  • What kinds of services and supports are needed?
  • How many hours per day and days per week?
  • Should it be a year-round program with no breaks or a year-round program with short breaks at the beginning and end of the summer? What should the summer program look like?
  • What qualifications should the teacher and support staff have?

School systems are required to reevaluate a child every three years. The school evaluation team might include a school psychologist, speech and language pathologist, occupational and/or physical therapist, social worker, special education teacher, and regular education teacher. While many of these professionals may be qualified, they vary dramatically in their ability to thoroughly and accurately assess children with developmental problems, particularly ASD. And with school districts under such extreme pressure to reduce costs, typically they will recommend only the services and supports the district is prepared to offer. I have witnessed more than once qualified school personnel take a strong position in support of the child and then two weeks later, in a subsequent meeting with the special education director present, advocate the complete opposite view.

For this reason, school personnel may not report on findings that an outside evaluator might, so consider getting updated evaluations from qualified professionals every two to three years from the following disciplines:

- ❍ neuropsychological evaluation: Neuropsychological tests are designed to measure and relate the child's mental (cognitive) and emotional capacities to specific brain structures and central nervous system pathways. This testing is based on traditional psychometric theory; scores are compared with the norms of the general population and adjusted for age, educational level, ethnicity, etc. Such tests may provide critical information about your child and how he or she will likely perform in school in terms of cognitive, perceptual, and motor skills.
- ❍ speech and language
- ❍ occupational therapy
- ❍ physical therapy (if needed)
- ❍ medical

Good reports from qualified professionals can carry a lot of weight and may be the ticket to getting the services and insurance reimbursements you need.

IN A SENTENCE

Remember that your team is essential to your success; be strategic in selecting team members, do your homework, and be persistent.

learning

Defining Your Role and Your Family's Role

WHEN YOU ARE managing any project or business, you have to define roles so you know what the responsibilities are for the day-to-day tasks.

If you are new to the world of autism, the number of roles might surprise you. On the following pages is a fairly comprehensive list with some comments and suggestions that might help you prepare yourself and your family for what will be required.

It is very important to discuss, reach an understanding, and establish agreements about the execution of these roles with your spouse or partner and, as possible, with your other children.

In an ideal world the responsibilities will be equally distributed, but often they fall to one individual. If at all possible, try to avoid this situation; otherwise you will be headed for burnout. Use this list of roles and responsibilities to plan and negotiate who does what.

Roles / Responsibilities	Comments / Examples / Notes
Team leader	This is the "captain of the ship" insofar as the child's recovery program is concerned—the person with the primary responsibility.
Deputy team leader	This person supports the team leader at key meetings and is able to stand in when the primary team leader cannot attend.
Researcher	This person researches prospective team members, new treatment approaches, therapies, programs, sources of aid and support, developments in the world of ASD, etc.
Peer models/ playmates	This can be a sibling and/or a child in the neighborhood.
	While it can be stressful for children to have a sibling with autism, it has been documented that siblings of children with autism have often gone on to do quite amazing things in their lives because they assume high-level responsibilities from an early age.
	Usually this is facilitated by ensuring each child gets his or her own one-on-one time with the parents and thereby feels included, equally important, and able to follow his or her own dreams and activities.
Team personnel: solicitation and interviewing	This involves contacting and interviewing candidate team members.
Appointments: coordination	This involves scheduling and coordinating appointments for visits with professionals, arranging child care for siblings if needed, and juggling the family's schedules.
Appointments: preparation	This involves checking for any documents that need to be copied and prepared for an appointment and preparing the child's travel/entertainment bag, if needed.
	This also involves preparing the child for evaluations and procedures (e.g., blood work, EEG, EKG, colonoscopy, endoscopy, etc.) and/or hospital visits with "social stories" (stories that explain an event or situation that would otherwise be difficult for a child to understand), incentives, role play, and discussions.
Appointments: attendance	This involves attending evaluations, assessments, observations, therapies, medical procedures, doctors' appointments, team meetings, and other meetings, as well as providing input and feedback, observing, taking notes, learning new information, etc.
Appointments: follow-up	This involves following up with team recommendations, such as additional evaluations or procedures, medications, therapies, etc.
Play dates: coordination and facilitation	This involves arranging and coordinating play dates, transporting, and facilitating social interactions with other children.

Roles / Responsibilities	Comments / Examples / Notes
Team updates	This involves preparing and distributing updates for team members on a continual basis and facilitating communication between team members.
Educational program: participation	This involves preparing, observing, and providing information and feedback to educational team members, as well as overseeing the child's educational program. Team members include regular and special education teachers, aides/paraprofessionals, therapists (speech/OT/PT), nurse, principal, special education director or co-ordinator, psychologist, etc. This also involves following up with team recommendations (for example, at-home therapies, techniques, or activities to work on); providing the team with daily notes from home; helping to prepare, edit, and review results from the child's educational plans; reviewing quarterly reports and providing feedback to team members; and initiating regularly scheduled meetings.
Therapy participation	Some therapies require at least one parent to participate. Take turns if possible. Perhaps an older sibling can be part of it as well. As Dr. Karen Levine, a developmental psychologist, observes, "Parents become the best therapists in many ways. They're the ones who have the strongest connections to the children. And once parents are able to see how much they can connect and help their child develop, I think that's the most therapeutic moment for a parent who is grieving. . . . It's like, 'Oh, I can have an influence. I can help my child develop. I can bring my child out.'"[1]
Medication and supplements dosages: daily preparation	There may be quite a lot of medication and supplements to sort out and prepare for daily use. Someone has to plan, purchase, prepare, and oversee that the child has taken the daily dosage(s).
Meals: planning, purchasing, preparation	The recovery program may include dietary restrictions that require careful thought, planning, ordering/purchasing, preparation, and cleanup.
Other home and community activities	This involves arranging, transporting, and observing outside community activities, such as swimming, karate, and gymnastics, and providing instructors with information regarding ASD and techniques that work best for the child. This also involves maintaining a consistent and calm environment to keep the child modulated; helping to calm the child down and redirect her when she is activated or having tantrums; implementing routines in a consistent fashion; preparing the child for what activities or demands are next; preparing the child for any dramatic changes in routine; coming up with alternate plans and strategies at a moment's notice when required; and preparing the child's snacks, meals, drinks, medications, and vitamins ahead of time when she is away from home.

Roles / Responsibilities	Comments / Examples / Notes
Case file binder maintenance	The case file must be updated and ready for use at all times.
Financial books and records	This includes handling any insurance transactions and coordinating with doctors' staffs, insurance companies, etc.
Siblings: child care	While one parent is caring for the child with ASD, another family member or friend should be available to give some special one-on-one time to the siblings. This is a very stressful time for them—especially in the first year—when you are trying to cope, adjust, and apply therapies to the child with ASD.
Breadwinning	It is entirely likely that one or the other of the parents will have to devote himself or herself full-time to caring for the family if one child has autism.

While being the sole breadwinner can be daunting for a parent who once participated in a dual working family, remember that a paid job away from home is often easier and less stressful than taking on all of these other responsibilities. |

If You Have More than One Child on the Spectrum

Having one child on the spectrum can be difficult enough, but when you have two or three children on the spectrum, it can be downright overwhelming. One parent with four children (three of whom are on the spectrum) makes these excellent suggestions:

"Of course, you make a list for everything you want to do and should do for each child, but at the same time you admit to yourself that completing that list can be challenging. So you have to approach it like you do everything else in life—by prioritizing.

This is not to say that one child is more important than another, but each child's needs and priorities are different. So after you make your list of what you would ideally like to do for each child, go back and number the priorities on each child's list. Pick the top priorities on each child's list, and start there.

Eventually you will get to most everything on your list, but it may not be on the timetable you like. You can only do so much, so don't beat yourself up for not doing as much as your friends or other parents are doing for their children. Your situation is different, and therefore your approach to treatment will be different.

When setting up your team of doctors for each child, try to pick the same team for each of your children. This is important because not only is the doctor familiar with the family situation, but you can often bring two or three kids in on the same day, saving time and money."[2]

The Family Working as a Team

The same parent goes on to add:

"It is so important that you and your spouse work together closely as a team, especially when you have more than one child on the spectrum. Although I always considered myself the general contractor of my team, I have nightly discussions with my husband about everything. We look at everything together, talk about everything, and listen to one another's thoughts and opinions. We feel this is important to keeping our marriage strong. If something goes wrong or doesn't work, we do not blame one another for trying it, as we come to all decisions together as a team and support each other in the process."[3]

Naturally, the same organizational skills you put to work when you have one child on the spectrum are even more important when you have two or more children to care for.

IN A SENTENCE

> *Treat the assignment of roles in your family with the importance you would in staffing an organization, and try to share the load.*

living

The Journey Ahead

NO MATTER WHAT your mission is, you need to view handling your child's autism condition as potentially a lifelong situation. I won't sugarcoat the fact that it can be a long and arduous journey. Here are a few points that will make it much easier:

○ If there is any magic to be found along the way, it will appear because you have taken the essential steps of preparation: getting organized, having your supports in place (particularly from your spouse or partner and other family members), getting the respite you need, finding the right team members, and all the other elements elaborated in this book. The more you put these pieces into place, the easier your journey will be. Get going immediately with Early Intervention services (see page 115). This is crucial.

○ Incorporate some home-based therapies into your program—such as **Floortime** play—that will help you to become more engaged and connected with your child. You don't have to be formally trained in Floortime. You can purchase the book *Engaging Autism* by Stanley I. Greenspan and Serena Wieder[4] and order a parent training DVD from http://ICDL.com. (See Month 3, "Living: Getting to Know the Treatments Available," for more information on Floortime.) If your child has challenging behaviors, the book *Replays* by Karen Levine and Naomi Chedd teaches you how to use play to address specific issues in different settings and circumstances.[5]

○ Get your child involved in a play group, one that has typical peer models about the same age. Just be sure it is not overwhelming for your child. If you can't find one in your community, ask your local school district or Early Intervention Program for suggestions.

○ Find a friendly, socially interactive child in your neighborhood who is interested in having play dates at your house, and schedule them. You will have to learn how to facilitate social interactions between the two children and know when to sit back and let nature take its course and when to help your child when he is struggling. Again, learning Floortime will help enormously with this.

○ Look for another family in your neighborhood or community who has a child with special needs and try to create your own built-in support group to share experiences, resources, information, strategies, and maybe even play dates.

○ Hire a teen or preteen from your neighborhood to come in and play with your child while you get some things done around the house.

○ Find a support group that gives you what you need, whether it's emotional support, referrals, resources, strategies, or how-to's.

○ Take time for yourself. As difficult as it may be to find, even thirty minutes can be enough time to take a deep breath, clear your head, relax, and regroup.

○ Find time to be with your spouse or partner; do everything possible to keep your relationship alive.

○ Of course, having the financial means to hire professional therapists and respite care will help enormously, but *nothing will substitute for your being an active, involved parent.*

Plenty of parents who cannot afford therapists get training for themselves, become actively involved with their children's recovery program, and end up deeply connected to their child for life. They develop the deepest understanding and are often tremendously effective.

○ The most fundamentally valuable time you can spend is in playing with your child and getting involved in her internal world. By doing so, her perceptions and values will become more meaningful to you, and yours to her. You will learn to read amazingly subtle nuances accurately, and she will know it. This alone has therapeutic benefits beyond what many people would expect.

❍ This can be an incredibly difficult, challenging, and depressing journey. Keep your eye on the prize (accomplishing your mission with respect to your child and your family), and remember to notice the little gains along the way. They will be there and must be acknowledged to keep your morale up. That's one reason your child's evaluations are important—to notice the changes that might be subtle or fall below your notice.

❍ Pace yourself. Space your battles, and choose them carefully. Don't schedule a fight with your school district and your insurance company in the same week. Don't try to accomplish two major goals in the same day.

❍ Limit your workload; prioritize your tasks and responsibilities, and work as efficiently as possible. You will not have time for everything. Eliminate what is not essential so you have just a little less pressure.

IN A SENTENCE

Prioritize, choose your battles and your timing carefully, conserve and protect your sources of strength, and pace yourself.

FIRST-WEEK MILESTONE

The first week can be particularly traumatic and overwhelming for any parent of a newly diagnosed child. But this week, you have already taken tremendous steps forward. This week you have learned that:

- ○ AUTISM IS A WIDE AND COMPLEX SPECTRUM OF NEUROBIOLOGICAL DISORDERS THAT AFFECT EVERY CHILD DIFFERENTLY.
- ○ YOU SHOULD NOT DELAY IN GETTING YOUR CHILD THE INTENSIVE INTERVENTION HE NEEDS.
- ○ YOU NEED TO DEFINE THE MOUNTAIN YOU ARE GOING TO CLIMB.
- ○ THE FIRST STEP IN THE ROAD TO RECOVERY IS TO UNDERSTAND AND ACCEPT THE DIAGNOSIS.
- ○ YOU MUST CHOOSE YOUR TEAM CAREFULLY.
- ○ MULTI- OR INTERDISCIPLINARY TEAM EVALUATIONS ARE VITAL.
- ○ YOU MUST TAKE THE DRIVER'S SEAT.

But above everything else, take care of yourself!

learning

Diagnosis Is Not Enough

YOUR CHILD HAS now been diagnosed with an autism spectrum disorder. But what does "diagnosed" really mean?

The word "**diagnosis**" has two basic meanings:

1. The identification of a disease or condition by its outward signs and symptoms
2. The analysis of the underlying causes for a disease or condition

At the present time, when the word "diagnosis" is used in connection with autism, we are referring to its first meaning. The etiology or causes of the disorder are suspected but not confirmed.

For this reason, when a child is diagnosed with the disorder, you cannot directly treat that condition since *"autism" is merely a label for a collection of symptoms of unknown causes.*

At some point in the future, it may well turn out that autism will be found to have a single cause that can be simply and directly treated. But until that day arrives, we have to deal with the fact that autism is a disorder of unknown causes with myriad manifestations, phenomena, and severities, all of which differ from child to child.

Comorbid Disorders

As discussed earlier, a comorbid disorder is defined as a medical condition a patient may have while also having some other primary disease or disorder.

Many professionals believe that the gastrointestinal disturbances, viral infections, seizures, and food allergies experienced by a child with ASD are *coincidental* and not central to the disorder.

Yet it is also true that many children with ASD have some of these "comorbid disorders" and, when these comorbidities are reduced through various forms of medical treatment, many of the symptoms can diminish significantly. Consequently, these children feel better and are in much better condition to participate in their therapeutic services and educational program. The gains can be huge.[1]

So are we really to believe this is a coincidence?

In fact, the model of autism as a genetic, brain-based disorder is maturing to encompass new discoveries about how body system dysfunctions contribute to brain dysfunction and together produce autism behaviors.[2] But regardless of whether or not all these various comorbid disorders are specifically part of autism per se, they clearly negatively affect the child and need to be reduced in order to treat autism.

Thus, what we have to treat are the individual issues or manifestations of the autism spectrum disorder itself—per the diagnostic criteria—and any comorbid disorders, including gastrointestinal disturbances, viral infections, seizures, food allergies, and so forth.

A Basic Treatment Development Process

So how does one figure out what to treat? Treatments are often based upon:

1. Analyzing a manifestation of the disorder
2. Looking for the likely trigger(s) of that event and any discoverable antecedent or preceding factors

3. Creating a hypothesis for why it is happening
4. Devising a way to test the hypothesis
   ○ When choosing a way to test the hypothesis, weigh the pros and cons of the test, including technical feasibility, duration, level of invasiveness, cost, insurance coverage, the doctor's willingness to prescribe, availability, prospective gain, and side effects.
   ○ If multiple tests are required, determine the proper sequence.
5. Conducting the test
6. Evaluating the outcome from the test

After completing these six steps, begin again with the first step, reanalyzing the manifestation in light of what is now known, and continue with steps 2 through 6, digging deeper and moving toward a more basic cause.

This is the process a good practitioner will use (often called a functional assessment); however, as the parent, you can also apply it in dealing with daily life problems that arise. For example, you see that your child throws tantrums frequently while out with you on errands:

1. **Analyze the manifestation.**	Your son becomes very cranky and throws a tantrum whenever you take him shopping.
2. **Look for likely trigger(s) and any discoverable antecedents.**	You notice this happens in only those stores that are large, crowded, and noisy and have lots of activity. He seems to do fine in smaller, less busy shops.
3. **Create a hypothesis for why it is happening.**	He gets triggered by large crowds, overwhelming activity, and loud noises.
4. **Devise a way to test the hypothesis.**	You decide to avoid these stores for a few weeks and see if tantrums continue when going into smaller stores with fewer crowds, lower activity, and less noise. You make sure he is fed and well rested before going out.
5. **Conduct the test devised in step 4.**	You avoid taking him to these types of stores for three weeks. You document the results weekly.
6. **Evaluate the outcome.**	He throws tantrums only twice while on errands with you. Once is in a large library, once in an auto parts store.

Now repeat the process:

1. Analyze the manifestation.	Tantrum levels were significantly reduced.
	The two instances occurred in the library (large room; high ceilings with fans; very long, high rows of bookshelves; fluorescent lighting; quiet environment) and in the auto parts store (not very large or crowded; long, low rows of parts; fluorescent lighting).
2. Look for the likely trigger(s).	On both occasions of the last two tantrums, the child was in a space with very long rows of shelving and fluorescent lighting.
	There were no tantrums while in small stores even when crowded, and some had typical fluorescent lights.
	The child is not bothered by fluorescent lights at school or in very small stores.
3. Create a hypothesis for why it is happening.	The child is triggered by a combination of aisles with long shelving and fluorescent lighting.
4. Devise a way to test the hypothesis.	You try to avoid all stores and other institutional spaces with aisles that have long shelving and fluorescent lighting.
5. Conduct the test devised in step 4.	You avoid such stores and spaces for three weeks, documenting the results weekly.
6. Evaluate the outcome.	No tantrums occur, except one time when you take the child into a very large furniture store, which was unavoidable. The theory is tentatively confirmed: the child is triggered by the combined presence of long shelving aisles and fluorescent lighting.

Certainly we did not get to the underlying cause in the example given above, and the test devised in step 4 provided only a temporary fix. We don't yet know why this type of experience triggers the child; however, we do know some of the physical and environmental triggers that affect him. Since the child can't go on forever avoiding long shelving aisles and fluorescent lighting, treatment will be needed for any long-term gain.

In simplified form, this is the general procedure for "peeling the onion"— that is, tracing effects back to causes and secondary causes back to more fundamental causes. Note that in this example, a "workable" cause was reached.

The analogy of "peeling an onion" to remove imperfections is appropriate because:

○ onions often have multiple imperfections ("issues")
○ some imperfections are more severe than others and so call one's attention more than others (prioritization)
○ as you peel, you really don't know at what level the last of the imperfections will disappear. Indeed, the imperfection may appear to get much worse the closer you get to it and will lessen only after you reach it (child appears to get worse before she gets better).

But alas, the analogy is not perfect. Onion imperfections usually stand alone; you rarely have to remove a "secondary" imperfection first before you can remove a "primary" one. Unlike onion imperfections, ASD issues often have interdependencies, requiring you to deal with one before you can even start to address another.

Here is an example: A child has severe tantrums and no language or social skills. Speech therapy is not working because the child is so upset that nothing is being accomplished and it's difficult to engage the child in play therapy. The therapy sessions are useless.

The child is having severe discomfort from gastrointestinal problems and constantly throwing himself against others or on furniture over and over again. Once the gastrointestinal problems subside through treatment, the child is much calmer and focused and able to attend to therapy sessions. The child begins to develop language skills, and the child is more engaged in social interactive play.

IN A SENTENCE

In the world of ASD, a diagnosis is really a statement of symptoms; you and your team have to work backwards from effects to causes in a repeating, cyclically progressive fashion.

living

Understanding Your Child's Individual Profile

THERE IS A common tendency among clinical practitioners to fit every child into a standard program of one type or another. This may be because the practitioner believes:

○ all children with autism should have a certain therapeutic or educational approach, and/or
○ children with the same diagnosis and even similar symptoms share similar underlying neurobiology and process information in a similar way

In fact, each child's underlying neurobiology, developmental patterns, and responses to environmental stimuli are often vastly different. Thus, if one operates on a "one size fits all" basis, a lot of potential gain is going to be missed.

Your child's **individual profile** is a thorough analysis of the unique characteristics and interests he or she demonstrates in the key developmental and biological domains (categories). This approach comes from leading child psychiatrist Stanley I. Greenspan.

Without having an in-depth individual profile, it is difficult to devise a truly comprehensive, effective treatment program for a child. Unfortunately, at this time, few clinicians understand how to profile children this extensively.

The Scope of an Individual Profile

The following reveals how you create an individual profile for a child.[3]

1. Social interaction
   - Does the child want to be with other children or adults? Is she able to indicate interests in appropriate ways?
   - In what situations does the child approach people or avoid them?
   - Does the child seem attached to parents or other caregivers?
   - Is the child more engaged with some people than with others?
   - Does the child read and understand subtle social cues and rules?
2. Communication
   - How well does the child understand and use nonverbal communication, such as gestures and facial expressions?
   - How much language does the child understand or use?
   - Is the child able to articulate words intelligibly?
   - Is the child engaging in sustained back-and-forth communication or using language or gestures only to make one-way demands?
   - Do the child's words, sounds, or gestures have meaning?
3. Emotional regulation
   - How well does the child regulate his emotions and moods?
   - Is the child generally happy and calm? Agitated and irritated? Anxious? Depressed?
   - Does the child swing rapidly from one emotion to another?
   - What triggers the emotional changes?
   - Does the child understand the emotions of others?
4. Sensory processing
   - How well does the child understand and use what she hears, sees, tastes, smells, and feels?
   - Does she learn better by seeing rather than by hearing? Or better by hearing (etc.)?
   - Does she touch objects to learn about them?

5. Sensory modulation
   - ○ Is the child over- or under-reactive to sounds, light, touch, movement, or other sensations?
   - ○ Is the child constantly seeking or avoiding certain situations?
6. Auditory processing and language
   - ○ When you ask a question, does the child pause or stall? How many times do you need to repeat it? Does the child understand only a portion of what you say? Does she understand the meaning of what you are saying?
7. Visual-spatial processing
   - ○ Body awareness: How aware is the child of his own sensations and movements?
   - ○ Body location: How well and in what ways does the child understand the parts of his body in relationship to each other? What is his sense of where his body is in the general environment?
   - ○ Relationship of objects to self, other objects, and other people: If you hide an object someplace obvious, can your child find it?
   - ○ Spatial relationships: How is the child's understanding of the difference between his moving through space and space itself changing?
   - ○ Visual-logical reasoning: How well does the child use logical thinking to solve problems and plan actions?
8. Representational thought
   - ○ How well does the child represent his thoughts, ideas, and desires through words, sounds, pictures, etc.?
9. Motor skills, planning, and sequencing
   - ○ How well can the child use her hands?
   - ○ Does the child have mouth control needed to eat and speak?
   - ○ How does she use larger muscles to walk, run, and climb?
   - ○ Does the child have trouble planning and carrying out complex sequences of action, like putting on shoes or washing and drying hands?
   - ○ Is the child able to imitate the actions of others?
10. Cognitive
    - ○ How easy is it for the child to learn?
    - ○ Can the child think and solve problems with logic and creativity?
    - ○ Does the child think only in concrete terms, or is he able to use abstract ideas and engage in symbolic play?
    - ○ Can the child understand and expand on the ideas of others?

11. Attention
    - ○ Does the child pay attention to the people and events around her?
    - ○ How hard is it to get and keep the child's attention?
    - ○ Can the child focus on activities she chooses? On activities initiated by others?
    - ○ Is the child easily distracted by sights and sounds in the environment?
12. Biological
    - ○ What is the state of the child's immune system, gastrointestinal system, nutrition, metabolic functions, and neurological system?
    - ○ Does the child have any other symptoms of biological disorders?

Mark Freilich, MD, a developmental pediatrician with Total Kids Developmental Pediatric Resources in New York, says it is important to look at not only each child individually but also the family dynamics, home environment, and classroom setting. Whenever he develops an individual profile for a child, he likes to visit the family in the home environment and the child in the classroom setting to observe the following:

1. Organization of the home and classroom; established routines and rituals:
   - ○ Is this a home or school that is disorganized and cluttered?
   - ○ Is it too organized?
   - ○ Is it a child-friendly home or classroom?
   - ○ Is the environment as chaotic as the child's inner workings?
   - ○ How much available space is there for the child to play?
   - ○ How much flexibility is there within the structure of the home or classroom?
   - ○ Does the family or classroom have routines or rituals?
   - ○ Are they predictable or, perhaps, too predictable?
2. Interactions and relationships with siblings and parents and with peers and teacher(s):
   - ○ Are the siblings, parents, peers, and teachers connected with the child?
   - ○ Are their relationships close?
   - ○ What is the quality and frequency of the interactions?
   - ○ What activities do they enjoy?
   - ○ Are the social interactions in the classroom facilitated by a trained professional? Only during classroom time or also during lunch, recess, library, and gym?

○ Does the child have a one-on-one paraprofessional or aide to facilitate with social interactions?

○ Do the parents roll up their sleeves and get down on the floor to interact with the child, or are they so busy planning and coordinating the child's treatment plan and therapies that they have no time left?

○ Are they possibly neglecting themselves physically or emotionally? Or are they taking the time to revitalize themselves?

3. Effects of child's regulatory and sensory systems on behavior:

○ How do the child's regulatory and sensory systems affect positive and negative behavior?

○ What approach do the parents and teachers use to address behavior? What are the outcomes?

○ Do the parents and teachers understand the etiology of the child's behavior and what that means?

○ Do the parents understand why, when, and how the child's body needs to be aroused or calmed?

○ Are there relatives or extended family members who are willing to pitch in and help? If not, are there any friends, neighbors, or school personnel you can recruit? Do they understand the situation and know how to interact with the child?

○ Is everyone on the same page with regards to goals and approaches?

But isn't this an awful lot of work? You bet it is.

Is it all necessary? It is hard to overstate the value of a thorough, accurate profile, since it is upon this analysis that all treatments and therapies will be based.

"Know your child" means knowing at *a very detailed* level those areas you will treat with therapies. But knowing your child also means knowing his strengths so a program can be designed *to treat the deficits by capitalizing on these strengths.*

For example, in the domain of communication, the profile may reveal that your child has a deficit in auditory (listening, hearing) processing skills but is a very strong visual learner. Let us say you want to explain to your child what the schedule will be for the day: "First we go to the doctor, then the playground; then we have lunch, and then naptime."

Instead of just trying (and perhaps failing) to get this across to your child with just words, you might use a visual display on your refrigerator laying out a sequence of pictures that relate to each activity:

- First point to a person with a white coat and stethoscope and say, "First, doctor."
- Next point to the picture of swing set and slide and say, "Then, playground."
- Then point to a picture of food: "Then, lunch."
- And then point to a picture of a child sleeping in bed and say, "And then, naptime."

You can show the child all four pictures at once and bring along each of the pictures to reinforce what is coming next, so the child knows what to expect and won't become dysregulated. In this way, you are using visual cues that are easy for him to grasp to reinforce auditory information, which can be much more difficult for the child to comprehend. For a young child, this is also a good way to teach the meaning of words.

I used to bring a camera with me wherever we went so I could take photos of doctors, therapists, activities, stores, parks, and playgrounds because my daughter had great difficulty understanding generic symbols or illustrations. The photos had to be specific to her frame of reference.

Without having a sufficiently detailed individual profile, like the one described above, you or a clinician might not have arrived at this simple but highly effective treatment for your child's auditory or language processing deficiency.

In a similar way, this kind of information will be invaluable when choosing:

- what kind of classroom and educational settings would work well
- what kind of educational therapies could be used for each developmental challenge and which should be avoided
- what types of supports may be needed in the classroom
- what style(s) of teaching may be most effective
- how to restructure your home environment and daily routine so it provides continuous support for the child's sensory or regulatory systems and reduces negative behaviors
- what kind of adjustments in the family dynamics will provide greater positive impact on the child and help to stabilize his emotional regulation
- how to incorporate the child's interests and strengths into daily activities and therapies and build on his developmental skills
- how to structure visits to the grocery store, playground, or anywhere in the community without experiencing tantrums
- strategies you can use when the child becomes dysregulated

Finding the Right Professional to Do This Profile

Finding the right professional to create this profile won't be easy, and chances are, it won't be inexpensive either. You may have to search far and wide, but it is well worth the time you take, and it will certainly be worth the investment you make. Look for a trained professional who has a broad perspective, someone who will look at the child and the family (ideally in their own natural environment at school, at home, or in the community)—someone who can go beyond the traditional (and arbitrary) boundaries between disciplines. The most likely candidate will be a developmental pediatrician, because he or she can bridge the medical gap you will have if you choose a professional from another discipline. But very few developmental pediatricians have their practice set up to make visits to your home, school, or community. Ideally this professional will visit the family's home and the child's school, meet with other team members on the phone or in person, and help the family put together a team of physicians, clinicians, and educators. He or she is a rare find! This could also be a psychologist, social worker, occupational therapist, or any other professional who is willing to provide case management support for you—someone who has an integrative approach and is open minded, and also willing to go the distance.

I strongly recommend this book for understanding and developing your child's individual profile: *The Child with Special Needs: Encouraging Intellectual and Emotional Growth*, by Stanley I. Greenspan and Serena Wieder with Robin Simons (Reading, MA: Addison-Wesley, 1998).

IN A SENTENCE

> *A comprehensive individual profile puts you in the position of really knowing your child and getting the kind of integrated treatment program that will truly meet his or her needs.*

Autism's Underlying Biomedical Factors

IN RECENT YEARS, most of the research on autism has been directed toward supporting the theory that autism is a genetic disorder. It is clear that genetics does play a role and is an important predisposing factor. However, there are several important reasons why allowing ASD to be thought of solely as a genetic disorder is doing a grave disservice to our children and to ourselves.

ASD Cannot Be Just a Genetic Disorder

The word "epidemic" means an outbreak of a disease in a given population that substantially exceeds expectations for an observed period of time. The increase in new cases of ASD over the last ten years has jumped from 3 in 10,000 to 1 in 150. This is not only unexpected but nothing short of staggering.

It is also well worth repeating here what has been noted by other researchers: *There is no such thing as a "genetic epidemic."* That is to say, it is impossible for there to be a rapid outbreak of a disease or disorder—such as we've seen with ASD—if it were passed only by inheritance. It is physically impossible for any outbreak to move with this speed if it depended solely upon the passing of genes to one's offspring.

A variety of arguments has been advanced to explain away this sudden increase of autism cases, most related to the claim it was the loosening of the DSM-IV criteria for what constitutes autism. A number of studies have looked into this question, including one commissioned by the California legislature and conducted by the University of California's Medical Investigation of Neurodevelopmental Disorders. The final conclusion of this multiyear study released in 2002 was that it was not just a matter of the redefinition of the disorder; the 210 percent increase in the number of cases between 1987 and 1998 was quite real.[1]

Two years later, in 2004, the Centers for Disease Control and Prevention determined that the current rate of ASD occurrence in the United States had reached 1 in 166, and that developmental disorders and/or behavioral problems in children were occurring at an even higher rate: 1 in 6.[2]

More recently, a 2006 study in Britain reported ASD occurrences at a rate of 1 in 86 in the South Thames region. There are also increases in Iceland, Sweden, Finland, Denmark, Canada, Australia, and Japan, as reported in their various professional journals.

If an outbreak of influenza had reached the level of incidence that autism did even eight years ago, an epidemic—even a pandemic—would have been declared long ago.

> For a very competent review of the various arguments and rebuttals, see Bryan Jepson, "The Autism Epidemic," chapter 4 in *Changing the Course of Autism* (Boulder, CO: Sentient Publications, 2007).

The Triggers Are External, Not Genetic

Genetic predisposition can increase risk for any disease or disorder—there is little disagreement about that. There may well be a trend in the general population toward the development of predisposing genetic factors. But this increase cannot possibly exceed the rate of population increase—which is exactly what is happening with the growth of ASD cases.

That is to say, even if there were a gradual general weakening of the genetic constitution of Americans, something else must be acting on those weakened bodies to manifest the various behaviors and impairments in development we are calling "autism" or "autism spectrum disorders."

Along the trail of investigating this "something else," the following becomes clear:

○ Many children with ASD are physically ill.

○ Many children with ASD, once specifically tested, are found to have compromised immune systems, abnormal detoxification systems, and imbalanced gastrointestinal systems.

○ Evidence shows that families of children with autism also have higher rates of autoimmune disease. This suggests that children with autism may have a genetic predisposition for immune system weakness. Indeed, a 2006 study by the University of California's Medical Investigation of Neurodevelopmental Disorders provides a strong argument for autism's immunological basis.[3]

○ Because of their much higher incidence of illness, children with ASD have a higher usage rate of antibiotics and other medicines. Combined with increasing levels of toxins in the general environment—taken in through air, water, foods, mother's milk, etc.—it is easy to see how young, developing immune systems can become easily overwhelmed.

For example, there is clear evidence that the beneficial bacteria found in the gastrointestinal (GI) tract are killed off rapidly by exposure to a wide variety of antibiotics and environmental toxins. With their loss, harmful bacteria and fungi are free to multiply and cause damage to the mucosal lining, which protects the intestinal walls. The weakened defenses in the GI tract permit the entrance into the bloodstream of foreign or incompletely digested substances that set off immune responses (allergies) or cause other complex physical disorders.

Many children with ASD have abnormal detoxification systems. This impairment or disabling of the system has been clearly associated with exposures to mercury—usually in the easy absorbed form of ethyl- or methyl-mercury. These highly toxic substances come from a variety of sources in the environment including some vaccination preparations that use these chemicals as a preservative.

The question of mercury exposure is especially important because there are extraordinarily close parallels between the consequences of mercury poisoning and the signs and symptoms of autism. These parallels are quite dramatic across a wide range of categories: psychological phenomena, sensory abnormalities, speech and language deficits, motor disorders, cognitive impairments, unusual behaviors, physical body disorders, biochemistry disruption, immune system dysfunction, central nervous system pathology, neurochemistry, and neurophysiology. Indeed, the evidence against mercury is quite damning.[4] Treatment through a large variety of methods can yield good results in mitigating impairments in behavior and development commonly associated with ASD.[5]

So what is this all telling us?

Dr. Jepson calls this the "**multiple hit hypothesis**": "The most likely scenario for the development of this disease involves a series of negative responses to the environment in a baby who is at risk genetically."[6]

IN A SENTENCE

ASD is probably best viewed as a disorder with a multiplicity of causes that, when combined, weaken your child's bodily systems in predictable ways.

living

Finding the Right Biomedical Specialist

WHAT I SAID before is undeniably true: every child's diagnosis is different. That is, signs, symptoms, and degree of severity vary widely. But what all these children have in common are physical systems in varying states of dysfunction. In all probability, your child will begin the recovery process as his or her system abnormalities are skillfully addressed.

But the task of finding the right biomedical specialist (a health care professional who employs biological and physiological healing methods in the treatment of symptoms and diseases) poses a number of difficulties:

- ○ The idea that autism is a biomedical condition with an environmental cause is relatively new—and still the subject of research.
- ○ Since autism is still officially classified as a psychiatric disorder, it is considered a mental health disorder and not a medical disease.
- ○ Specialists in the field of autism are just beginning to accept the evidence of environmental causation.

- Because children with ASD manifest dysfunctions or abnormalities across multiple bodily systems, integrating many medical disciplines and treatment approaches is necessary for a successful recovery program.
- Those doctors who do work to correct multiple biological system failures are few and far between. Those who are truly knowledgeable and experienced with this integrated approach are even fewer.
- Virtually all treatments are still experimental.
- Some of the best results have been obtained using approaches and therapies that have only slight or no acceptance in the traditional medical community.

The Autism Research Institute (ARI), founded by the late Dr. Bernard Rimland in 1967, is "a non-profit research, resource, and referral organization. . . . Since 1995, ARI has convened recurring meetings for carefully selected physicians, researchers, and scientists committed to finding effective treatments for autism. Their work has become known as Defeat Autism Now!"[7] This initiative has expanded considerably since that time and has become the focal point for health care practitioners seeking to find biomedical treatments for autism. These practitioners span a wide range of disciplines including traditional medical doctors, nutritionists, chiropractors, doctors of naturopathic medicine, osteopaths, registered nurses, and other specialists, all of whom subscribe to this philosophy.

While many avoid developing a "one size fits all" protocol, Defeat Autism Now! practitioners in general do engage in treatments that address the biomedical areas mentioned earlier:

- food sensitivities, diet, and nutrition
- immune system repair
- gastrointestinal system repair
- general, integrated biological systems support

An outline of the recommended practices can be found on the ARI website.[8]

All of these treatments fall somewhere on the "evidence-based treatments" scale discussed in Day 4. The scientific foundations for these methods are well documented and can be found on the ARI web page *Scientific Foundations of a Defeat Autism Now! Protocol*: http://autism.com/dan/scientificfoundations.htm.

In general, Defeat Autism Now! practitioners endorse a philosophy that includes the following ideas:

1. Autism encompasses a spectrum of disorders with multiple provoking stressors and multiple possible susceptibilities.
2. There is no fixed protocol for treating autism because the approach is based on paying careful attention to the unique symptoms, history, examinations, and data of each child.
3. Autism and related problems reflect dysfunction of the neural, metabolic, immune, and/or digestive systems in individuals genetically predisposed to such problems as sub-optimal nutrition, food intolerances, microbial overgrowth, metabolic abnormalities, immune dysregulation, and reduced ability to eliminate toxins.
4. Appropriate treatment involves identifying and alleviating the problems causing symptoms in a particular individual, rather than attempting to suppress symptoms through the use of psychoactive drugs.
5. Practitioners should conduct collaborative conversations with an abiding respect for the intelligence and intuition of parents and their children.
6. Practitioners should involve families as full participants in the search for answers and recognize that the child is often listening, even when he or she appears inattentive.
7. There are no one-size-fits-all strategies, so practitioners use a broad range of diagnostic and treatment methods that are appropriate to each patient.
8. Practitioners should look for opportunities to collaborate with our educational, behavioral, physical, and speech therapists and colleagues.[9]

When seeking medical advice, diagnosis, and treatment for matters related to nutrition and possible effects on your child of exposures to environmental toxins, be sure to carefully examine the physician's education and experience in specifically these areas. Both subjects require *considerable* expertise and are often insufficiently addressed in medical schools. The doctors you choose should demonstrate strong personal interest in these topics and should have ambitiously pursued continuing education in these areas of knowledge.

Finding Defeat Autism Now! Practitioners Near You

The Autism Research Institute maintains an online registry by state of clinicians who implement the Defeat Autism Now! methods. Go to http://www.autism.com/dan/danusdis.htm, or search on "Defeat Autism Now! Clinician Registry."

You can also find physicians in your area who practice integrated medicine by searching the American College for Advancement in Medicine (ACAM) website: http://www.acamnet.org.

I would not just select any practitioner from either of these two lists. Be sure to examine their credentials, expertise, and reputation, as you would any medical professional. The best way to make contact with top pros in the field and connect with other involved parents is by attending one of the regularly scheduled ARI conferences. Go to http://www.defeatautismnow.com, or search on "Defeat Autism Now! Conference."

The Parent's Role in Integrated Medicine

The strengths of integrative medicine and Defeat Autism Now! treatments lie in:

1. Viewing the patient and his or her body as a composite of interacting systems and influences
2. Performing comprehensive examination, testing, and evaluation
3. Selecting treatments based on 1 and 2 above and on state-of-the-art treatments (which treatments are available and their level of proven safety and effectiveness per the evidence-based treatment scale)
4. Coordinating and balancing the implementation of the treatments with each other so they do not conflict but maximally support one another

As the team leader, you should make every effort to educate yourself on these methods. *But do not get drawn into dabbling with treatments or attempting to create a treatment program on your own.* Do not get into a "try this, try that" mode; the likelihood of failure or doing harm is high without comprehensive knowledge and experience. You need the guidance of a trained professional!

On the other hand, your role of providing oversight and coordination will be of great importance because, generally at this time, the Defeat Autism Now! biomedical approaches are not particularly well integrated with the other nonmedical therapies—an issue we shall examine in more detail later.

IN A SENTENCE

When proper functionality is restored to the body's key systems, the signs, symptoms, and severity of ASD can diminish.

WEEK **4**

learning

Early Intervention

IN DAY 2, you learned about Early Intervention (EI)—the statewide, federally funded program for infants and toddlers with disabilities and their families—and how vital it is to get your child enrolled immediately at the first sign of developmental delay, even before a diagnosis is made.

Now let's take a closer look at Early Intervention, its services, and how it is structured.

Introducing IDEA

In 1975 the U.S. Congress passed the Individuals with Disabilities Education Act (IDEA), which established federal standards for the provision of special education services to children with disabilities. Until that time, public schools either excluded these children or segregated them into separate facilities with little or no appropriate instruction or assistance.

IDEA contains many initiatives, but three key programs critical to the expansion and improvement of services to children with disabilities are:

○ Part B of IDEA, Assistance for Education of All Children with Disabilities, which governs services provided by public school districts to children from ages three to twenty-one

○ Part C of IDEA, The Program for Infants and Toddlers with Disabilities, which governs services provided by the Early Intervention Program to children from birth to age three (and in some states through age five)

○ Part D of IDEA, National Activities, which "authorizes a variety of activities to help states and local communities facilitate systemic change toward improvement and positive results for children, youth and families, from birth through 21. These activities include research, training and professional development, parent training and information centers, demonstration and outreach projects, state improvement projects, dissemination, technical assistance and technology applications. Often called 'discretionary projects,' these are supported by competitive federal grants, cooperative agreements or contracts by the U.S. Department of Education."[1]

In this book, we will focus on Part B and Part C of IDEA. Part B will be discussed in Month 2, "Learning: Part I: Know Your Rights" (page 123).

What Is Early Intervention?

IDEA Part C services are provided to infants and toddlers from birth to age three (and in some states through age five) with disabilities, as well as their families. The goal of Early Intervention (EI) is to provide quality, early support services to enhance the capacity of families to meet the developmental needs of children within the specified ages who have delays and disabilities.

Each state submits to the federal government an application on a yearly basis for funding an EI program of coordinated and comprehensive services. Although it is not mandatory, all states participate in this program. The governor of each state or jurisdiction appoints a lead agency within the state to administer the program; in many states it is the Department of Health or the Department of Education. Each state develops its own criteria for eligibility within the federal IDEA parameters.

There is an EI program in every county of every state. The services provided vary from state to state; however, in general they will provide:

- screening
- evaluation and assessment
- service coordination
- family training, counseling, and home visits
- speech, occupational, and physical therapies
- psychological, vision, and audiology services
- social work services
- assistive technology
- nursing services
- nutritional counseling
- transportation
- other services

Initially, these services were provided only in center-based facilities. Now, however, Early Intervention services are provided in the child's home or community-based environments.

Early Intervention services are

"designed to meet the developmental needs of each eligible child and the needs of the family related to enhancing the child's development. Services are:

- Selected in collaboration with the parents
- Provided in accordance with an **Individualized Family Service Plan (IFSP)**, under public supervision, and by qualified personnel (as defined in Sec. 303.21)
- Provided at no cost, unless, subject to Sec. 303.520(b)(3), Federal or State law provides for a system of payments by families, including a schedule of sliding fees
- Provided in natural environments, including the home and community settings in which children without disabilities participate; and they must meet the standards of the State."[2]

Who Is Eligible for Early Intervention?

Each state must provide services to children with significant developmental delay or to those who have a diagnosed mental or physical condition (such as autism, Down syndrome, spina bifida, blindness, deafness, etc.) that has a high probability of resulting in a developmental delay.

Eligibility criteria are different in every state but may be based upon the level of delay in one or more of the following developmental areas:

○ adaptive skills—self-help, such as dressing or feeding
○ cognitive skills—thinking, including the ability to absorb, process, and understand information
○ communicative skills—receptive and expressive language, including understanding what is being said, following directions, and making needs known
○ physical skills—gross motor, fine motor, vision and hearing, motor planning, and sensory integration (the ability of the central nervous system to receive, process, and learn from sensations, such as touch, movement, sight, sound, smell, and the pull of gravity, in order to develop skills)
○ social / emotional skills—interacting with other children, adults, and the environment[3]

At the discretion of each individual state, they may also provide services to children who are considered at risk for developmental and learning delays because of situations in the child's environment (lack of adequate parenting, dangerous home environment, etc). Currently, only seven states offer services to at-risk children.

See the NECTAC website for links to each state's rules, regulations, and policies: http://www.nectac.org/partc/statepolicies.asp.

Early Intervention Program Costs

Federal law requires that the following services be provided at public expense to children and families who are eligible:

○ child find/referral
○ assessment
○ IFSP development and review
○ procedural safeguards (family rights)
○ service coordination

Depending upon the state in which the family resides, the family may have to assume some, all, or none of the costs for other EI services, depending upon the resources available and the parents' ability to pay. Medicaid, private health insurance, and state-funded health insurance can sometimes be accessed as payment sources. (For more information about insurance, see Month 2, "Learning, Part II: Know Your Insurance.")

IN A SENTENCE

Become knowledgeable about Early Intervention and what it has to offer.

living

How to Access Early Intervention Services

ANYBODY CAN PICK up the telephone and make a referral for a child to receive services: a physician, parent, grandparent, teacher, friend, etc. As long as the parent or guardian grants permission for the child to receive services, the process can begin.

The process is quite simple:

1. To find out how to contact and make a referral to Early Intervention in your state, visit the National Dissemination Center for Children with Disabilities (NICHCY) website: http://www.nichcy.org/states.htm.
2. Once a referral is made, the Early Intervention Program collects information as to the reason for the referral and the results of any screening tests or assessments.
3. A service coordinator is assigned, and the child's record is established.
4. The service coordinator contacts the family to gather basic information about the child, the family, and the concerns;

provide basic information about the program; and determine the family's interest in scheduling an initial visit.

5. The service coordinator schedules a visit with the family and determines the need to conduct screening.

6. The service coordinator meets with the family and conducts a screening, if appropriate, then explains the program and determines with the family if they wish to have their child evaluated and assessed.

7. If they do, the service coordinator explains their rights, obtains written parent consent for evaluation and assessment, and provides prior notice for the evaluation.

8. The service coordinator gathers information about the child, discusses routines and activities for the child and family, identifies parental concerns and priorities, and identifies family resources to assist in addressing these priorities and concerns.

9. The service coordinator will request existing developmental and medical information.

10. The service coordinator then determines if the child is automatically eligible, based on a diagnosed condition. She will also determine if an evaluation and assessment are needed based on the child's needs in each of the developmental domains. She will determine the composition of the evaluation and assessment team, schedule a date and time convenient with the family, provide prior written notice, provide an explanation of their rights, and prepare the family for the evaluation and assessment.

Neither the evaluation nor the assessment provides a diagnosis; both are used to identify the needs and strengths of the child who is at risk for developmental delays or disorders, as well as the needs and strengths of the family. They may include both formal and informal procedures to evaluate the child's ability in all areas of development, including cognitive, language, motor, social, emotional, behavioral, and self-help skills.

Often the team of professionals, which may include an educator, social worker, nurse, speech-language pathologist, and occupational and/or physical therapist, will perform the evaluation and assessment in your home.

An evaluation and assessment will help to determine if your child is eligible for services and, if so, which services can best meet his needs and be provided by your local Early Intervention program. Keep in mind that this evaluation or assessment is an adjunct and not a substitute for (or equivalent to) an evaluation or assessment conducted by a developmental pediatrician or other developmental professional described in previous chapters.

The service coordinator's role is described in the National Early Childhood Technical Assistance Center's NECTAC Notes issue on service coordination caseloads (http://www.nectac.org/~pdfs/pubs/nnotes8.pdf). See the section "Service Coordination Under the IDEA Regulations for Part C."

11. The team, including the family, conducts the evaluation and assessment and then determines eligibility.

12. If your child is eligible for EI services, an Individualized Family Service Plan (IFSP) meeting is scheduled. The service coordinator will prepare the family for this meeting.

13. The IFSP team meets to develop the IFSP, which includes:
    - reviewing parents' concerns and priorities
    - establishing measurable outcome goals
    - identifying strategies
    - identifying necessary services to support achieving the outcome goals and the timeline for beginning services
    - how the services will be provided. (Normally they will be delivered in the child's natural environment—at home or in the community.)

    Keep in mind, as parents you are an integral part of the IFSP team, and the team determines the number of hours of services per week based on the defined outcomes.

14. The service coordinator obtains the parents' written consent for IFSP services, and a date is scheduled to begin delivery of services.[4]

Getting the Most Out of Your Local Early Intervention Program

The quality of each EI Program and service is highly variable. Every state, county, and local EI Program is different. The training of each service coordinator, program therapist, and clinician varies, and the quality of the service largely depends upon their skill sets, their levels of experience, and their personalities.

Sometimes it is hard to find out what your local EI Program offers until you ask. Much depends upon your particular EI coordinator and how well he or she informs you of what is available.

There are several things you should do to ensure you receive all the services you are due:

1. Ask lots of questions of your EI service coordinator.
2. Learn your rights.
3. Talk to other families who are also receiving services from your local EI Program. Find out what they know about the program and what is offered; compare notes.
4. Be sure to inquire about:
   - speech and language therapy
   - occupational and physical therapy
   - oromotor therapy (for children with feeding problems)
   - getting the help of a social worker or family therapist
   - support and play groups, and other community activities
   - respite
   - referrals for developmental specialists (some EIPs contract with developmental pediatricians or other developmental specialists)

   Don't wait to be offered these services; unless you ask, they may not be offered to you!
5. Keep in mind: EI personnel are usually well-intentioned individuals; however, their program often has limited funds. As service access providers, they are often caught between wanting to help as much as they can and having to stretch federal monies as far as possible. It helps to understand the forces at work from their side of the table, but you still need to advocate for what your child needs.

   Each state and county permit service coordinators different latitudes of permission to make recommendations or *even to mention what services might be available* to the child and family. So ask for what you need; do not wait for it to be offered to you.

   In some states, coordinators are not allowed to even mention the word "autism"—only "developmental delays." The sole basis of their discussions with you is a strict interpretation of the language of their state's criteria.
6. From other parents in your local EI program, find out:
   - who are the program clinicians you really should get in to see and who you should avoid
   - what their experience has been navigating the local EI program
   - what are the available resources

Ask your service coordinator to introduce you to an experienced parent who can show you the ropes.

7. Contact your statewide parent training and information center. State parent centers provide free services to families of children with disabilities. To find the center in your state, go to the Parent Center Directory of the Technical Assistance ALLIANCE for Parent Centers (the ALLIANCE): http://www.taalliance.org/ptidirectory/pti_list.pdf.

Another important service your EI coordinator will provide is helping you make the transition from EI to your local public school district (by your child's third birthday or in some states by your child's sixth birthday). As your child approaches age three, the EI coordinator will assist you in getting your child into a preschool program and/or in obtaining other support services that your child or your family may need.

When Early Intervention Will Not Provide What Is Required

EI is required to abide by the various state and federal laws regarding the provision of services. But there may be times when they do not—because of underfunding and/or understaffing. For all states, the number of days between the time of the initial referral and the initial IFSP meeting must be within forty-five days.

To find the regulations and policies for your state, visit NECTAC's website: http://www.nectac.org/partc/statepolicies.asp.

If your local EI Program is not adhering to your state's policies, you may have to file a complaint with the lead state agency and get its help in resolving the matter. How to deal with these types of situations is discussed in Month 2.

Specialty Providers for Children with ASD

In some states, if a child has a diagnosis of ASD, he may be eligible to receive individualized, autism-specific services provided by ASD specialty providers—state-funded direct service agencies that provide specialized services to children with ASD. These specialty providers have expertise in using different methodologies and structured, individualized treatments to improve social skills and communication and to manage behaviors that interfere with learning. They collaborate with EIP to deliver the IFSP services to the child and family. To find out if your state offers this, check with your local EIP.[5]

IN A SENTENCE

Build good, solid relationships with your Early Intervention coordinator and clinicians—learn as much as you can from them, and let them help you learn the lay of the land.

FIRST-MONTH MILESTONE

As difficult as the first month must have been, you learned that a diagnosis by itself is not sufficient. You need to have a complete understanding of your child's individual profile. You also learned:

- ○ WHAT'S INVOLVED IN AN INDIVIDUAL PRO-FILE
- ○ ABOUT UNDERLYING BIOMEDICAL FACTORS AND POSSIBLE TRIGGERS
- ○ HOW TO FIND A BIOMEDICAL SPECIALIST
- ○ ABOUT EARLY INTERVENTION AND HOW TO ASSESS YOUR EI SERVICES

Now take a well-earned break, and go do something nice for yourself!

Know Your Rights;
Know Your Insurance

Part I: Know Your Rights

YOUR RIGHTS UNDER
FEDERAL AND STATE LAWS

AS DISCUSSED IN Week 4, the basis of your rights to services for a child with developmental delays and/or disabilities are detailed in the Individuals with Disabilities Education Act (IDEA) and the various local state laws that implement this federal act. To ensure your child gets the medical, therapeutic, educational, and other supports and services he is entitled to, you *must* know your rights. The two best sources of information on this topic are:

- ○ Wrightslaw.com (www.wrightslaw.com), which provides a huge amount of valuable, free material on all aspects of the law and your rights
- ○ Lawrence M. Siegel's *The Complete IEP Guide: How to Advocate for Your Special Ed Child*, 5th edition (Berkeley: Nolo

Press, 2007), which provides complete, thorough, and highly readable coverage of the ins and outs of the federal special education program and your rights under IDEA

Consider *The Complete IEP Guide* required reading if you are serious about understanding and invoking your rights.

Your Rights Regarding Early Intervention

Problems with Early Intervention do occur, but they rarely become complex and are normally easily resolved. Usual issues involve delays in

- conducting an intake once you have placed the initial call to EI
- assessing your child upon completion of the intake
- developing an Individualized Family Service Plan (IFSP)
- beginning services on time and at the level specified

Some parents are kept waiting for months, and although this is rarely intentional and most often due to a high influx of children into the EI system and lack of available staff, it is still against the law. Your first step should be to contact the director of your local EI program and if the situation is not immediately rectified, your recourse is to file a complaint with the state agency that hosts your EI program.[1]

YOUR RIGHTS REGARDING SPECIAL EDUCATION

IDEA is quite explicit about your rights to services through your local public school system, once your child is of age.

1. The right to speedy professional evaluations to determine your child's eligibility for special education programs, known as an **Individualized Education Program (IEP)**

2. The right to **Free Appropriate Public Education (FAPE)** at no cost to you
3. The right to an education specifically designed to meet your child's unique needs

To learn about the additional provisions under the laws of your state for either Part B or Part C of IDEA, go to http://nectac.org/.

THE INDIVIDUALIZED EDUCATION PROGRAM (IEP)

Often referred to as the "Individualized Education Plan," the IEP defines the educational program that is designed to meet your child's individual needs. Every child who receives special education services must have an IEP. It is a legal process that consists of:

○ meetings and assessments with a variety of professionals to determine if your child is eligible for special education services and which service(s) would be most appropriate
○ meetings with school representatives to develop your child's educational plan
○ development of the actual document, which contains the prescribed educational plan. This document addresses parent concerns, student strengths, parent vision statement, measurable goals, benchmarks/objectives, strategies, the type of program needed, the classroom setting, classroom and other accommodations, curriculum modifications, peer needs, teacher and staff needs, frequency of therapies needed, other services and supports needed, transportation, the length of school day and year, and so forth
○ the actual delivery of services called for in the educational plan

FREE APPROPRIATE PUBLIC EDUCATION (FAPE)

IDEA requires your state's schools to provide a free educational program that is "appropriate" for your child. "Appropriate" may be a bit of a loaded term, but the word has been clearly determined to speak to:

- ○ the child's unique needs
- ○ the child's evaluations
- ○ the physical classroom location, setting, and class makeup
- ○ the teaching services and methods provided
- ○ the curricula
- ○ any additional special education supports and services that may be required among other elements.

All of these considerations and more should be delineated in your child's IEP document.

SHOULDN'T MY CHILD GET THE BEST EDUCATION POSSIBLE?

Yes, of course. However, the law mandates only an *appropriate* education. As Nolo's *Complete IEP Guide* explains, "The law does not require that your school district provide the very best possible education, but an appropriate education. 'Appropriate' is an elusive but tremendously important concept. It is used throughout IDEA and frequently in the IEP process. For one child, an appropriate education may mean a regular class with minor support services, while a hospital placement might be appropriate for another."[2]

LEAST RESTRICTIVE EDUCATIONAL ENVIRONMENT

The Act also requires your child's education to occur in the "least restrictive environment."

"IDEA does not tell you or the school what specific program or class your child should be in; that is a decision for the IEP team. IDEA does require school districts to place children with disabilities in the least restrictive environment (LRE) that meets their individual needs. What is LRE for a particular child, like what constitutes an 'appropriate education', will depend on that child's abilities and disabilities. Although Congress expressed a strong preference for mainstreaming (placing a child in a regular classroom), it used the term LRE to ensure that individual needs would determine each individual placement decision—and that children who really need a more restricted placement (such as a special school) would have one."[3]

WHAT IDEA COVERS IN TERMS OF
YOUR RIGHTS IN THE IEP PROCESS

Part B of IDEA details your rights concerning:

- ○ eligibility and evaluations
- ○ the nature of special education to be available
- ○ educational placement and the child's program
- ○ supports and related services
- ○ any required assistive technology
- ○ transition services
- ○ due process
- ○ suspension and expulsion
- ○ summer school
- ○ private schooling
- ○ special education in prison

CHECK THE EXTENT OF LOCAL
COMPLIANCE TO IEP RULES

Once you've come to understand the laws, the next step is to find out the level of compliance to these laws within your state, county, and school district. There are two ways to do this, and you should do both.

1. Contact your school district's Special Education Parent Advisory Council (SpEd PAC—pronounced "sped-pack"). This is a committee or council of individuals interested in improving special education services in their district. Their contact information should be available from your school district's special education office. From them you can get the "lay of the land":
   - a parent's-eye-view of how easy or difficult it may be to work with your school district and the best way to proceed
   - what special education programs are offered
   - the quality and expertise of personnel and the education in this district
   - the effectiveness of the Special Ed team members

- the number of children in the district who receive out-of-district placements and, of these, the number of cases litigated

  Out-of-district placements occur when the district cannot meet the needs of the child within the district, so the child is placed in a school out of the district—public or private. Under these circumstances, the district is required to compensate the school the child is placed in. Needless to say, they strongly prefer to avoid paying this out, so the issue can become quite contentious.

- whether parents are happy with the Special Ed programs and whether they are meeting their children's needs (whether the program has adequately skilled occupational therapists, speech-language pathologists, physical therapists, etc.)

- the school district's policy in regards to allowing parents to observe classrooms

  Most schools will allow you to observe some classrooms, as long as you reside in the district. Other schools will *not* allow you to observe any classrooms, even if you do reside in that district. If this is the case with your school district, you may want to seek advice from an attorney.

  If you are considering moving to another district, the special education director might be willing to meet with you and have you observe a classroom or two, but that school district is not obligated to do so.

  In addition to the above, you should also establish many good contacts with parents within the special needs community. Be discerning, and learn whose opinion you can trust.

2. Consult with a good, local special education attorney (covered later).

KNOW YOUR RIGHTS REGARDING STARTING THE IEP PROCESS

There is much to know about this, and it is well covered in the *Complete IEP Guide*. However, in the early stages of engaging the IEP process for your child, you will be concerned with your rights regarding the list below. Each right has specific compliance deadlines that vary from state to state.

- getting a copy of your child's school file
- providing you with an explanation of your rights under IDEA

○ amending your child's file because it contains false, inaccurate, misleading, or privacy-violating information

○ responding to requests for developing or updating an IEP document

○ performing your child's evaluation for determination of eligibility for special education programs

○ convening an IEP team meeting

○ IDEA also mandates specific guidelines for the development of IEPs. The IEP team must consider:

- the child's strengths
- the parent's concerns for enhancing the child's education
- the results of the initial evaluation or most recent evaluation
- the child's academic, developmental, and functional needs[4]

To learn about the additional provisions under the laws of your state, do an internet search on "[your state's name] + IEP + parents' rights."

PARENTS AS WATCHDOGS

IDEA establishes the rights of your child when it comes to education and ensures that parents have a say in all decisions that affect their child's education. However, parents really need to be vigilant and think of their role as watchdogs over the full use of IDEA in their own school districts.

FINDING A LOCAL SPECIAL EDUCATION ATTORNEY

It is wisely said that the best way to avoid a battle is by being fully prepared to wage it. While your attitude should never be adversarial when dealing with school personnel, there may arise circumstances that require you to be well informed on the means of recourse available and times you may have serious difficulties securing your due under IDEA.

Thus, *right at the outset* you should find a good special education lawyer who has a lot of experience with children on the autism spectrum, preferably one who is familiar with your school district. Get referrals from other parents even if they reside in other districts. If you can afford it, consider buying an hour of his or her time early on in the process to help guide you, so you can be fully prepared and fully armed. It may very well be the best hour ever spent.

The best advice on finding a special education attorney is given on the Wrightslaw.com website: http://www.wrightslaw.com/info/advo.referrals.htm. To summarize and add to its list:

1. Visit the Wrightslaw.com Yellow Pages for Kids with Disabilities: http://www.yellowpagesforkids.com.
2. Ask other parents—once again, frequently your best source of advice.
3. Contact your state Parent Training Information Center: http://www.yellowpagesforkids.com/help/ptis.htm.
4. Contact your local autism organizations.
5. Contact the Protection and Advocacy organization for your state. You can use the National Disabilities Rights Network website for this search: www.napas.org or http://www.napas.org/aboutus/PA_CAP.htm.
6. Get referrals from other members of your team.

Next, research your candidates by searching their names online, by talking with other parents, and by conducting telephone interviews with the candidates. Find out the answers to the following from each one:

1. Does she have a special interest or area of specialization?
2. Does she have a lot of experience handling cases with children on the autism spectrum?
3. What is her fee? Retainer? How does she like to work?
4. What is her style like?
5. What is her success rate?
6. Is she responsive to calls and emails? Typically, how long before she responds to calls and emails?
7. Are parents happy with her? Why?
8. How familiar is she with your school district and the opposing counsel?
9. How many cases within your district has she taken? (Note: although 8 and 9 are not critical to finding a good attorney and, in the end, these answers may not weigh heavily in your final decision to hire him or her, they are questions you should ask.)
   - How difficult was it to reach an agreement?
   - Of these cases, how many settled out of court?

- How many litigated? (It can be very costly to go to litigation.)
- Did the parents get what they wanted?
- How difficult was it to settle?
- How long did it take?
- How much did it cost?

10. If applicable, were there any cases filed against Early Intervention for noncompliance?
     - How many?
     - What were the problems?
     - How were they resolved?
     - What was the process for resolution?
11. What percentage of all her cases settled before going to litigation?
12. Is she taking on any more cases at this time?

After you have gathered and digested all this information, list the candidates in order of preference. At this point you can go ahead and schedule at the appropriate time a face-to-face meeting with your top choice.

PREPARING TO MEET WITH AN ATTORNEY

If you want to get the most out of your meeting with your selected attorney, it is important to already know before you meet with him or her:

1. The relevant laws (do all the homework suggested above so you are not wasting the precious time you have with the attorney by having him explain basic laws to you)
2. The problems within your school district and, if applicable, your Early Intervention Program (based on feedback from parents and your local PAC)
3. Your child's specific needs (be brief in your description)
4. Based on #2 and #3, how difficult it might be to get what your child needs

You should arrive at your scheduled appointment as an educated parent. In your hand should be a list of topics or questions that will help you:

- ❍ find out more about him
- ❍ learn how he works

○ understand what issues exist in your local district

○ decide, based on your needs, the best way to proceed

Be prepared to conduct the interview as succinctly as possible.

The attorney should help define the process you will have to go through for your child specifically. He or she should be able to tell you specifically what you need to do to be properly organized; what reports, evaluations, and processes you need to pursue as a matter of immediate need and *just in case* there should be a problem later on.

The attorney should also review your team member list and make recommendations about who else to add. A good attorney knows which professionals will do well in court, should it ever come to that.

Naturally, this would be the best time to decide if this is the attorney you might want to use if you ever need legal assistance. You will want someone who is masterful at working with other attorneys to settle whenever possible. What is his or her experience in this regard?

KNOW YOUR NATURAL RIGHTS

In addition to your rights (entitlements) protected under law, you also have rights that, while not necessarily defended by any government, are nevertheless yours to claim.

These rights (sometimes called "natural rights") are not granted; they simply exist for you to use or not use. Natural rights can be declared or stated by a proclamation (such as a "Bill of Rights"), but it isn't the bill that gives them to you, and cancelling the bill does not cancel the existence of the rights.

If you are a parent concerned about your child's development, you have:

1. The right to receive complete and accurate assessments, diagnostic evaluations, and reports

2. The right to receive full information about your child's diagnoses and developmental and medical condition(s)

3. The right to receive full information about the medical, therapeutic, and educational services most beneficial to your child. Stay informed: some clinicians will prescribe certain medications and treatments over others because of the reimbursement factor.

4. The right to adequate and appropriate therapeutic and educational services. In the event full therapeutic and educational services are not available, you have the right to receive the tools and training needed to provide your child with those services yourself.

5. The right to speak up and express your views and opinions to health care providers, clinicians, and educators about your child and his or her needs and treatments.

6. The right to be listened to and taken seriously during discussions with professionals, even if your views are contrary to theirs. As your team's leader, you have the duty to take effective action to bring about the best result for your child.

   You have to remember that it is *you* who is hiring the professional.

7. The right to have your child receive appropriate, complete medical treatment even if it means being referred to a specialist. You have the *right* to receive a referral. If you do not feel your doctor has the qualifications to make a proper judgment—for example, if he adopts a "wait and see" attitude or if you feel she is not examining your child's condition far enough, you should persist until you are given a referral even if it is out of your health plan's network. (Some doctors will stonewall you because they will receive more compensation if you stay within their network.)

8. You always have the right to a second opinion.

9. You have the right to expect support from your family, friends, and community. Failing to find this support, you have the right to go where you must to find it.

10. You have the right and duty to be outspoken in defense of your child's well-being.

11. You have the right and duty to take all ethical actions necessary to bring about your child's most rapid and complete recovery.

Part II: Know Your Insurance

In the absence of insurance coverage, families often pay as much as they can out of pocket—for services that can easily cost upwards of $70,000 per year. In this process, many families risk their homes, their retirement funds, and the educations of the children who are not affected.

Surprisingly, most states do not require private insurance companies to cover even the most essential services and treatments for ASD. Thus, many insurers even at this date do not provide this coverage. However, even if your carrier is one of those that does not, there are many ways to get what you need, but you need to be creative.

GET TO KNOW YOUR INSURANCE POLICY

It may not seem fair, but parents who know what benefits their children are entitled to, and who work hard to get them, get more from their insurers than parents who remain passive. It's so easy to accept what they tell you and assume that is all you are entitled to, but that is not the case. There are always exceptions to the rules. Get to know your insurer and work hard to get the coverage your child deserves.

1. Find your benefits package, and read through it thoroughly.
   - If you are unable to locate it, look for it online at your insurer's website, or call the member services number on the back of your insurance card and request another copy.
2. Make sure you learn the basics—for example:
   - whether your child always needs a referral to see a specialist
   - whether you will pay more if she sees someone outside the plan's network or at a "nonparticipating" hospital or clinic
   - whether some procedures or therapies need to be preapproved
   - if there are any exceptions to these basic rules. For example, some plans will pay for out-of-network specialists if the care you need is not provided by anyone in their network or if there are no providers within a certain radius. Don't assume your insurance company won't approve it; you never know until you ask.
3. As you read through your benefits package, look for the language it uses to describe the services your child needs. For example:
   - You may find that the plan covers "occupational therapy" but not "sensory integration therapy" (which is a specific kind of therapy offered by many occupational therapists). So, when you are speaking with the insurer, refer to "occupational therapy," not "sensory integration therapy." And be sure your therapist bills it that way.
   - You may find the plan specifically excludes certain diagnoses (such as "PDD" or "autism") but does allow coverage for unspecified encephalopathy, which can refer to a wide variety of brain disorders or

an unspecified condition of the nervous system. Because autism is so complex and affects so many bodily systems, you can find a number of diagnoses that will be covered by your policy. Remember, autism is just a diagnosis—it doesn't define what the deficits are. Insurance companies work by both diagnoses and deficits. Know which they will cover, which they will not, and under which circumstances they will cover something that under other circumstances they might not. Don't assume that the doctor or clinician is familiar with your insurance policy, so be sure to discuss this in advance. Talk with the person who bills insurance for that doctor or clinician, and see if he or she can suggest the best diagnostic and procedural codes to use. If your benefits package does not provide specific enough information about the coverage you are seeking, you may have to contact member services to get this information. Or, better yet, go to step 4.

4. Get a case manager assigned to you.

- A case manager (some health plans call this a "nurse care manager") is a single point of contact for the insurance company who helps individuals and families with complex health care needs. Often the mental health services are handled separately, so you may need to have two case managers assigned—one for the medical side and one for the mental health side. But you must call up and request one. This way, you will be speaking with one person (either a medical or mental health professional) and not thirty different clerks. Sometimes you have to jump through hoops to get a case manager assigned, but be persistent.

- Don't dump a lot of information about your child's condition on the insurance clerks or case manager without first doing your homework. Everything you say to the case manager (or clerk) will be transcribed into your file. So study your policy, and go over the possibilities with your providers. You should also make good use of your time in waiting rooms by speaking with other parents who may have the same policies you do.

- In speaking with the case manager, take a team approach. Try not to be adversarial; try to enlist his help. Try to put a personal touch into your communication with him. Without getting into a long history, let him get to know a little about you and your child. You are just trying to find some way for that person to connect with you.

- When speaking with a case manager, ask some "what if" questions as opposed to saying "my child has autism." For example, you might ask under what circumstances would the company cover listening therapy. If the case manager says it never would, check under what circumstances it would cover occupational therapy. Ask in general about the insurance company's policies before you make specific statements about your child's condition. Keep in mind that your conversation may be recorded or documented, so unless you want this information in your permanent record, be careful what you say.

5. Find out which doctors, clinicians, labs, clinics, and hospitals are within your network. Most health insurance companies have websites where you can search online to see if your providers are covered under your plan.
   - Do they have the expertise your child needs? If not, you may be able to build a case for why you should go out of network. Enlist the help of your case manager so you can obtain prior approval. Be sure to push for as many visits as you need and know which procedural codes it covers. Don't forget to get the authorization code from your case manager.

6. Gather whatever forms you need for prior approvals, reimbursement, appeals, etc.
   - Organize your forms and files so they are available when and where you need them.
   - Keep copies of everything you submit, and indicate the date it was mailed in.

7. Enlist your providers to help you get the services you need covered. Before you begin using a provider, find out the following:
   - What is the maximum coverage they've seen a child get within their practice, and under what circumstances can that occur?
   - What were the diagnostic and procedural codes used?

   Often practices will have a staff member who is willing to assist families to obtain coverage by placing a call to the insurer. Other practices may subcontract to an experienced insurance billing professional to submit and process their claims. You should ask if you can speak with this person. She may know how best to describe your child's diagnosis and treatments in terms understood and accepted by your insurer and the professionals involved. She may also know when an alternative but equally valid diagnostic code might make the difference between coverage and denial.

8. Follow the process for prior approval.
   - Find out the process for prior approval with your insurer. Can the provider handle this for you? If not, perhaps the case manager can.
   - If not, and you are told to call the member services number at your insurance company, remember you are talking to a clerk, not a medical expert. Don't get into a complex discussion about your child's condition and treatment options. Stick to the questions you need to ask about coverage, and, again, try to use language that is in the written policy.
   - Keep a log of all calls: date, time, discussion notes, and the name of the person you spoke with. Be assured that the insurance company is doing the same. Your records could be important if you need to appeal a decision or correct an error. *Document everything.*
   - Be polite, but if you feel you need to, don't hesitate to ask to speak with the person's supervisor. If you find yourself unable to communicate with a particular insurance company employee—and especially if you are getting angry on the phone—end the call. Call back later, and talk with someone else. Avoid getting into adversarial situations.
9. When providers won't take insurance, there are steps you can take.
   - Many providers today refuse to accept insurance simply because they find it is too difficult to stay in business with the high cost of insurance and limited reimbursement rates. If this is a doctor or clinician you really want to see and you are willing to submit the claim yourself, then be sure to find out from your insurance company if this is acceptable. If you have a PPO (preferred provider organization), it should not be a problem, but if you have an HMO (health maintenance organization), you will need prior approval. Make sure the provider gives you an invoice or statement that includes their name, address, tax ID number, name of the patient, date of service, diagnostic code, service provided (including the CPT code), and the fee. You will then need to complete the proper insurance form and submit it to your insurer for reimbursement.
10. Always submit your reimbursement forms soon after the date of service.
   - Be sure you keep a copy of what you mail in, and indicate on the form the date you mail it. Keep a log of what was submitted for reimbursement so you can track it in case it is detained or lost. Most insurers have websites and systems for tracking online the claims you submit.

11. If coverage is denied, you have the right to appeal.

- Ask the insurer to explain the appeals process to you. With the amount of documentation you will have to provide, the process will likely be very time consuming. You may want to ask a few members of your team to write a letter supporting the treatment, or you may want to find a few research studies that show this type of therapy for *this* diagnosis can yield a positive outcome. Your appeal will be sent to doctors who are not expert in your child's condition, so you may have to pull out all the ammunition you can find and be as thorough as you can. Parents often give up during the appeal process—and maybe sometimes they should. You will have to weigh how great the reimbursement potential is for you.[5]

SUPPLEMENTARY HEALTH INSURANCE

Some states offer special health plans for children and families with disabilities, often through the Division of Medical Assistance. However, only certain providers will accept this supplementary insurance, so be sure to check to see if they do. You can search online under "[your state's name] + Division of Medical Assistance."

SUPPLEMENTAL SECURITY INCOME (SSI) BENEFITS

Your child (from birth to age eighteen) may be eligible for SSI benefits provided certain requirements are met. According to the Social Security Administration (SSA) starter kit, "Social Security has a strict definition of disability for children. The child must have a physical or mental condition(s) that very seriously limits his or her activities; and the condition(s) must have lasted, or be expected to last, at least 1 year or result in death."

Furthermore, it has to be demonstrated that the child has "little or no income and resources." The administering agency will evaluate "the family's household income, resources and other personal information" when making this determination.[6]

The above information comes from the SSA's Child Disability Starter Kit Fact Sheet: http://www.ssa.gov/disability/Child_StarterKit_Factsheet.pdf.

MEDICAID: THE "KATIE BECKETT OPTION"

Some states provide Medicaid assistance to families of children with mental and physical disabilities who would otherwise be unable to obtain services because of their insurance coverage limitations.

Under the Federal Tax Equity and Fiscal Responsibility Act of 1982 (TEFRA), states are allowed (not mandated) to extend Medicaid coverage to children who qualify as disabled according to the SSI definition above. Known as the "Katie Beckett option," this optional Medicaid eligibility category allows states to waive parental income and resources for any child under nineteen years of age who is "disabled" and meets qualifications as requiring a level of care that would make him or her eligible for placement in a hospital, nursing facility, or intermediate care facility for the intellectually disabled.

TEFRA coverage can make a huge difference to a family, since it will often cover intensive therapies (occupational therapy, physical therapy, speech-language therapy) that other insurance policies will not. Information about TEFRA can be found through your Early Intervention office or by searching on the web for "[your state's name] + Tax Equity and Fiscal Responsibility Act of 1982 Katie Beckett option."[7]

MEDICAID WAIVER PROGRAMS

Section 1915(c) of the Social Security Act, Medicaid law permits the U.S. Department of Health and Human Services to waive certain portions of Medicaid rules under specified circumstances. These waivers are relevant to substituting home-based and community-based services for patients who would otherwise be eligible for institutionalization. These waivers are used at the discretion of each state and can cover a very wide variety of services not covered under state plans or other forms of insurance. These services can include special training, many therapies not otherwise covered, respite care, and environmental modifications.[8] This is well worth your checking into. Search on the terms "[your state's name] + Medicaid Waiver Programs."

Medicare Coverage is important to research. The U.S. Department of Health and Human Services maintains a website to educate you about this resource: www.medicare.gov.

A Medicaid website is also maintained by the U.S. Department of Health and Human Services that covers information you should be familiar with: http://www.cms.hhs.gov/home/medicaid.asp.

GET HELP THROUGH YOUR EMPLOYER

If you or your partner works for a large corporation, tell the human resources department about your situation, and ask whether the company offers any assistance outside of the insurance plan. Some companies have set up special funds to cover certain employee expenses that are not covered by insurance. Sometimes there is flexibility in the plans you can join, or there are multiple plans. They might have a plan that better fits your needs.

Take advantage of flexible spending accounts—money you can set aside, tax-free, from your paycheck and then use to cover medical expenses, including co-payments and deductibles that are not covered by insurance.

Find out if there are other employees in the company with a similar situation—you could ask them what they are doing in terms of insurance.

When you have an opportunity to switch insurers or jobs, make sure you know how your child's coverage will be affected and whether you will be able to keep using current providers.

GET YOUR EMPLOYER INVOLVED

Educate your employer about the needs of families raising children with disabilities. This is especially valuable if you work for a company that runs its own health insurance program and has the power to make positive change. Consider that at a minimum, 1 out of every 150 children are on the autism spectrum; thus in a company with ten thousand employees, there are going to be a lot of families in the same situation as yours. From the perspective of the company wanting to retain good employees, health care for children with autism is an ever-increasing issue.

GETTING COVERAGE FOR NEW TREATMENTS

Few of the treatments for ASD have complete evidence provided through comprehensive clinical studies; thus many are still considered experimental, and most insurance plans will not cover them. Some insurance companies will allow "compassionate care exceptions" in cases in which regular treatments have not worked and the provider's medical advisors give permission for an alternative or experimental treatment. This exception is usually granted only in cases of life-threatening illnesses; however, if all other avenues to get coverage for a particular treatment are unavailable, you can try this approach.

A "Letter of Medical Necessity" will be needed to support your treatment request. This letter should include:

1. The diagnosis for which the service or equipment is needed
2. The specific symptom or function the service or equipment will help
3. A full description of the service or equipment and how it will help the patient
4. Supporting evidence (medical studies, journal articles, etc.) if the service or equipment is new or experimental
5. Well-supported reasons why any less expensive, traditionally used alternatives are not appropriate for the patient[9]

GETTING STUCK BETWEEN THE CRACKS

Despite your best efforts, you may find that some of the treatments you feel are absolutely needed for your child will not be covered by insurance. You may have to redouble efforts to get services included or increased in your child's Early Intervention or school system program. But you may find yourself in a common bind: the same service that is considered educational (and therefore not covered) by a medical insurer may be considered medical (and therefore not provided) by a school system. Parents and advocacy groups nationwide, like Autism Speaks, are working to improve this situation. In the meantime, many parents will find themselves digging deeper into their own pockets.

HMO VERSUS PPO

The choice of having coverage with an HMO versus a PPO comes down to balancing out-of-pocket costs that you will recover versus the amount of work it will take to get these reimbursements. Operating within an HMO's network is easier because there is less paperwork involved. You know what it will cover as long as you keep to professionals within the network. Many of the specialists you will need, however, may be out of network. As described earlier, it is possible to use an out-of-network doctor or clinician as long as you have solid justification (for example, there is no professional within the network who has the expertise or services required) and obtain prior approval in advance. With a PPO, you can select your specialists, but you will have to deal with a lot more paperwork and potentially more battles to recover costs.

In general, my advice is this: when you get the diagnosis, if you possibly can, get out of your HMO and into a PPO so you can more easily go out of network and have many more options available to you—unless you subscribe to a large network and the majority of the specialists you would like to see are covered under your current plan.

WHERE TO GO TO GET MORE INFORMATION AND HELP

Insurance Help for Autism maintains a listing of useful information for parents seeking insurance coverage, especially for California: http://www.insurance helpforautism.com/index.html. Be sure to check its "Tips" page (http://insurancehelpforautism.com/tips.html), which contains valuable information on how your insurance company is likely to respond to requests for coverage for autism treatments.

The organization Talk About Curing Autism (TACA) includes on its website the document "Health Insurance Reimbursement Tips and Tricks," which provides a lot of specific information on health insurance codes that can be used for autism treatments. Go to http://www.talkaboutcuringautism.org, and under the menu Help for Families, look for "Health Insurance" and then "Reimbursement Tips." TACA's website is filled with excellent information.

A posting on the blog Autism Bulletin, "17 States Require Some Insurance Coverage for Autism Services, Recent Survey Finds" (May 7, 2007), provides summary information on which states require some insurance coverage for autism services: http://autismbulletin.blogspot.com/2007/05/17-states-require-some-insurance.html.

Health Rights Hotline (http://www.hrh.org/cag.html) publishes "Consumer Action Guides," which cover a range of topics informing people of their rights within the health care system and assisting them with navigating the system. The focus is on California, but the information can be helpful to those in other states.

Insure Kids Now! is a website run by the U.S. Department of Health and Human Services that provides information by state on eligibility for free or low-cost health insurance: http://www.insurekidsnow.gov.

IN A SENTENCE

Learn to use the system by becoming an expert on your rights.

living

The Financials:
Planning Ahead

THIS SECTION WILL examine the topic of your finances and help you to adjust to the new reality of having a child with ASD. It may be difficult for many parents, so you may not want to read this entire chapter at once. Take as long as you need to get through it.

The information in the sidebar on the following page is not difficult to understand. But you are going to be asked to do what most people prefer to avoid: face your finances. By avoiding them, parents bury themselves in debt that gets only worse with each passing year. On the other hand, by gradually facing your financial situation, you will eventually unravel those knots that are so difficult to confront.

Take this chapter as slowly as you need. It will be here waiting for you when you are ready.

Often after a child is diagnosed with autism and the parents begin to understand the time involved and the scope of the recovery process, one parent—more often than not the mother—quits her job. Given no other support systems (grandparents, extended family, close-knit community), someone almost certainly has to become a full-time parent to manage this process successfully. Adding to the situation is a potentially expanding list of expenses, easily upwards of $70,000 per year.

"It can cost about $3.2 million to take care of an autistic person over his or her lifetime. Caring for all people with autism over their lifetimes costs an estimated $35 billion per year. Those figures are part of the findings in the first study to comprehensively survey and document the costs of autism to U.S. society. Dr. Michael Ganz, Assistant Professor of Society, Human Development, and Health at Harvard School of Public Health, authored the study, which appears in the newly published book, *Understanding Autism: From Basic Neuroscience to Treatment* (CRC Press, 2006).

Ganz broke down the total costs of autism into two components: direct and indirect costs. Direct costs include direct medical costs, such as physician and outpatient services, prescription medication, and behavioral therapies (estimated to cost, on average, more than $29,000 per person per year) and direct non-medical costs, such as special education, camps, and child care (estimated to annually cost more than $38,000 for those with lower levels of disability and more than $43,000 for those with higher levels).

Indirect costs equal the value of lost productivity resulting from a person having autism, for example, the difference in potential income between someone with autism and someone without. It also captures the value of lost productivity for an autistic person's parents. Examples include loss of income due to reduced work hours or not working altogether. Ganz estimates that annual indirect costs for autistic individuals and their parents range from more than $39,000 to nearly $130,000."[10]

For families accustomed to having two income sources, this is going to be a big readjustment. It can quickly become overwhelming and crush your marriage if you don't take some measured, well-coordinated steps. So pay attention, and do not neglect the following steps.

Assess Your Current Financial Position

First, comprehensively assess your current financial position as it is, at this very moment, before any changes occur as a result of autism recovery planning.

If you don't already have a good system for evaluating your finances, the tables below should help you out. I recommend re-creating these tables using a spreadsheet program.

Current Cash Flows			
Income Source	**Monthly**	**Quarterly**	**Annually**
Totals			
Expenses (not related to autism recovery)	**Monthly**	**Quarterly**	**Annually**
Set-asides:			
Children's college fund			
Vacation			
Totals			
Net Cash Flow			

Value of Property Owned			
Item	Current Sale or Cash Value	Amount Owed	Net Value (current sale value minus amount owed)
Cash on hand			
Stocks, bonds, etc.			
Auto			
House			
Boat			
Life insurance			
Other saleable items:			
1.			
2.			
3.			
4.			
5.			
Set-asides:			
1. Children's college fund			
2. Vacation			
3.			
Totals			

Estimating Recovery-Related Expenses

Now let's assess the expected autism recovery costs plus some potential sources of support. If you have more than one child on the autism spectrum, you can either enter costs for both into the following table or create one table for each child.

At this point, a lot of the expenses will be difficult or impossible for you to estimate. Just do the best you can at this time; you will be able to refine it later.

Year 1—Estimated Out-of-Pocket Autism Recovery Costs			
	Child 1	Child 2	Total
Medical			
Office visits			
Lab tests			
Procedures (EEGs, MRIs, IVs, etc.)			
Medication/supplements			
Misc. supplies/equipment			
Clinical/Therapeutic/Educational			
Evaluations			
Consults			
Sessions			
Misc. supplies/equipment			
Legal/Advocacy/Insurance			
Attorney			
Advocate			
Filing/court fees			
Supplemental insurance			

	Child 1	Child 2	Total
Self-Education			
Conferences (fees, travel expenses)			
Books/DVDs/CDs/audiotapes			
Subscriptions (newsletters, magazines)			
Membership fees			
Counseling/support groups			
Child Care			
Babysitter			
Respite provider			
Recreation			
Play groups			
Summer camp			
Special activities (swimming, karate, etc.)			
Travel (for out-of-town provider visits)			
Gas			
Parking/Tolls			
Hotel			
Food			
Miscellaneous			
Special foods, equipment (food processor, yogurt maker, etc.), and supplies			
Special toys and equipment			
Modifications to home			
Office supplies (binders, folders, pens, tape, sticky notes, stapler, etc.)			
Photocopying or copier (plus paper, ink)			
Computer			
Software			

Reducing the Costs of Recovery

There are many ways to reduce the costs of a recovery program.

1. Get trained in how to administer some of the therapy techniques yourself. You will find many training seminars offered inside and outside the United States. If you are unable to attend any of these seminars, check the internet for online training courses. More and more organizations are offering online training. Dr. Stanley Greenspan offers online and certificate training on DIR/Floortime through his organization; see the website http://www.stanleygreenspan.com.

2. Ask family members to help you out.

3. Look to foundations or agencies to get supplemental insurance, respite care, or flexible spending dollars. Some states have agencies that offer these benefits to qualifying families; every state is different, however, and some don't offer them at all.

4. In some states, the Department of Mental Retardation offers flexible spending for families with children who are diagnosed with autism. For example, in Massachusetts, on average $600 to $800 per year is available through these types of programs and can be used for respite care (through a child care provider) or recreational activities.

5. AutismCares provides up to $1,500 per family in crisis; see the web page http://www.autismspeaks.org/press/autism_cares_family_support_awards .php.

6. Try the National Autism Association's Family First program: http:// www.nationalautismassociation.org/familyfirst.php.

7. Apply for grants from biomedical treatment foundations such as 4-A Healing Foundation (http://www.4ahealingfoundation.org).

8. Move in with your sibling or your parents until you get on your feet.

9. Eliminate nonessential expenses. For example, instead of taking that long-distance vacation, find a way to cut it back to something more local and less costly. Or instead of setting money aside for your child's college education, use it for treatment. After all, if the various therapies and treatments are not undertaken now, there is a good chance your child will never have the capacity to attend college. Discern what you *want* from what you really *need*.

10. Prioritize the services your child needs; choose your targets carefully. Of course you will do this in collaboration with your team, but you must always focus on what will get you the best result at any given time.

11. Look for tax benefits. According to a January 2007 posting by Michael O'Connor on Wrightslaw.com, "It's likely that 15–30 percent of families with a disabled child have one or more unclaimed tax benefits." Here are some of the potential benefits he cites:

    • Tuition costs for a special school that has a program designed to educate children with disabilities and amounts paid for a child's tutoring by a teacher specially trained and qualified to deal with severe disabilities may be deducted.

    • Special instruction, training, or therapy, such as sign language instruction, speech therapy, and remedial reading instruction may be deductible. Related books and materials can qualify for the medical expense deduction.

    • As of 2006, parents may deduct some of the costs of attending a medical conference related to the treatment and care for their child with a disability.[11]

As tax laws change frequently, be sure to check current resources (tax guides, IRS, etc.) to see if these deductions are still allowed.

Building a Local Autism Community Self-Sufficiency Cooperative

A cooperative is "an autonomous association of persons united voluntarily to meet their common economic, social, and cultural needs and aspirations through a jointly-owned and democratically-controlled enterprise."[12]

If ever there were a group of people desperately in need of voluntary cooperation to meet their common needs, it is the parents and families of children with autism!

At the signing of the Declaration of Independence, Benjamin Franklin famously declared, "We must all hang together, gentlemen. . . . Else, we shall most assuredly hang separately." What I'm claiming is that we are in a similar position, particularly in terms of finances. If we hope to give our children the care they truly need without going massively into debt (even bankruptcy) in the process, we will have to get inventive in how these costs are to be covered—very inventive, indeed.

So consider this: At least 1 in 150 children in your local community has autism. What does this mean? Well, in a medium-sized city and its immediate environs near where I live, there is a population of about 118,000 with about 46,000 households and about 30,000 children under age eighteen. If only 1 in 150 children have autism, then that amounts to about 200 cases spread over perhaps 120 families. *Think about how much collective purchasing power that is!* With even just 40 participating families, even less, this group might afford to hire its own therapist and pay him or her $50,000 per year (each family paying $172 per month, potentially reimbursable by insurance).

Or they could arrange for treatments for which reimbursement is sometimes difficult. What if a sympathetic, trusted local primary care provider became part of this cooperative and was sponsored by the cooperative to obtain special Defeat Autism Now! training? What if, in exchange for greatly reduced rates, the co-op worked out various ways to cover that practitioner's expenses—such as services provided by members with expertise in law and accounting; auto repair; construction and home repair; arts, sports, social activities, and other activities for children; advertising and marketing; computer maintenance; organic farming; and so forth.

With the group sponsoring professionals, there would be more local services, more tailoring to your child's specific needs, and more control over how services are performed.

In other words, *the cooperative would set up its own internal economic system*, as all cooperatives basically do to a greater or lesser degree. The difference in this case is that the cooperative would not just focus on food purchasing or the like. This co-op would bulk-purchase any item or service the group held to be important (as determined by extensive and continuous surveying).

Similarly, families could reduce their overhead by giving their business as much as possible to other people within the co-op. In this way, the group itself could ensure its members' employment and continuation of services, even in hard times. A good example of how this was successfully applied *by an entire* city is the "Ithaca Hours" program created by visionary urban planner Paul Glover in Ithaca, New York, in the 1980s (see http://www.ithacahours.com).

Since local people would deliver all these services, there would be a natural regrowth of local support services and networks. It would even be possible for this cooperative to apply for 501(c)(3) status and become eligible for grants and model programs funding.

With a little initial success, the cooperative could grow to surprising proportions. Perhaps a site in a tranquil rural area could eventually be established where therapeutic arts, sports, occupational therapy, and medical treatment programs and other activities would operate on a seven-days-a-week, year-round basis.

Do you think this is a good idea? If so, bring it up at your local autism support group meeting, and see if the other members share this vision. It can start with simple actions the majority feels are vitally in the common interest.

IN A SENTENCE

There are many ways in which you can reduce your expenses; be open-minded, resourceful, and creative.

MONTH **3**

Taking a Balanced, Integrated Approach to Intervention

SOMEONE ONCE SAID, "We've gotten to the point where all the little problems are someone's concern but none of the big problems are anyone's."

Suppose you want to build your dream home—the house you'd like to live in for the rest of your life. So you hire some good tradespeople, but you schedule each to arrive when none of the others are there. Furthermore, you provide no blueprints, and you neither hire a general contractor nor act as one, so there is no coordination or timing of the build sequences. Given these conditions, it shouldn't be surprising when the outcome falls far short of what was originally desired.

Well, this is somewhat like what parents of children with autism are faced with. There are some very good "tradespeople" out there—good doctors, good clinicians, good therapists, and good educators. But in the world of autism recovery, unless you find that one rare professional I described in Week 2, there is no equivalent to an architect, general contractor, or job site superintendent. And believe it or not, like it or not, there is no one to wear these hats but you, the parent. You are the case manager.

Just because you have a team doesn't mean an integrated approach will magically emerge. The integration will happen *only if you facilitate it.* Some of your team professionals will be able to see beyond their own disciplines; however, don't count on it. And even if they do, don't assume that they are expert enough to know how to integrate different disciplines. It is unfortunately true that in the world of autism, because the coordination or integration hat is not professionally worn by anyone, the various disciplines can end up somewhat at odds with one another.

Even some of the best professionals on your team—even those who believe the most in an integrated approach—cannot make recommendations about therapies or treatments in which they have no experience. So it will be up to you to do this research and to figure out how best to integrate them.

The Case Manager as Intervention Integrator

In Day 5 you were introduced to a recovery management plan. Now you are going to get to use it. Here is a little drill to get you started.

If you haven't done so already, complete at least the section on long- and short-term goals. What are the most important goals at this point (both yours and those offered by your professional team members)? Examples include learning to talk, building nonverbal skills, developing social interactions with peers, improving self-help skills (dressing, toileting, etc.), and reducing tantrums.

Now fine-tune your goals, and make them as specific and measurable as possible; then turn them into outcome goals, and prioritize them. For example:

1. Eric will learn to use and understand twenty words by [date].
2. Cathy will use one showing gesture to draw attention to something of interest to her by [date].
3. Jeff will exchange ten back and forth interactions in a row with a peer by [date].
4. Mark will be learn to dress himself without any assistance or prompting by [date].
5. Jenny will be able to transition from one activity to another without having a tantrum by [date].

Learn as much as you can about the different treatments, therapies, and supports available. Start with the list on the following pages. For a brief description of each, see the Living section, and visit the treatment section of the ASD Video Glossary on the First Signs website for brief video clips of many of these treatments. Based on your child's unique profile and underlying biomedical factors, you and your team must choose the treatments that can best help you achieve your goals.

Treatments to Be Used:	Goal #1:	Goal #2:	Goal #3:
Medical			
Biomedical			
Nutritional Therapy			
Supplementation Therapy			
Detoxification			
Medication			
Developmental Therapies			
DIR/Floortime			
RDI			
SCERTS Model			
Son-Rise Program			
Hanen/More than Words			
Behavioral Therapies			
Applied Behavioral Analysis (ABA)			
Discrete Trial Training (DTT)			
Verbal Behavior (VB)			
Pivotal Response Training (PRT)			
Picture Exchange Communication System (PECS)			
Positive Behavior Support			
Incidental and Milieu Teaching			

Treatments to Be Used:	Goal #1:	Goal #2:	Goal #3:
Structured Teaching and Environmental Supports			
TEACCH			
Social Stories, Social Movies			
Augmentative Communication			
Clinical Therapies			
Speech-Language Therapy			
Occupational Therapy/ Sensory Integration			
Physical Therapy			
Social Skills Training			
Listening Therapy			
Vision Therapy			
Music Therapy			
Art Therapy			
Animal Therapy			

While you should be able to rely on your team members to make recommendations for treatments and therapies, and impart their knowledge to you, *you* must be the one to

- understand what each treatment is and what it does
- know what intensity of treatment is needed to reach the best outcome
- know the pros and cons of each treatment
- know about any science supporting the effectiveness of the treatment
- find out in advance if a treatment can possibly change or alter your child's personality and, if so, how
- find out about any dangers involved with using the treatment
- know how progress with the treatment can be measured

- ○ find out how each treatment can be complemented or be integrated with other treatments that may be working toward the same goal
- ○ find out if the selected treatments can be "layered" (run simultaneously or in timed, coordinated sequences) and, if so, how and when

For each treatment, you will also have to get answers to the following questions:

- ○ Who should conduct the treatments?
- ○ What qualifications should the professional have?
- ○ What is the availability in your area?
- ○ What is the cost?
- ○ Will insurance cover it? If not, what do you have to do to get it covered?
- ○ How long should you stay with a particular treatment?
- ○ How do you know if it is effective?
- ○ Is the clinician promising that this is the only treatment needed? (If it sounds too good to be true, it probably is. Do not work with this clinician.)
- ○ How long should you continue it before concluding it isn't getting the desired result?

Ultimately, you must be the one to:

- ○ know the facts
- ○ manage the details
- ○ ensure that information is shared with team members
- ○ track what works and what doesn't

You will be the constant thread of connection as your child goes through interventions, classrooms, and therapists.

Another guiding rule has to do with drawing solutions from multiple wells of knowledge. Think of it this way: Our understanding of autism is fairly limited at this point; however, we do have a wide variety of approaches that can be classified under three general categories:

- ○ those that address the body—such as traditional and nontraditional medicine, nutrition, detoxification

○ those that address the mind—such as developmental and behavioral therapies and the educational program

○ those that address the individual's interaction with his or her environment (people, groups, animals, objects, etc.)—such as social skills training, animal therapy, socially interactive activities, and occupational and physical therapy.

Within each category there is a wide assortment of possible approaches and tools. Of course, many therapies cross these somewhat arbitrary category boundaries, but here is the point: Some parents may try to put all their eggs in one basket by hoping just one method will provide the total solution, while others will try everything all at once to see what works. What seems to work best is finding the correct balance of approaches in each of the categories that works for you and works for your child and trying them slowly and methodically.

Some of the best outcomes I've seen have been with families who are not relying on one particular treatment but are taking this kind of balanced, integrated approach: judiciously layering and spacing (for example) play therapy with a biomedical program, occupational therapy, speech and language therapy, a social skills group, and a well-integrated program at school or home.

As much as possible, you want to include on your team professionals who buy into the idea of integration. It can often be difficult finding professionals who will look broadly at the issues and the goals and think in terms of methodologies appropriate for those goals, but this is where your talents as an integrator will be most necessary.

Conducting team case management conferences on a regular basis can help with the integration process. Everyone can walk away energized and on the same page.

IN A SENTENCE

Solving the big problem of integration becomes your specialty.

living

Getting to Know the
Treatments Available

THE FOLLOWING IS an overview of each of the therapies mentioned in Month 3, "Learning." This is by no means a complete summary of your options; these are merely the therapies commonly in use at this time.

It is important that you get to know the treatments and understand what they can do for your child before selecting them. Remember that no two children are alike, so it is important that you choose treatments with your team that are tailored to your child's needs. While many of the following therapeutic methods are used routinely with children on the autism spectrum, they may not be appropriate for some children and in fact may be counterproductive.

Biomedical Treatment:
Nutritional Therapy

Nutritional therapy uses changes in diet to reduce medical conditions. Such treatment is called for when disorders are diagnosed as being caused or worsened by nutritional imbalances, or when a disorder is depleting the body of essential nutrients. Though many doctors may discourage parents from trying dietary interventions because they have not been proven, several peer-reviewed reports support the use of dietary interventions for children with autism spectrum disorders.[1]

Kenneth Bock, a biomedical specialist in what he terms the "4-A disorders" *(autism, ADHD, asthma, and allergies)* believes that diet plays a major role in the treatment of ASD but that there is also no single, magic bullet on this subject. In his own clinic, he has seen great improvements in children when prescribing diets that eliminated or reduced:

- foods containing gluten (protein found in wheat, barley, rye, and other grains) and/or casein (protein found in milk)
- foods to which the child was found to be allergic and/or sensitive
- foods that provoked the growth of intestinal yeast
- specific carbohydrates to which the child is found to have an adverse reaction
- foods that induce hypoglycemic reactions (extreme decreases in blood sugar levels)
- foods high in oxalates[2]

For more information on nutritional therapy, see these resources:

- Kenneth Bock and Cameron Stauth, *Healing the New Childhood Epidemics: Autism, ADHD, Asthma, and Allergies: The Groundbreaking Program for the 4-A Disorders* (New York: Ballantine Books, 2007)
- Jaqueline McCandless, *Children with Starving Brains: A Medical Treatment Guide for Autism Spectrum Disorders*, 2nd ed. (Putney, VT: Bramble Books, 2007)
- Karyn Seroussi, *Unraveling the Mystery of Autism and Pervasive Developmental Disorder: A Mother's Story of Research and Recovery*, 2nd ed. (New York: Broadway Books, 2002)
- Karyn Seroussi and Lisa S. Lewis, *The Encyclopedia of Dietary Interventions for the Treatment of Autism and Related Disorders* (Pennington, NJ: Sarpsborg Press, 2008)
- Autism Research Institute, http://www.autism.com

Biomedical Treatment: Supplementation Therapy

Supplementation therapy is the use of supplementary vitamins, minerals, amino acids, essential fatty acids, and herbal preparations to assist in remedying nutritional deficiencies or to otherwise assist the body to recover its natural biochemical balance.

Biochemical imbalances are extremely common in children with autism; in fact, it seems to be the rule rather than the exception. Nutritional supplementation has been found to be an effective component in a well-coordinated biomedical treatment program.[3]

Supplementation therapy is not a matter of just "throwing vitamins at the problem" but rather a skilled use of supplements in an orchestrated manner. For example, it may be best to administer several different groups of supplements, one after the other, but only after specific results have been achieved by the preceding group.

Dr. Kenneth Bock writes:

"Deficiencies, and sometimes excesses—particularly when they are present in numerous combinations—can create vast cascades of dysfunction in each of the three major systems involved in autism and ADHD:

- The gastrointestinal system
- The immune system
- The nervous system

Some parents, however, are resistant to the concept of supplementation therapy, because they often hear presumed experts in the media saying that a healthy diet is sufficient to provide all necessary nutrients. This sounds reasonable—but it's not. Kids with the 4-A disorders have specific, elevated needs. These heightened needs require full-scale, comprehensive nutritional and supplementation therapy—not just a wholesome diet. These kids need more than minimum daily requirements, or a one-a-day type of supplement."[4]

For more information about supplementation therapy, see these resources:

❍ Kenneth Bock and Cameron Stauth, *Healing the New Childhood Epidemics: Autism, ADHD, Asthma, and Allergies: The Groundbreaking Program for the 4-A Disorders* (New York: Ballantine Books, 2007)

○ Jaquelyn McCandlesss, *Children with Starving Brains: A Medical Treatment Guide for Autism Spectrum Disorders*, 2nd ed. (Putney, VT: Bramble Books, 2007)

○ Autism Research Institute, http://www.autism.com

Biomedical Treatment: Detoxification

Detoxification is the removal of foreign substances that are antagonistic toward the body and its various systems. Toxic substances, such as heavy metals (lead, mercury, cadmium, etc.), find their way into the body through any number of means: food, water, air, medications, and so forth. Other environmental poisons (such as pesticides, chemicals that comprise plastics, and hydrocarbons) commonly show up as deposits in the various tissues of the body.

As noted earlier in this book, these toxins are strongly suspected to play a primary role in the creation of conditions that bring about what we call autism.[5] Dr. Bock believes that:

Toxins, as much as any other single, isolated element, are a primary driving force of the 4-A epidemics.

Toxic heavy metals and environmental chemicals are the two most destructive toxic forces. They are, in my opinion, the greatest contributors to the epidemic of autism. In addition, they often play an important role in ADHD, and are often involved in the onset of asthma and allergies.

Many other factors contribute to the 4-A epidemics, including:

- Poor nutrition
- Immune dysfunction
- Gastrointestinal distress
- Genetic vulnerabilities
- Assaults by viruses, bacteria and fungi

However, many of these factors could be overcome or successfully endured by most children if it were not for the role played by toxins, and especially heavy metals.[6]

For more information on detoxification, see these resources:

○ Kenneth Bock and Cameron Stauth, *Healing the New Childhood Epidemics: Autism, ADHD, Asthma, and Allergies: The Groundbreaking Program for the 4-A Disorders* (New York: Ballantine Books, 2007)
○ Jaquelyn McCandless, *Children with Starving Brains: A Medical Treatment Guide for Autism Spectrum Disorders*, 2nd ed. (Putney, VT: Bramble Books, 2007)
○ Autism Research Institute, http://www.autism.com

Biomedical Treatment: Medication

There is an intense and long-running dispute about what constitutes a "drug" or a "medication." At one extreme are the interests that would classify any natural or synthetic substance that cures physical disorders or improves health as a "drug"—to the extent that many common wild and cultivated plants and vegetables could become subject to controlled usage. At the other extreme are those who would use no human-made substance of any kind.

Somewhere in between would lie, for example, "nutraceuticals," which are substances, often plant extracts, that may be considered foods or parts of food and that provide medicinal or health benefits, including the prevention and treatment of disease.

For the sake of the next few paragraphs, let's use the term "pharmaceutical" to represent highly processed medications or drugs manufactured by pharmaceutical firms and "nutraceuticals" to be that fuzzy zone somewhere between foods and pharmaceuticals.

That said, there are two general categories and several subcategories into which fall the various medications used in the treatment of autism and related disorders:

1. Comorbid disorder medications
   - antibiotics: Many different forms of antibiotics (to treat bacterial infections) appropriate for children are well-known and easily administered once the condition that calls for their use has been properly diagnosed.
   - antivirals: Long-term viral infections can contribute heavily to immune system dysfunctions. For example, live measles virus from the measles-mumps-rubella vaccination can take up residence in the gut

and thereby enter other systems of the body. Appropriate antivirals are often available for the treatment of children.[7]

- antifungals: *Candida albicans* is a fungus that commonly infects the gastrointestinal tract and can spread to other systems of the body, provoking many kinds of disorders, including imbalances of the bowels, allergies, immune dysfunction, and—directly or indirectly—the entrance of neurotoxins into the brain.[8] Antifungal medications are also well-known and tested.

- anti-inflammatories: Inflammations of various tissues and membranes in the body can contribute heavily to phenomena identified with autism. Inflammation can be initially specific to a particular organ (for example, the bowels) but can spread more widely throughout the body, including the brain. Though there are many pharmaceutical anti-inflammatories, "the best medications for long-term treatment of widespread inflammation are the nutraceuticals, accompanied by nutritional therapy."[9]

- other medications specific to particular comorbid disorders (e.g., diabetes, allergies, high blood pressure, etc.)

2. Psychoactive medications

Psychoactive medications (also referred to as psychiatric or psychotropic medications) act primarily on the central nervous system and alter brain function. These medications consist of the following categories:

- stimulants: a class of medications used to treat ADHD and narcolepsy by increasing alertness and wakefulness

- antidepressants: a class of medications used to treat depression, anxieties, and obsessive behaviors

- mood stabilizers: a class of medications used to reduce volatile behavior and emotional outbursts and the symptoms of sudden and unpredictable mood shifts

- anti-anxiety medications: a class of medications used to reduce symptoms of fear and anxiety

- anti-psychotics: a class of medications used to treat the symptoms of psychosis (persons who are considered to have "lost contact with reality") and also used to stabilize moods and reduce hyperactivity, tics, and self-injurious behaviors

- anticonvulsants: a class of medications used to treat seizure disorders. A large percentage of children with autism suffer from seizure disorders at some point in their lives. Medications may be necessary to control the seizures, but, as with other psychoactive pharmaceuticals, these drugs do not cure the condition. Anticonvulsants are also used to treat mood disorders and pain.

- miscellaneous psychoactive pharmaceuticals used for sleep, bed-wetting, and other problems.[10]

For more information on medication, see this resource:

○ Timothy Wilens, *Straight Talk about Psychiatric Medications for Kids*, 2nd ed. (New York: Guilford Press, 2004)

Developmental Therapy: Developmental, Individual-Difference, Relationship-Based (DIR) / Floortime

DIR/Floortime is a comprehensive framework and holistic approach that enables clinicians and parents to construct a program tailored to the child's unique challenges and strengths. Developed by pediatric psychiatrist Stanley Greenspan and clinical psychologist Serena Wieder, DIR/Floortime is "based on the theory that children with autism have biologically based processing difficulties that affect their ability to have relationships with others. This approach focuses on helping children to master the building blocks of relating, communicating, and thinking, rather than on individual symptoms."[11] The heart of the DIR program is Floortime, a technique that encourages you to seek out what the child is currently willing to give her attention to and use that to engage her emotionally. Once this much has been accomplished, the next step may be to gradually shift her attention to other objects or aspects of life that up to this point she might not have been interested in or even aware of.

The primary means of accomplishing this are two-way communication, social reciprocity, and starting with or building on what the child is already capable of doing. By meeting the child at her own developmental level, a firm connection is established between the child and the parent or therapist.

Another key principle is to use the child's motivations as opposed to something the parent or teacher wishes to impose upon her. By following the child's lead, the adult can entice the child to engage in interactions and thus "climb the developmental ladder"—that is, establish a stronger bond to the world and reality of other people around her. This therapy is inherently spontaneous, flexible, and warm, and it deals with subjects deeply meaningful to the child.

DIR/Floortime strongly encourages a cross-disciplinary approach, integrating speech, occupational, and other therapies together with educational programs, biomedical intervention, problem-solving exercises, and so on. Floortime professionals also consider the parents and other family members' emotional relationships with the child to be of paramount importance and strongly encourage activities that support those relationships.[12]

For more information on DIR/Floortime, see these resources:

○ Stanley I. Greenspan and Serena Wieder, *Engaging Autism: Helping Children Relate, Communicate, and Think with the Floortime Approach* (Cambridge, MA: Da Capo Lifelong Books, 2006)
○ Interdisciplinary Council on Developmental and Learning Disorders, http://www.icdl.com

Developmental Therapy: Relationship Development Intervention (RDI)

RDI was developed by pediatric psychologist Steven Gutstein "in response to concerns about older methods of ABA [Applied Behavioral Analysis] . . . [and its] strict impersonal approach to teaching. . . . Because of the inflexible and often counterproductive procedures used in ABA during that time, children were not encouraged to seek or desire social interaction nor did the method foster interaction or experience sharing." (See page 171 for a description of ABA.) RDI's goals "include helping children with autism become more flexible thinkers and to adapt more easily to ever-changing environments . . . [so they can] gain the important missing pieces that allow [them] to truly understand the shared benefit of being with others."[13]

According to RDI Connect, RDI is

a program for educating and coaching parents and teachers of children with Autism Spectrum Disorders (ASD) and others who interact and work with the child. . . . The mission of RDI is to develop the most effective methods to remediate those specific deficits which impede people on the autism spectrum from productive employment, independent living, marriage and intimate social relationships. . . .

RDI empowers families and those who are primarily involved in caring for and educating the child. The bulk of resources are invested in preparing parents and teachers to act as participant guides, creating daily opportunities for the child to respond in more flexible, thoughtful ways to novel, challenging and increasingly unpredictable settings and problems. Both fathers and mothers are essential participants in the treatment process.[14]

For more information on RDI, see these resources:

○ Steven E. Gutstein and Rachelle K. Sheely, *Relationship Development Intervention with Young Children: Social and Emotional Development Activities for Asperger Syndrome, Autism, PDD and NLD* (Philadelphia: Jessica Kingsley Publishers, 2002)
○ Relationship Development Intervention (RDI), http://www.rdiconnect.com

Developmental Therapy: The SCERTS Model

The SCERTS Model was developed by Barry M. Prizant, PhD, CCC-SLP (Certificate of Clinical Competency in Speech-Language Pathology); Amy M. Wetherby, PhD, CCC-SLP; Emily Rubin, MS, CCC-SLP; and Amy C. Laurent, EdM, OTR/L (Occupational Therapist, Registered, Licensed). The SCERTS Model is a comprehensive, multidisciplinary educational and treatment approach to enhancing social communication and emotional abilities of children with ASD in everyday activities across home, school, and community settings.

The model was developed to address the critical foundations that best support children with ASD across a range of abilities, as well as specific intervention goals and priorities based on our most current understanding of ASD as a developmental disability.

The SCERTS Model prioritizes social communication, emotional regulation, and transactional support as the primary domains that must be addressed in a comprehensive program. The social communication domain focuses on building spontaneous, functional communication abilities and relationships across a variety of partners and activities.

The emotional regulation domain teaches strategies to help children to be most available for learning and engaging and for preventing the development of problem behavior.

Transactional support focuses on implementing appropriate strategies for supporting children interpersonally, for supporting children's learning, and for enhancing parent-professional relationships. Family members are considered experts on their children and collaborate closely with professionals to build the most functional and meaningful skills that will enable children to develop warm and trusting relationships with others and to actively participate in daily activities at home, at school, and in the community.[15]

For more information on the SCERTS Model, see these resources:

○ Barry M. Prizant et al., *The SCERTS Model: A Comprehensive Educational Approach for Children with Autism Spectrum Disorders* (Baltimore: Brookes Publishing, 2005)
○ SCERTS website: http://www.scerts.com

Developmental Therapy: Son-Rise Program

The Son-Rise Program was originated in 1974 by two parents, Barry Neil Kaufman and Samahria Lyte Kaufman, for their son, Raun, who was diagnosed with autism before the age of two. The Son-Rise Program is taught at the Autism Treatment Center of America, part of a nonprofit organization founded by the Kaufmans in 1983.

Their organization's website describes the program as "stimulating, high-energy, one-on-one, home-based, and child-centered." Their operating principles include:

"Joining in a child's repetitive and ritualistic behaviors supplies the key to unlocking the mystery of these behaviors and facilitates eye contact, social development and the inclusion of others in play.

Utilizing a child's own motivation advances learning and builds the foundation for education and skill acquisition.

Teaching through interactive play results in effective and meaningful socialization and communication.

Using energy, excitement and enthusiasm engages the child and inspires a continuous love of learning and interaction.

Employing a nonjudgmental and optimistic attitude maximizes the child's enjoyment, attention and desire throughout their Son-Rise Program®.

Placing the parent as the child's most important and lasting resource provides a consistent and compelling focus for training, education and inspiration.

Creating a safe, distraction-free work/play area facilitates the optimal environment for learning and growth."[16]

The pace and subjects are determined by the child's interests, and they are then used as an entrance point into the child's private world. The idea is that by undertaking interactions of this nature, the child begins to find success and pleasure in engaging the external world, thus making it more attractive to the child than the objects and topics he or she may be obsessed with.

For more information on the Son-Rise Program, see these resources:

- ❍ Barry Neil Kaufman, *Son-Rise: The Miracle Continues* (Tiburon, CA: H. J. Kramer, 1995)
- ❍ Autism Treatment Center of America, http://www.autismtreatment.org

Developmental Therapy: Hanen / More than Words

The Hanen Center's *More than Words* is a speech and language pathology program that identifies its goals as:

- ❍ improved two-way interaction
- ❍ more mature and conventional ways of communicating
- ❍ better skills in communicating for social purposes
- ❍ an improved understanding of language

The program "emphasizes the child's everyday activities as the context for learning to communicate."[17]

"The program's philosophy is that because parents are the most important people in a child's life, they are the best people to help the child learn to communicate. Your child will learn to communicate when he or she:

- • Pays attention to you
- • Finds enjoyment in two-way communication
- • Copies the things you do and say

- Understands what others say
- Interacts with other people
- Has fun!
- Practices what he or she learns often
- Has structure, repetition and predictability in his or her life"[18]

For more information on the Hanen Centre and More than Words, see these resources:

- ❍ Jan Pepper and Elaine Weitzman, *It Takes Two to Talk: A Practical Guide for Parents of Children with Language Delays* (Toronto: Hanen Centre, 2004)
- ❍ Hanen Centre, http://www.hanen.org

Behavioral Therapy: Applied Behavioral Analysis (ABA)

Behavioral therapies in general follow the principles of behavioral science and are thus grounded in the work of researchers Edward L. Thorndike and B. F. Skinner. ABA is the application of these basic principles toward the end of modifying undesirable behaviors. In simplest terms, the therapies included under the banner of ABA operate on a stimulus-response basis—positively reinforcing (teaching) socially appropriate behaviors whose delays are associated with the diagnosis of autistic disorder (speech, communication skills, play skills, social skill, self-help skills, etc.) and withholding reinforcement of (ignoring or redirecting) behavioral excesses (tantrums, aggression, self-injury, etc.). This basic approach has led to the development of a whole range of applications for children with autism, some of which are listed on the following pages.

The Lovaas Model of Early Intensive Behavioral Intervention is a specific behavioral treatment method employed by the Lovaas Institute and other Lovaas replication sites around the country. The Lovaas model was initiated by clinical psychologist Ole Ivar Lovaas beginning in the 1960s.

The method is targeted for children between the ages of two and eight. Lovaas intervention is behavioral; the procedures used and specified and the objective data are collected to evaluate the efficacy. Treatment requires family participation, and parents become part of the treatment team assisting in goal selection, choosing interventions, and direct teaching and evaluation of procedures. Lovaas treatment is intense not only in terms of the number of hours per week of structured intervention but also initially with one-to-one instruction to address developmental delays. Treatment is comprehensive in curriculum content to address language, social skills, play skills, self-help skills, pre-academic skills, and behavioral excesses; additionally treatment is conducted in all significant settings, including home, community, and school.

Therapy generally begins in the child's natural play environment and gradually transitions him or her to a structured environment where more complex aspects of the therapy can be conducted. Therapies use the Discrete Trial Teaching and Incidental Teaching methods, among others (see below for a definition of Discrete Trial Teaching and page 177 for a definition of Incidental Teaching). The overall goal of Lovaas therapy, as with ABA therapies in general, is to increase socially appropriate behaviors, skills, and relationships.[19]

For more information on ABA and the Lovaas model, see these resources:

○ Albert J. Kearney, *Understanding Applied Behavior Analysis: An Introduction to ABA for Parents, Teachers, and Other Professionals* (Philadelphia: Jessica Kingsley Publishers, 2007)

○ Catherine Maurice, Gina Green, and Stephen C. Luce, *Behavioral Intervention for Young Children with Autism: A Manual for Parents and Professionals* (Austin: Pro-Ed, 1996)

○ O. Ivar Lovaas, *Teaching Individuals with Developmental Delays: Basic Intervention Techniques* (Austin: Pr-Ed, 2003)

○ Lovaas Institute, http://www.lovaas.com

Behavioral Therapies: Discrete Trial Teaching (DTT)

The discrete trial is a general ABA teaching method that seeks to teach complex skills and behaviors by breaking them down into subcomponents and teaching them with behavioral analysis methodology. B.F. Skinner is credited with coining the term "discrete trial" as a way of studying the interaction of a speaker and a listener. Discrete Trial Teaching is a procedure commonly used in many behavioral treatment regimes.

The basic steps are:

1. The skill or item to be taught is broken down into small steps or elements (such as "touch your shoulder" or "find a friend to play with").

2. A prompt is given by the teacher or therapist to help the child respond correctly (the teacher touches the child's shoulder or gestures to peers on the playground).

3. When the child does carry out the instruction, he or she is rewarded with an acknowledgment, physical object, or any reinforcer individualized to the child.

4. There is a slight pause given to separate trials. Data may be collected at this time, and then the exercise may be repeated again for further practice or another skill may be interspersed.

5. Gradually the teacher's prompts are reduced until the child can perform the skill independently.

Gradually these simple tasks are compiled into accomplishing some larger, more complex tasks or chains of behaviors.[20]

For more information on Discrete Trial Teaching, see these resources:

○ Sandra L. Harris and Mary Jane Gill-Weis, *Right from the Start: Behavioral Intervention for Young Children with Autism* (Bethesda, MD: Woodbine House, 1998)

○ Suzannah Ferraioli, Carrie Hughes, and Tristram Smith, "A Model for Problem Solving in Discrete Trial Training for Children with Autism," *Journal of Early and Intensive Behavioral Intervention* 2 (Winter 2005): 224–246

○ O. Ivar Lovaas, *Teaching Individuals with Developmental Delays: Basic Intervention Techniques* (Austin: Pr-Ed, 2003)

○ Lovaas Institute, http://www.lovaas.com

Behavioral Therapy: Verbal Behavior (VB)

The analysis of Verbal Behavior (VB) is the behavioral psychology approach to language instruction. B.F. Skinner's text *Verbal Behavior*, published in 1957, provides a conceptual guide for the development of language.

More recently, behavior analysts involved in education and the treatment of children with autism have adopted Skinner's theories as an approach to teaching language and social interaction to children with autism.

An example of application of the Verbal Behavior approach to teaching the concept of "cookie" requires that the child be able to:

- ❍ "Ask for a cookie when it is wanted . . .
- ❍ Find the cookie when it is asked for . . .
- ❍ Select a cookie if asked:
  - What do you eat? . . .
  - What has chocolate chips? . . .
  - Find the food . . .
- ❍ Answer questions about the cookie when it is not present: . . .
  - Tell me what you eat.
  - What has chocolate chips?
  - What's crunchy?"[21]

Many ABA providers are making use of Skinner's conceptual guide to teach language within their existing programs. The application of the behavioral approach to language learning may result in even the most difficult-to-teach learners acquiring language skills.

For more information about Verbal Behavior, see these resources:

- ❍ Mary Barbera and Tracy Rasmussen, *The Verbal Behavior Approach: How to Teach Children with Autism and Related Disorders* (Philadelphia: Jessica Kingsley Publishers, 2007)
- ❍ Robert Schramm, *Educate Toward Recovery: Turning the Tables on Autism* (Morrisville, NC: Lulu Press, 2007)
- ❍ Carbone Clinic, http://www.drcarbone.net
- ❍ VBN Training, http://www.vbntraining.com

Behavioral Therapies: Pivotal Response Training (PRT)

Developed by Robert L. Koegel, PhD, and Laura Schreibman, PhD, PRT is a behavior treatment based upon the principles of ABA.

"Researchers have identified two pivotal behaviors that affect a wide range of behaviors in children with autism: motivation and responsivity to multiple cues. These behaviors are central to a wide area of functioning, so positive changes in these behaviors should have widespread effects on other behaviors. Thus PRT is able to increase the generalization of new skills while increasing the motivation of children to perform these behaviors being taught to them. PRT works to increase motivation by including components such as child choice, turn-taking, reinforcing attempts and interspersing maintenance tasks. PRT has been used to target language skills, play skills and social behaviors in children with autism."[22]

In its application, PRT consists of specific, practical guidelines for how to teach verbal or other types of skills while engaging in some natural activity. Guidelines include:

1. Ensure that you have the child's full attention before asking a question or giving an instruction. (For example, touch the child on the arm gently until you have his attention.)
2. Give clear, unambiguous, situation-appropriate instructions or questions. ("Please put the forks on the table" instead of "Help me with the table.")
3. Use natural opportunities to teach verbal behavior. (Child is banging on the door, obviously wanting to go out but does not speak what she wants. Her brother goes over to her, gets her full attention, and then asks her what she wants to do. The child responds, "Out!" Her brother responds by opening the door.)
4. Teach only one thing at a time ("acquisition tasks"), and intersperse repetitions of the teaching with other activities he can already do ("maintenance tasks") so as to not overwhelm the child with too much too fast.
5. Give "reinforcement" (full acknowledgments for correct responses) immediately but only if the tasks are correctly carried out.[23]

For more information on PRT, see these resources:

- ○ Robert L. Koegel and Lynn Kern Koegel, *Pivotal Response Treatments for Autism: Communication, Social, and Academic Development* (Baltimore: Brookes Publishing, 2006)
- ○ UCSC Autism Research Program, http://psy.ucsd.edu/autism/prttraining .html

Behavioral Therapy: Picture Exchange Communication System (PECS)

PECS is a training protocol based upon the principles laid out in B.F. Skinner's book *Verbal Behavior*, as well as principles of ABA combined with typical language development. The principal text on the subject is the *PECS Training Manual* (second edition), written by Lori Frost, MS, CCC/SLP, and Andrew Bondy, PhD, who developed and published the technique in 1985.

There are six phases to learning PECS. In the first phase a child is taught to initiate communication by exchanging a picture for a favorite food or toy. The "communication partner" (a parent, therapist, caregiver, or another child) hands the child the food or toy. This exchange reinforces the communication. Phase two teaches the child to actively seek out a desired picture and to take it to the "teacher." In the third phase the child is taught to discriminate among pictures and select the one that represents the item he or she wants.

Over time, the complexity of the exchange increases to include sentence structure and more advanced language concepts. In phase four the child learns to construct an entire sentence strip ("*I want book*") to make a request. Once basic sentence structure is mastered, the child will begin to add attributes into the sentence (color, shape, size). Phase five teaches the child to respond to the question "What do you want?" By the time the child advances to phase six, PECS can be used to make comments about things seen or heard in the environment spontaneously and in response to a question.[24]

The system is used to teach functional communication (getting across one's needs and wants) at a wide range of ages, from preschool children to adults.

For more information on PECS, see these resources:

○ Andy Bondy and Lori Frost, *A Picture's Worth: PECS and Other Visual Communication Strategies in Autism* (Bethesda, MD: Woodbine House, 2001)
○ PECS, http://www.pecs.com

Behavioral Therapies: Positive Behavior Support (PBS)

Positive Behavior Support (PBS) is a behavior modification technique that is especially targeted for children with challenging types of behavior patterns. The first step is a "functional behavior assessment" (FBA), which includes:

1. Describing the problem behavior and the general environment in which it commonly occurs

2. Identifying the events, situations, conditions, persons, etc., associated with the behavior that might be used to anticipate a reoccurrence
3. Identifying the consequences or outcomes that might maintain the behavior
4. Determining the functional use or possible motivation of the behavior

Once these steps are completed, various strategies may be used to change the child's behavior including:

○ teaching new behavior skills
○ preventing the occurrence of the undesirable behavior by ensuring that the challenging behavior is no longer permitted to be functional (i.e., the child can no longer use it to get what she wants)
○ modifying the child's exposure to the environment in which the behavior is likely to occur.[25]

For more information on PBS, see these resources:

○ Lynn Kern Koegel, Robert L. Koegel, and Glen Dunlap, *Positive Behavioral Support: Including People with Difficult Behavior in the Community* (Baltimore: Brookes Publishing, 1996)
○ University of South Florida Center for Evidence-Based Practice: Young Children with Challenging Behavior, http://challengingbehavior.fmhi.usf.edu/pbs.html

Behavioral Therapy: Incidental and Milieu Teaching

Incidental teaching is a behavioral method that seeks to encourage the child's language capabilities in their natural environments (hence "milieu teaching"). In general the steps are:

1. Observe that the child is in some fashion signaling he wants something.
2. Verify what the child is requesting.
3. Prompt the child to become more descriptive about what he desires, getting him to exercise his use of communication skills and language.
4. The child responds by becoming more descriptive in his request.
5. Confirm with the child his elaboration of the request.
6. Give the child what he has requested as reinforcement.[26]

These procedures are intended to be used within the context of the child's normal, daily interactions—with his parents, teachers, siblings, friends, etc. Typically the child's interests are followed in selecting the situation to be used in teaching. Thus, in preparing for the steps above, the parent or teacher might arrange the room with various preferred toys within sight but out of reach. Once the child shows some interest in one of the items, she uses these steps to provoke the child into communication so he can obtain what he wants.[27]

For more information on incidental and milieu teaching, see this resource:

❍ Interactive Collaborative Autism Network (ICAN), http://www.autism network.org/modules/academic/incidental/index.html

Structured Teaching and Environmental Support: TEACCH

The Treatment and Education of Autistic and Related Communication-Handicapped Children (TEACCH) method was developed in the early 1970s by the late Eric Schopler, PhD, at the University of North Carolina at Chapel Hill. TEACCH approaches individuals with ASD as a group with a distinct culture. Instead of trying to "normalize" the individual's behavior to a predefined educational method, TEACCH seeks to adjust the educational approach to the individual. For example, the physical teaching environment is adjusted until it works for the person or persons involved; schedules and other systems are adapted to support what works best for the students. Expectations are at all times clear and explicit, often using many visual materials. Heavy emphasis is placed upon helping students develop skills that support self-determined actions and independence of direct adult prompting or cueing. These accommodations are made because individuals with ASD process information differently from those who develop typically.

To avoid dwelling on deficits, strengths and interests are given priority. For example, "extraordinary attention to detail" could be viewed as a maladaptation and something to be eliminated, or it could be viewed as a strength to be used and refined and to propel the student along her chosen educational pathway.

TEACCH believes that "these strategies enhance efforts to work positively and productively with these people, rather than coercing and forcing them in directions that do not interest them and that they cannot comprehend."[28]

For more information on TEACCH, see these resources:

○ Gary B. Mesibov, Victoria Shea, and Eric Schopler, *The TEACCH Approach to Autism Spectrum Disorders* (New York: Springer, 2004)
○ TEACCH, http://www.teacch.com

Structured Teaching and Environmental Support: Social Stories and Storymovies

Social Stories was developed in 1991 by author Carol Gray, PhD. Gray later developed Storymovies, which use a video format but have the same basic design and intent as Social Stories.

"A Social Story describes a situation, skill, or concept in terms of relevant social cues, perspectives, and common responses in a specifically defined style and format. The goal of a Social Story is to share accurate social information in a patient and reassuring manner that is easily understood by its audience. Half of all Social Stories developed should affirm something that an individual does well. Although the goal of a Story should never be to change the individual's behavior, that individual's improved understanding of events and expectations may lead to more effective responses.

Although Social Stories were first developed for use with children with ASD, the approach has also been successful with children, adolescents, and adults with ASD and other social and communication delays and differences, as well as individuals developing normally."[29]

These stories deal with subjects ranging from waiting in lines, eating a meal, toileting, speaking up for oneself, sharing toys, etc. The stories are written using very specific guidelines that seek to ensure the quality and effectiveness of the material. In some ways this technique is similar to how a person might learn about the "do's and don'ts" of a foreign culture.

For more information on Social Stories, see these resources:

○ Jed Baker, *The Social Skills Picture Book: Teaching Play, Emotion, and Communication to Children with Autism* (Arlington, TX: Future Horizons, 2003)
○ Carol Gray, *The New Social Story Book* (Arlington, TX: Future Horizons, 2000)

○ The Gray Center, http://www.thegraycenter.org
○ Storymovies, http://storymovies.com

Structured Teaching and Environmental Support: Augmentative and Alternative Communication

Augmentative and alternative communication (AAC) is a general term that includes any system that may be used to assist a person to communicate effectively with others. The system can be as simple as sketching a stick drawing on a pad of paper, communicating with sign language, or using a picture book to indicate what he wishes to say, or it can be as complex as computer-based speech synthesis audio equipment.

For more information on AAC, see this resource:

○ Joanne Cafiero, *Meaningful Exchanges for People with Autism: An Introduction to Augmentative and Alternative Communication* (Bethesda, MD: Woodbine House, 2005)

Clinical Therapy: Speech and Language Therapy

The difficulties a child with autism has with speech and language can run in two directions: (1) Speech and the use of language can be physically difficult for them, thus inhibiting their social involvements. (2) They can have a withdrawal from social involvements for reasons having nothing to do with physical speech; however, this reluctance to be involved with others can reduce their interest in speaking. A failure to develop communications skills can then feed back into becoming even more socially withdrawn, creating a downward spiral.

Speech therapy seeks to help the child improve her communication abilities in all respects: comprehension, expression, sound production, and social use of language. The therapy itself may be conducted using whatever means of communication the child is physically able to master. Thus speech therapy can be accomplished with picture symbols and sign language as well as with common verbal speech. To be effective, this therapy should begin as early as its need is detected; it should be conducted frequently and become integrated into the child's normal life through the use of play.[30]

For more information on speech and language therapy, see this resource:

○ The American Speech–Language-Hearing Association, http://www.asha.org

Clinical Therapy: Occupational Therapy (OT) and Sensory Integration (SI)

Occupational therapy consists of a diverse set of techniques that seek to improve an individual's physical, fine motor, perceptual, and sensory capabilities through the medium of productive and creative activities. For young children, their creative activities are largely play, and their productive actions generally concern caring for themselves (bathing, feeding, dressing, etc.); thus these activities are those most commonly used. OT can help to decrease developmental delays; improve strength, coordination, visual skills, and the ability to manipulate objects; coordinate motor actions; and improve the child's confidence in handling the world around him.

Sensory integration (SI) was originally developed by A. Jean Ayres, PhD, OTR, who was both an occupational therapist and an educational psychologist. Sensory integration therapy is a specialty area of OT and seeks to improve a child's ability to process sensory information and coordinate it with other, simultaneous activities. For example, a child may be encouraged to fish through a tub filled with ping pong balls to find a wooden block hidden somewhere within it or, while swinging in a hammock, to sense how the pull of inertia feels as her body moves back and forth.

The idea is that children with autism often do not seem to process or integrate sensory information as neurotypical children do. This can result in an inability to bridge the gap in perceptual reality between themselves and other "normal" children. By having them experience a few enjoyable streams of perceptions simultaneously, children with autism can be led into experiencing the world as others around them do.[31]

For more information on OT and SI, see these resources:

○ A. Jean Ayres, *Sensory Integration and the Child* (Prescott, AZ: Western Psychological Services, 2005)
○ Paula Aquilla, Shirley Sutton, and Ellen Yack, *Building Bridges through Sensory Integration: Therapy for Children with Autism and Other Pervasive Developmental Disorders* (Arlington, TX: Future Horizons, 2003)

- Lucy Jane Miller and Doris A. Fuller, *Sensational Kids: Hope and Help for Children with Sensory Processing Disorder* (New York: Perigee, 2007)
- Lindsey Biel and Nancy Peske, *Raising a Sensory Smart Child: The Definitive Handbook for Helping Your Child with Sensory Integration Issues* (New York: Penguin, 2005)
- Carol Stock Kranowitz and Lucy Jane Miller, *The Out-of-Sync Child: Recognizing and Coping with Sensory Processing Disorder* (New York: Perigee, 2006)
- American Occupational Therapy Association, http://www.aota.org

Clinical Therapy: Physical Therapy (PT)

Physical therapy generally addresses matters involving gross (large) motor skills and balance, such as crawling, walking, running, jumping, climbing, etc. The physical therapist coaxes and assists the child to perform actions that stimulate his progressive coordination and integration of large motor actions with the goal of his achieving mastery over these activities commensurate with neurotypical children of his age.

As with many other therapies, physical therapists often specialize in working with particular age groups, since the approach and techniques can be rather different as a child gets older. The therapist may also be involved in suggesting and selecting assistive devices appropriate for the condition of the child.[32]

For more information on physical therapy, see this resource:

- American Physical Therapy Association, http://www.apta.org

Clinical Therapy: Social Skills Training

Often children with autism have a difficult time grasping the social skills that neurotypical children learn intuitively. Thus it can be helpful to provide them with special training (appropriate to their age and development) that will help them interact more comfortably with children who have acquired these social protocols without conscious awareness.

Social skills can be broken down to basic verbal and nonverbal activities that are quite teachable: how to speak so you are understood, how far to stand from someone while speaking, what body language is and how to use it, and so forth.[33]

For more information on social skills training, see these resources:

○ Ann E. Densmore, *Helping Children with Autism Become More Social: 76 Ways to Use Narrative Play* (Westport, CT: Praeger Publishers, 2007)
○ Kelly McKinnon and Janis L. Krempa, *Social Skills Solutions: A Hands-on Manual for Teaching Social Skills to Children with Autism* (New York: DRL Books, 2005)

Clinical Therapy: Listening Therapy

Listening therapy was invented by Dr. Alfred A. Tomatis, an internationally known otolaryngologist (or ENT—ear, nose, and throat specialist). Starting with his discovery that "the voice can only produce the harmonics that the ear is able to perceive," he invented methods of training or "reeducating" the ear as means to rehabilitate persons with speaking, singing, or language difficulties. Later he extended the application of his discoveries to improving the functions of alertness, attention, and coordination, which in turn strongly affect the domains of thinking and therefore perception in general.

Several different schools of therapy have since descended from his seminal work. These methods can be characterized (and enormously oversimplified) as the structured use of tones, sounds, and music to accomplish a wide variety of therapeutic ends, including improved emotional state, better self-regulation, and improved motor coordination among others.

In addition to the Tomatis Method, another popular listening therapy is called Auditory Integration Training (AIT), which was developed by French ENT physician Dr. Guy Berard as a means to help individuals who have suffered losses, hypersensitivities, or distortions of hearing. Later it was found that these techniques could be successfully applied to persons on the autism spectrum who had various auditory, language, and other sensory problems.

For example, children with hypersensitivity to sounds at certain frequencies can be desensitized using these methods. Or a child could have asymmetrical hearing—perceiving better out of one ear than another—that can lead to various learning difficulties, which can be mistakenly attributed to other reasons and thus never get resolved.[34]

Subsequently, additional methods of listening therapy were developed by other practitioners, including Ingo Steinbach's Samonas Sound Therapy.

For more information on listening therapy, see these resources:

○ Dorinne S. Davis, *Sound Bodies through Sound Therapy* (Mt. Arlington, NJ: Kalco Publishing, 2004)
○ Paul Madaule, *Listening Training for Children with Autism*, The Listening Centre, Toronto, 2004, http://www.listeningcentre.com/pdf/15autism.pdf

Clinical Therapy: Vision Therapy

"Vision therapy is a series of treatment procedures prescribed by optometrists to improve certain types of vision problems that cannot be helped with only glasses or contact lenses. Vision therapy is much akin to physical therapy for the eyes, during which vision disorders are corrected to improve patients' visual function and performance.

Vision therapy treats vision problems children have when using their eyes up close, especially at school. Problems with tracking, eye teaming, and focusing make it impossible for children to read, learn, and remain on task. . . .

Before a child can begin a vision therapy program, he or she must be seen by the doctor for a complete developmental vision evaluation and diagnostic workup. In addition to checking the child's eye health and sharpness of vision (visual acuity as measured by the eye chart), the doctor will complete a comprehensive assessment to evaluate the child's eye teaming, tracking, focusing, visual perception, and eye-hand coordination skills."[35]

Thus, while it is not necessarily a direct treatment for autism as a disorder, it might be appropriate and helpful in cases in which a child is diagnosed with vision difficulties.

For more information on vision therapy, see these resources:

○ Children's Vision Information Network, http://www.childrensvision.com
○ Optometrists Network National Directory of Vision Therapy Providers, http://www.visiontherapydirectory.com

Clinical Therapy: Music Therapy

Music as a means of human improvement is actually quite ancient and has often been mentioned as "therapy for the soul." In more recent times, the study and practice of music have been used to treat a wide range of problems and disorders that are nonmusical in nature.

For example, playing music has been used as a therapy for people with arthritis, anxiety, or motor coordination difficulties. The rhythmic nature of music can be very calming; the challenge of learning to play an instrument in which one has interest can serve to focus the attention of a mind that would otherwise be dispersed. Learning musical skills can provide an environment of structure, with one-on-one interactions and reciprocating communication, thus potentially aiding in cases of communication disorders. Music therapy has become a standard therapeutic technique in the toolbox of professionals who treat children with ASD. Certification of a music therapist is performed by the Certification Board for Music Therapists.[36]

For more information on music therapy, see these resources:

- ❍ Dorita S. Berger, *Music Therapy, Sensory Integration and the Autistic Child* (Philadelphia: Jessica Kingsley Publishers, 2002)
- ❍ American Music Therapy Association at http://www.musictherapy.org/

Clinical Therapy: Art Therapy

"Art therapy is the therapeutic use of art making, within a professional relationship, by people who experience illness, trauma, or challenges in living, and by people who seek personal development. Through creating art and reflecting on the art products and processes, people can increase awareness of self and others, cope with symptoms, stress, and traumatic experiences; enhance cognitive abilities; and enjoy the life-affirming pleasures of making art.

Art therapists are professionals trained in both art and therapy. They are knowledgeable about human development, psychological theories, clinical practice, spiritual, multicultural and artistic traditions, and the healing potential of art. They use art in treatment, assessment and research, and provide consultations to allied professionals. Art therapists work with people of all ages: individuals, couples, families, groups and communities. They provide services, individually and as part of clinical teams, in settings that include mental health, rehabilitation, medical and forensic institutions; community outreach programs; wellness centers; schools; nursing homes; corporate structures; open studios and independent practices.

The American Art Therapy Association, Inc. (AATA) sets educational, professional, and ethical standards for its members. The Art Therapy Credentials Board, Inc. (ATCB), an independent organization, grants credentials."[37]

For more information on art therapy, see these resources:

○ Cathy Malchiodi, *Art Therapy Sourcebook* (New York: McGraw-Hill, 2006)
○ American Art Therapy Association, http://www.arttherapy.org

Clinical Therapy: Animal Therapy

Animal therapy is based upon the natural therapeutic effects that result from forming close relationships with animals. While this phenomenon has been known for ages, it was only in the 1990s that formal standards were established for the clinical use of horseback riding therapy (hippotherapy) in treating children with mental disabilities. Hippotherapy has evolved to the point where it is considered an advanced physical therapy and has its own licensing and certification board (the American Hippotherapy Board).

Aside from the healing nature of the emotional connections made between child and animal, the physical motions of (for example) riding a horse can:

○ provide deep pressure to the skeletal and muscular systems, simultaneously stimulating them and soothing them
○ improve posture
○ improve motor coordination
○ improve muscle strength and balance

Additionally, the interest many children naturally have in forming relationships with animals causes them to be more observant of consequences and motivates them to learn how to communicate and interact better.[38]

For more information on animal therapy, see this resource:

○ Merope Pavlides, *Animal-Assisted Interventions for Individuals with Autism* (Philadelphia: Jessica Kingsley Publishers, 2008)
○ North American Riding for the Handicapped Association (NARHA), http://www.narha.org/

These are just a handful of the various approaches out there. There are many more possibilities—some that have been scientifically evaluated and many more that have not. Do not be afraid to turn over a few stones yourself and look outside the box. Remember, all of the treatments listed in this chapter, at one time or another, were also considered "outside the box."

Here is one more book to check out:

○ Lisa A. Kurtz, *Understanding Controversial Therapies for Children with Autism, Attention Deficit Disorder, and Other Learning Disabilities: A Guide to Complementary and Alternative Medicine* (Philadelphia: Jessica Kingsley Publishers, 2008)

IN A SENTENCE

> *What is most important is that you find treatments best suited to your child and family's circumstances.*

MONTH **4**

Making Observations and Understanding What They Mean

ONE OF THE best things you can do is to train yourself to become an expert observer of your child. When my daughter was young, I observed her every chance I could during therapy sessions. Sometimes there were one-way mirrors that would make this easy, and other times I would just sit as unobtrusively as possible. When there were changes in diet, medication, and routines, I took notes, recording her reactions and behaviors. This became part of a way of life: watching for changes in behavior and development (good and bad), and tracing them back to what may have brought them about. Sometimes I'd notice something that most people don't think about: that is, *no change* for an extended period of time when you might have expected some.

I drew up charts to organize these observations, and this made it easier to link them with events just prior to the change—events that may have caused or reinforced what I was now observing.

In many cases, I could figure out what precipitated the changes; in other cases, the causes were simply mysterious. Nevertheless, the exercise made me an excellent, instinctual observer and detective. It also made it possible for me to teach others how to observe my child—be it a grandparent, child care provider, or teacher. This is something I would like to share with you.

Age	Fifty-one months
Date	June 15, 2000
Medication	Risperdal, (low dose) twice daily
Vitamins/supplements	Twice daily (dissolved in grape juice and put into sippy cup):
	Antioxidants, vitamin supplements, Omega-3 Essential Fatty Acids, Cod Liver Oil, Calcium/Magnesium, Zinc
Food/drinks/snacks	(Note: all foods are gluten-, casein-, soy-, dye-, and additive-free)
	Breakfast (at home): banana, cereal, apple juice
	Snack (at school-brought from home): grape juice, strawberries, raisins
	Lunch (at school-brought from home): chicken, rice, carrot sticks, cookie, grape juice
	Snack (in car-brought from home): pretzels, juice, fruit (apple)
	Dinner (at home): hamburger (no bun), sliced cucumber, carrots, raw broccoli, pineapple
Elimination (character of stools)	Normal
Therapies	Occupational and speech therapy at school: Working on writing her name. Confusion about which hand to use. Seemed to enjoy it, as always.
	After school, social skills group with speech and language therapist: speaking in short sentences; great affect (emotional expression), though speech is very scripted. Tried to take the toys from another child. Perseverated on playing with toy grocery store—a little difficult to redirect her.
	Late afternoon, 20 minutes of Floortime. Great session. Lots of exchanges, wonderful affect; noticed that her tactile defensiveness has decreased significantly.
	Evening, very little time left so did Floortime in bathtub. Played with bathtub set of Teletubbies. Had a good time; completed 15 circles of communication. Worked on gestures and hide and seek. Nice affect, a lot of eye contact, great laughter.
Recreational activities	Watched *Mister Rogers* for 15 minutes before dinner.
Play dates	Played with 1 peer (4 years old) during social skills group and played with neighbor (5 years old) for 30 minutes while I made dinner.
Self-care activities	Dressed self as usual, toilet use okay.
General observations	In school until 2 pm. Was happy, mildly hyper.
	Did usual bedtime routine—went okay.

Two days passed with events not so different from this one. Then on June 18, the following happened:

Age	Fifty-one months
Date	June 18, 2000
Medication	No change
Vitamins/supplements	No change
Food/drinks/snacks	(Note: all foods are gluten-, casein-, soy-, dye-, and additive-free unless noted)
	Breakfast (at home): banana, waffle, syrup, apple juice, strawberries
	Snack (at home): grape juice, banana, cereal
	Lunch (at restaurant): homemade chicken nuggets, restaurant French fries, ketchup, salad with olive oil and balsamic vinegar
	Snack (at home): grapes, apple juice
	Dinner (at home): pasta with tomato sauce, cooked peas, apple sauce, cookie
Elimination (character of stools)	In morning, normal.
	15 minutes after lunch, diarrhea. Lasted 3 hours.
	In evening, normal.
Therapies	(Sunday schedule)
	Two 30-minute sessions of sensory integration (SI): ball pit, trampoline, swing, rice/sand bin, music, reading
	Four 20-minute sessions of Floortime.
	Morning sessions: Went well. She was perseverating on using toy foods in a basket (taking the exact same foods each time). Managed to bridge her to using more objects in her play and feeding it to a doll. Pretended to be a checkout person. Did very well with ball pit and trampoline. Had difficulty sitting for music and reading.
	Afternoon sessions: Couldn't get her focused at all; extraordinarily hyper, impossible to redirect, and went into a tantrum.
Recreational activities	Tried taking a walk but went into tantrum and took half an hour to get her back up the driveway.
Play dates	None
Self-care activities	Fine in morning. In evening she was over-stimulated and tired. She wouldn't undress herself so I had to do it. Didn't attempt to bathe her.
General observations	15 minutes after lunch she had severe diarrhea and out-of-control behavior. Running around manic, giddy, climbing on everything, in perpetual motion.

Since the days immediately preceding had been relatively uneventful, the phenomena of the day seemed to occur immediately following lunch. I brought chicken and salad with homemade dressing from home. I was careful in choosing the restaurant (never "fast food"). The only things she'd eaten at the restaurant were French fries and ketchup. The waitress assured me the fries were homemade with only potatoes and olive oil (no spices or additives), and the pan was washed before using it. The ketchup was a brand we'd often used without any problem, one that was supposedly gluten-free. I investigated further by reading the helpful website www.gfcfdiet.com and discovered that this particular batch of ketchup had been produced on machinery also used for processing other foods containing wheat. What happened made sense: The ketchup was cross-contaminated with traces of wheat. Sarah was very sensitive to gluten, and this was how she typically reacted when she ate wheat; gluten was the cause for the day's events.

As a result of the last day's experience, her nutritionist suggested we add digestive enzymes to her diet as a safeguard, and that helped.

You Can Use the Daily Logbook to Test New Treatments

One important use of this method of observation will be trying out treatments that are low on the evidence-based treatment scale (see Day 4). Some practitioners may throw up roadblocks to trying things, stating (accurately) that there are no formal, double-blind placebo studies on this or that treatment. When I encounter this situation, I tell the doctor that I don't need a double-blind study to know what is working with my child and what is not. I am the best observer of my child; I can anticipate her needs and wants, and I know what all her indicators mean. I know what the signs are long before she is about to "fall off the edge," and I know when she is starting to feel better—before even she realizes it.

With this kind of skill and with note taking, the parent-observer can much more easily suggest modifications to the child's program, since the suggestions are now based upon documented cause-and-effect evidence.

The same idea applies to any of the therapeutic methods. You can normally trace back both good and bad phenomena to one or more changes just prior to the phenomena emerging.

The Ideal: One Change at a Time

Being able to trace phenomena back to specific causes means that it is important not to make a lot of changes in your child's program all at once. The best method is to introduce only one change at a time. By allowing enough of an interval to pass to permit sufficient observation, you can have a clear view of the consequences of that one change, untainted by other changes. And since so many children with autism are extremely sensitive to changes, this is good advice to guide you. Of course in the real world this is not so easy to arrange; it can be hard to know the real cause of change in your child's behavior when she is going through a necessary change in her school program while at the same time alterations are made in her diet or supplementation levels. Nevertheless, the principle of controlling or limiting the number of changes is something you should aim for, since it will make correcting the program much easier.

IN A SENTENCE

Patient, careful observation is the essential groundwork for any effective treatment program.

living

An Example of Integrated Therapy

NOW THAT WE'VE gone over many of the vital pieces of "integrated therapy," let's look at how these elements might come together for a particular child.[1]

Remember: This is only one unique example. Your child's program will be very different. However, the following should give you some idea as to how integrated therapy can work.

Characteristics and Diagnoses

A thirty-month-old boy diagnosed with moderate ASD presented the following issues:

SOCIAL INTERACTION

- ○ exhibits minimal facial expressions, no pointing or showing gestures
- ○ has only limited use of eye contact
- ○ interacts very little with family members or peers (prefers to be alone)
- ○ has minimal social reciprocity (two-way exchanges with others)

COMMUNICATION

- O speaks only a few words and comprehends very little
- O doesn't respond to his name or to questions
- O can carry out simple, single-step actions with parental gestures but not actions that require multiple steps. For example, when a parent points to a toy and says, "Get your toy, and bring it to me," he can retrieve the toy, but he cannot bring it to the parent.
- O does not engage in social imitative play (play that mimics the interaction of people in real life)

REPETITIVE BEHAVIORS AND RESTRICTED INTERESTS

- O lines up trains obsessively, peels crayons repetitively, repeats same two words over and over again (however, words are not used in a meaningful way)
- O does not use objects functionally: wobbles bowls, rolls cups, and spins wheels on trains instead of using them appropriately

REGULATORY AND SENSORY SYSTEMS

- O experiences frequent mood swings and tantrums, from which he has trouble recovering
- O is extremely hyperactive (like a wind-up toy)
- O has a limited ability to focus
- O is over-reactive to or intolerant of many forms of sensory input, such as the low-pitched hum of a window air conditioner, the flushing of toilets, the tactile quality of sticky or gooey surfaces, and others, and does not like to be touched or held
- O has trouble understanding and following directions

BIOMEDICAL

- O has frequent diarrhea, skin rashes, and circles under the eyes

On the positive side:

- His **visual spatial memory** (ability to remember the placement of objects in space) is excellent: he can remember easily which box a certain toy is in, and he can put together a forty-five-piece puzzle very quickly.
- He seeks out parents for comfort when he is upset.
- He has emerging interest in establishing social interactions with his parents and siblings.
- He has a good range of affect and emotions.
- He demonstrates interest in a variety of toys (very skilled in manipulating mechanical toys) and activities (enjoys music and likes to sing).
- He has spontaneous vocalizations (babbling).
- He has a history of eating a variety of healthy foods.
- His parents have a strong determination to help.

FURTHER OBSERVATIONS AND EXAMINATION

The developmental pediatrician observed that the parents are very loving and affectionate with the child; however, they struggle when it comes to understanding how to engage his attention, keep his interest, and interact with him. They need to learn how to participate in his world and play with him.

Changes in the family's routines and environment were assessed as possibly contributing to the fluctuations in the child's mood and attention. Possible exposure to antagonistic environmental factors (such as toxins, dust, mold, noises, smells, foods, conflicts, and threatening circumstances) was considered.

Thorough biomedical testing was completed, and an analysis by team professionals concluded that gastrointestinal dysfunction and allergies might be the cause of:

- frequent diarrhea
- skin rashes
- circles under the eyes

and a contributing factor to:

- mood swings
- tantrums
- hyperactivity

Prioritization of Immediate Issues

While the team acknowledged the probability of several more comorbid issues, they felt no time should be lost getting treatment started for the obvious gastrointestinal dysfunction and allergies.

In addition to deficits in social reciprocity, they felt the following issues should also be addressed as soon as possible:

- ○ expressive language delay
- ○ severe auditory processing challenges
- ○ difficulty with motor planning
- ○ dysfunction with sensory modulation

Initial goals were identified for each of the following areas of concern:

Area	Goal
Social interactions	Create the condition in which the child is motivated to connect with the world around him.
	Get the child to engage and follow simple directions and commands.
	Maintain shared attention through back and forth continuous flow of communication (through either words, gestures, or play).
Communication	Use pretend play and one-word utterances to convey emotional intention ("happy," "sad").
Regulatory and sensory systems	Desensitize to specific sensory input, and begin to regulate attention and behavior while encouraging interest in a full range of sensations (sounds, sights, smells, movement patterns, etc.).
Biomedical	Reduce GI dysfunction and exposure to allergens and the damage these cause.

Recommended Treatments

Based on extensive testing, evaluations, and observations, the team considered a number of treatments from the list of possibilities and selected the ones listed in the table on pages 197–199.

> While many of the following therapeutic techniques are used routinely with children on the autism spectrum, they may not be appropriate for some children and in fact may be counterproductive for some children. Any recommendations for therapies or treatments (including medication) and its frequency are specific to this case example *only*. *The real needs of each case must be determined on a purely individual basis and never copied from some generalized example.*

	Goal: Create the condition in which the child is motivated to connect with the world around him.	Goal: Get the child to engage and follow simple directions and commands.	Goal: Maintain shared attention through back and forth continuous flow of communication (through words, gestures, or play).	Goal: Use pretend play and one-word utterances to convey emotional intention ("happy," "sad").	Goal: Desensitize to specific sensory input, and begin to regulate attention and behavior while encouraging interest in a full range of sensations (sounds, sights, smells, movement patterns, etc.).	Goal: Reduce GI dysfunction and exposure to allergens and the damage these cause.
Medical						
Biomedical						
Nutritional Therapy		YES ✓			YES ✓	YES ✓
Supplementation Therapy		YES ✓			YES ✓	YES ✓
Detoxification						
Medication						
Developmental Theories						
DIR/Floortime	YES ✓		YES ✓	YES ✓	YES ✓	
RDI						
SCERTS Model			YES ✓	YES ✓		
Son-Rise Program						
Hanen/More than Words						

continued

	Goal: Create the condition in which the child is motivated to connect with the world around him.	Goal: Get the child to engage and follow simple directions and commands.	Goal: Maintain shared attention through back and forth continuous flow of communication (through words, gestures, or play).	Goal: Use pretend play and one-word utterances to convey emotional intention ("happy," "sad").	Goal: Desensitize to specific sensory input, and begin to regulate attention and behavior while encouraging interest in a full range of sensations (sounds, sights, smells, movement patterns, etc.).	Goal: Reduce GI dysfunction and exposure to allergens and the damage these cause.
Behavioral Therapies						
Applied Behavioral Analysis (ABA)						
Discrete Trial Training						
Verbal Behavior						
Pivotal Response Training		YES ✓				
Picture Exchange Communication System (PECS)						
Positive Behavior Support						
Incidental and Milieu Teaching						

Structured Teaching and Environmental Support					
TEACCH					
Social Stories, Storymovies					
Augmentative Communication					
Clinical Therapies					
Speech-Language Therapy	YES ✓	YES ✓	YES ✓		
Occupational Therapy/ Sensory Integration	YES ✓	YES ✓		YES ✓	
Physical Therapy					
Social Skills Training					
Listening Therapy					
Vision Therapy					
Music Therapy					
Art Therapy					
Animal Therapy					

General Treatment Guidelines and Recommendations

Based on evaluations and observation, general guidelines were developed by the developmental pediatrician for the child's treatment plan. It was clear that the child needed to receive a lot of one-on-one support and intervention at home and in school. Particular focus needed to be given to:

- overcoming sensory processing difficulties
- improving ability to self-regulate his moods
- improving attention span
- improving ability to engage with other people
- improving motor planning skills

Therapies would be tailored to the child's specific interests and circumstances. For example, since his favorite activities are music, singing, puzzles, and mechanical toys, his parents and therapists planned to find ways to incorporate these interests into the various therapies.

Everyone involved in his care (parents, teachers, therapists, clinicians, other professionals) were advised to use increased affect (emotion) and gestures to attract and sustain his attention. On the other hand, his relatively short attention span and tendency to become overwhelmed by too much motion suggested his caregivers should slow down their communications with him so he could easily grasp what was being said. This would give him a chance to digest incoming information and not feel too pressured to give responses.

Examination of his home and school environments suggested that the child would benefit if they were physically reorganized to permit more frequent interaction with peers, family members, and others. (For example, his "designated" play area was in the basement. This arrangement physically isolated him from the rest of the family. His play area needed to be more centrally located so as to be more connected to the normal comings and goings of others in the household.)

The examination also revealed that the child's schedule was a bit erratic with the current babysitting arrangements. It was strongly recommended that his care become a more predictable routine, with easier transitions between his being "handed off" from one activity to another (school to babysitting, etc.). These steps alone would probably go far to reduce his tantrums.

As a general rule, he was to be given advance warning about upcoming activities or what was expected of him. Showing him pictures or acting out events with dolls (like "going to the doctor") would be used as a means of graphic communication.

Specific Recommendations

○ Sensory integration therapy was considered crucial and would be given at least three to four times per week. For this purpose, it was recommended that a "sensory gym" be constructed in the home. This would consist of lots of touchable objects with different textures, such as sand, rice, smooth balls, rough and soft materials, etc. There would also be objects he could safely climb on top of, into, or through, as well as objects in which he could bounce on or spin. A "sensory diet" would be composed by the therapist, consisting of textures, sights, smells, movement, and so forth, that he could experience so as to (1) provoke his involvement in the external world and (2) help him gradually overcome any aversions he has to specific sensory experiences. The therapist would also train all caregivers, teachers, and clinicians on how to use this "diet" as a routine part of his handling.

○ Speech and language therapy was recommended for three to four sessions per week. These would be given in a relatively unstructured but distraction-free play environment, preferably at home.

○ Pivotal Response Training (PRT) was suggested to help the child learn how to follow two-step directions. For example: "walk over to your sister, and tell her hi." However, if at any time it was observed that his actions were taking on an unnatural "robotic" character, PRT would be stopped, and its continued use reevaluated.

○ To enhance motor skills, encourage social communication, improve problem solving and abstract thinking, and give an outlet for imaginary play, DIR/Floortime and SCERTS therapies were recommended four to six times per day, with sessions running fifteen to twenty minutes each.

○ Under the supervision of a nutritionist, the child should begin a casein-free, dye- and additive-free diet along with a daily "cocktail" of vitamins, supplements, and digestive enzymes. Based on results, consideration should be given to removing gluten from the child's diet in four weeks.

Some Immediate Results

Within three weeks, the diarrhea and skin rashes cleared up completely, and the child showed a significant increase in his ability to focus.

As the parents and family members became more comfortable in their ability to follow through with the therapies at home and saw firsthand the positive results, it became easier for them to engage and interact with their son. Almost immediately, the child came "alive" and showed a real gleam in his eye. His eye contact improved, and he began to increase his vocabulary.

As this initial phase is the basic foundation for the child's treatment program and a critical time in which to observe and evaluate how he reacts to different styles, personalities, and treatments, it is important to measure the child's progress and determine what is most effective and what may be ineffective and/or having a negative impact. Once this has been determined, and it is apparent that the child is progressing, consideration should be given to listening therapy and music therapy. In addition, it is critical that the parents begin to evaluate preschool programs right away so they can secure a placement for when the child turns three. Follow-up evaluation and observation with the developmental pediatrician should be conducted in two months, and the team should meet to review goals and progress and to formulate a comprehensive developmental, medical, therapeutic, and educational plan.

IN A SENTENCE

> *The keys to successful integration are establishing the priorities, selecting the correct targets, sequencing treatments, and harmonizing the treatment regimes.*

MONTH **5**

Understanding Your Child's Educational Needs

ONCE YOU HAVE your evaluations and unique profile in hand, it's time to start thinking about the process of transitioning from Early Intervention to your local school district. There will be a great deal of prep work involved, and it's never too early to start. Remember, Early Intervention is responsible for helping with the transitional process, so enlist the aid of your EI coordinator as early as possible. Some EI coordinators will do just what is expected, while others will go well beyond the call of duty. Hopefully your coordinator will fall into the latter category.

How to Avoid Falling Through the Cracks: Children Turning Age Three

If you have a child who will turn three years old during the summer months, you really have to plan at least six months in advance—farther in advance if at all possible. If you haven't planned carefully, you may find that your child with his or her third birthday in June or July (for example) will no longer be eligible for EI services—unless you are able to obtain an extension from your EI provider—and may not be able to start school district services until September.

Defining What Your Child Needs

The first step in the process is to determine if your child will soon be ready for a school program and, if so, to define the characteristics of a program that would be most appropriate for his needs. Some children do better with a home-based program until they are ready. With what you now know and with the help of your team members, you must begin getting answers to the following questions:

1. TYPE OF CLASSROOM

- ○ Is your child ready for a classroom? Or does she still need one-on-one attention? Or a combination of both? A classroom setting may be too overwhelming for a child who is not yet ready.
- ○ What type of peer models would benefit the child, and how many? "With proper planning and implementation by well-trained staff, typically developing peers can be very effective in modeling positive behavior and eliciting social, play, and communicative responses from young children with autism."[1]
- ○ What type of classroom would be most appropriate for your child?

"**Mainstreaming**" is the practice of educating children with special needs in regular education classrooms based on their skills and ability to keep up with the work assigned by the regular education classroom. Any special education services they may receive are delivered outside the regular education classroom in smaller instructional or therapeutic settings. "**Inclusion**" is the practice of giving a child the special services required by his IEP in the regular classroom setting. This means integrating him into a regular education classroom in a natural manner that does not call attention to the child's special needs in any embarrassing or obvious way. "**Partial inclusion**" means delivering some services in the regular classroom while other services are delivered in separate classrooms or settings.[2]

There is a something of a philosophical difference between the ideas of "inclusion" and "mainstreaming." Special education professionals who speak of "mainstreaming" tend to believe that the child with special needs belongs in special education classes and enters mainstream classes only as he becomes more typical in his behavior. On the other hand, professionals who speak of "inclusion" or "full inclusion" generally support the notion that the child should always be in regular education classes unless any required additional services cannot be supplied in the regular classroom environment.[3]

Self-contained ASD classrooms are often made up of a small number of children—perhaps six to ten total. Some schools will bring one or two typically developing children into the classroom for brief periods of time to serve as peer models, mostly for demonstrating social skills. Self-contained classrooms can work well for children who are not ready to move into a regular education classroom or who need a lot of specialized attention. These classrooms may have a wide variation in skill levels, so it is important that they meet the individual needs of every child in them.

Keep in mind, if you feel your child would be better served in a full-inclusionary classroom and the school wants to place him in an autism-specific classroom, this battle should be reasonably surmountable, since federal IDEA laws require a "least restrictive environment."

2. PHYSICAL ENVIRONMENT

○ What size classroom would be most appropriate for the child? What should the maximum number of children be?

○ Are there any potential environmental issues? Some schools are old and may still have lead paint. Most classrooms use products that have gluten or other potential allergens in them (clay, markers, paint, etc.), and even if the child does not ingest them, they can be absorbed into the skin and cause a reaction (physical or behavioral). Are there any potential exposures to allergens that may affect your child?

○ Is the classroom suited for a child with sensory problems? Are there too many visual stimulations or clutter? Too many audio stimulations and not enough visual supports? Smells in or near the classroom that might bother your child? Is the environment calm or frenetic? Is there anything in a classroom that might trigger a child to shut down or become dysregulated?

3. ADULT-CHILD RATIO

○ Based on the individualized needs of the child, what is the recommended adult-child ratio for the classroom? Staffing of classrooms adequate to provide a high level of support for children on the spectrum vary depending upon the program format, class size, and children's developmental and chronological ages. However, recommended staff-to-children ratios can run from 1:1 to 1:8, depending upon the needs of the child.[4]

Get recommendations from the team members who know your child best and keep in mind, depending upon how well trained the classroom staff is, a lower staff-to-children ratio with a more highly trained staff may be better for your child than a higher ratio with an unqualified staff.

4. EXPERTISE AND TRAINING OF TEACHING STAFF

○ What level of expertise and training is required for the teacher and/or paraprofessional to meet your child's needs? Not all teachers and paraprofessionals have training and experience with children on the autism spectrum. Depending upon the severity of your child's issues, you may need one or more trained professionals (teacher and/or paraprofessional) who understand your child's needs and have expertise in the methodologies used that will best meet those needs. (See sidebar on page 207.)

5. TYPE OF STRUCTURE AND LEARNING ENVIRONMENT

○ Does your child require a highly structured environment? Semi-structured? No structure?
○ What is the recommended teaching approach?
  • A developmental approach is child-centered and based on the child's interest. Typically, the child leads, and the adult follows, using activities, tasks, and toys that are developmentally appropriate.

- A behavioral approach is based on reducing inappropriate behaviors while increasing communication, learning, and appropriate social behavior.
- An organizational approach focuses on creating a physical environment and routine that maximizes a child's ability to function and learn.
- An integrated approach uses a combination of two or three of the above approaches as appropriate for the individual needs of the child. (Example: A developmental approach may be used to develop social interactions with other children, a behavioral approach may be used to get a child to sit in a chair for longer periods of time or to develop writing skills, and an organizational approach may be used to teach independent life and work skills.)

See Month 3 for a further discussion of intervention approaches and methods.

"The challenge for states and communities and the children and families they are serving is to choose and implement effective approaches for personnel preparation, beyond a single training effort, to provide a continuum of services across time.

Teachers must be familiar with theory and research concerning best practices for children with autistic spectrum disorders, including methods of applied behavior analysis, naturalistic learning, incidental teaching, assistive technology, socialization, communication, inclusion, adaptation of the environment, language interventions, assessment, and the effective use of data collection systems. . . . To enable teachers to adequately work with parents and with other professionals to set appropriate goals, teachers need familiarity with the course of autism and the range of possible outcomes."[5]

6. SERVICES AND SUPPORTS PROVIDED

- ❍ What kinds of therapies are needed: occupational therapy, physical therapy, speech-language therapy, counseling, social skills group?
- ❍ What kinds of supports and accommodations are required: adaptive technology; preferential seating; sensory breaks; modifications to the curriculum,

homework, and/or test taking; special transportation; nursing care; daily communication book; home training; others?

○ Your team members should provide all the reports needed to support what your child needs.

7. LENGTH OF THE SCHOOL DAY

○ Half day? Full day? Does your child need a full day in one classroom setting? Or would it be better for her to be half-day in an inclusionary classroom and half-day in a self-contained ASD classroom, where she could get more specialized attention?

8. LENGTH OF THE PROGRAM DURING THE YEAR

○ Nine-month program with breaks during the winter, spring, and summer? Additional summer program? Year-round program with no breaks? Most public school programs run from September to June and break for two to three weeks during winter and spring. Many public schools offer separate four- to six-week summer programs that vary from three half days to five full days. Some private placements offer year-round programs with no breaks.

- Catherine Lord, PhD, director of the University of Michigan Autism and Communication Disorders Center and lead author of *Educating Children with Autism*, says, "Year-round programming is critical for students with ASD. Research has shown that children with autism who have made significant gains during intensive intervention often lose skills when such interventions are stopped abruptly."[6]

- Some summer programs in the public schools can be poorly staffed with untrained and inexperienced teachers and paraprofessionals. They may hold the summer program at another school, use a different curriculum, and offer reduced therapies, modifications, and supports. Don't accept this!

- In addition to year-round programming, Lord says, "Most children need equal levels of staffing and experience in their teachers through the year, though activities in the summer may move outdoors or take advantage of other age appropriate opportunities, as long as the student's individual goals are addressed. One way I think about year-round programming is that planned, individualized opportunities for social engagement and communication provide, for children with ASD, the same support as a hearing aid provides for a child with a hearing impairment. We would not decide that a child needs hearing aids, and then take them away in the summer because she 'needs a break.'"[7]

This book is a must read: Catherine Lord and James P. McGee, eds., *Educating Children with Autism*, (Washington, DC: National Academies Press, 2001).

IN A SENTENCE

Taking a methodical approach to defining your child's needs will prepare you for the next step: evaluating school programs.

living

Finding the Appropriate School Program

IN A PERFECT world, your local school district would provide all the services necessary to serve your child's special education needs appropriately. But the reality is that nearly all public schools are terribly underfunded, even for their regular academic programs. Every school district has to fight to do what they can to service typical children. So adding a full assortment of complex special education services on top of that is often an extraordinarily difficult task. School administrations can end up in the unenviable position of trying their hardest but ending up beset by parents who (rightfully) expect and demand more.

In the next few chapters, you will learn about many of the vital tools needed to get your child into a program appropriate for his situation. Some of these steps may involve potentially confrontational situations with school personnel who, for the most part, really deserve respect and admiration for doing the best they can under impossible circumstances.

This does not mean you should not try your hardest to stand by your rights and get what is appropriate. It means that in your dealings with school personnel, you should never fail to give them the respect they deserve for the jobs they do on their side of the school-house walls, even if you are forced to oppose decisions they may make about your child's services.

Initially, many parents believe they have two choices only: put their child in a private school and pay for it, or put her into their local public school system, accept what they are given, and the district pays for it. This is not the case. Federal law states the school system must provide "free, appropriate public education" in the "least restrictive environment" that is "specially designed . . . to meet the unique needs" of your child.[8]

But how do you judge the quality or "appropriateness" of what your school system has to offer unless you see what else is available and you have a basis for comparison? You need to investigate what is out there. Do not underestimate the importance of the following steps!

The Process

1. Establish your personal criteria for the program you are seeking. In addition to considering your child's unique profile and your team's recommendations, the criteria should also include answers to questions such as:
   - Are you willing to move to another district or state? What is the acceptable geographical radius?
   - Should this be a school for typically developing children, a school for children with special needs, or a school specifically for children with ASD?
   - What kind of experience and expertise should the school personnel have?
   - What should the classroom be like?
2. Build your list of possible programs using input from other educated and experienced parents, team members, parent organizations, attorneys, advocates, and educational consultants. Of course, include in this list whatever schools are in your local district (there may be three or four elementary schools within your district, and each may offer significantly different services and environments), but put these schools aside for later.
3. Go online, and research the schools and programs. Narrow down the choice based upon your list of criteria. See what they all have to offer.
4. Based on what you now know and using the questions posed in the first section of this chapter, compile a list of questions that still need answering.

5. Call and interview the principal or the school's program director on the phone.

6. Your list should be narrowed down by this point. Now it is time to organize visits to the schools remaining (just remember to set aside the schools in your local district for later). If possible, arrange to have your Early Intervention coordinator, educational assistant, psychologist, or other professional team member accompany you. This should be someone who knows your child and her unique profile.

    You should even visit schools that may be beyond reasonable driving distance, if you hear they are good. What is important in this step is not that you visit prospective schools for your child, but rather that you *get a sense of what is possible*, of what might suit your child's profile.

    Within each school, insofar as possible, visit a sampling of classrooms to see the range of educational environments (from full-inclusionary to self-contained ASD classrooms) and the different styles of teaching.

7. Once you find a program or classroom that potentially meets your child's needs, ask yourself: How does this program meet my child's needs? Be very specific and factual.

    At this point you should have a pretty good idea as to what kinds of programs are currently available and what is within your reach. The next step is to research the schools in your local district.

The reason for not doing this until now is twofold:

1. Some school systems, knowing you are within their district, will not let you check out their programs until you have formally begun the IEP process with a referral from Early Intervention (more about this in Month 6).

2. It is in your best interests to be as educated as you possibly can be before approaching your school district. By knowing what alternatives are potentially available to you, you will be better prepared to evaluate the quality of the special education services it is prepared to offer you.

If your school district allows you to visit your local schools now, schedule an appointment to visit a sampling of classrooms and bring along the same member of your professional team who accompanied you earlier.

- Be sure to visit full-inclusionary classrooms, partial-inclusionary classrooms, self-contained classrooms, and resource rooms. Your school district must have a continuum of the types of environments or placements needed to accommodate all children with special needs. Consider the general education setting first, and then decide if the goals of the general education setting can be accomplished. If they cannot, what accommodations will have to be made? Be sure to have firmly in mind (or on a piece of paper) your list of characteristics for a school program that would be most appropriate for your child.
- Now compare what your local school district has to offer to the schools and programs you visited outside of the district.
- Ask yourself what differences you see between the schools. Be specific and factual.

If your school district insists that you wait until after you are referred formally by EI, wait until then. More on this subject in Month 6.

An important point to remember: Before you set your heart on a school program outside of your district, you must first consider your home school and have *solid justification* for why your child should not be there, before you should consider asking for an out-of-district placement. Out-of-district placements can be very difficult to obtain (though not impossible) even with solid justification, unless you have good legal representation.

IN A SENTENCE

> *By educating yourself about comparative school programs, you will be in a much stronger position to evaluate what your school district has to offer.*

MONTH 6

learning

Preparing for the Educational Planning Process: Getting Your Ducks in a Row

BY NOW, YOU should be feeling less like a neophyte and much more knowledgeable about the disorder, your child's unique profile, and the services and treatments your child needs. You should be ready to take the reins, if you haven't already. If you have been working with your local Early Intervention Program, hopefully you had a helpful EI coordinator who has provided some valuable assistance along the way.

Now, get ready to learn about the transition from Early Intervention to the public school system.

You need to be prepared because, depending on your district, you may no longer have the sense of personalized attention you have grown accustomed to in Early Intervention.

That is why you must be fully prepared to deal with what lies ahead and assume the role of the coordinator, navigator, and parent advocate. Your skills in dealing with procedures and bureaucracy will be especially important.

On paper it looked really good.

My daughter was transitioning from Early Intervention to the public school system. The district I lived in at the time proudly presented me with its plan. They were just beginning to assemble a special class for children on the autism spectrum. There were to be six children with ASD and four typically developing children (as role models). The qualifications of the teacher looked appropriate, and a full complement of paraprofessionals was assigned to work full-time with the kids in addition to the teacher and clinicians. It sounded great, but I was a complete neophyte.

I did not have Sarah's unique profile in hand, nor was I able to visit the classroom, since there was nothing to see just yet. I accepted the school's word that this would be appropriate for her. But that was a mistake.

As it turned out, there was no individualized education going on. The paraprofessionals did not have experience or skills relevant to special education; the teacher was unable to bring any focus to the environment. The physical classroom was chaotic, and there was no facilitation of interactions between the kids; usually they were left to their own devices. My daughter was given tasks far below her capacity. Bored and hating disorder, she made it her job to walk around the room with her little red wagon in hand, collecting up the clutter and finding places to put it.

And so it went, from bad to worse, for months. Parents were seeing behaviors at home that they had never seen before. My daughter was very unhappy, and as she left school each day, she began a tantrum as soon as she reached the car. She could no longer hold it together.

A few parents asked to observe the classroom so they could see firsthand what was going on, but our requests were denied each time. Eventually we had to organize and exert some pressure to get the school to listen.

The moral to the story: *Do your homework, pay attention, and be prepared!*

Learn the Lay of the Land

In Month 2, "Learning: Part I: Know Your Rights," we discussed how you can get the inside scoop about your school district by speaking with the local Special Education Parent Advisory Council (PAC), parents of children with special needs, and perhaps an attorney who is familiar with the inner workings of your district. Your local EI Program and other parent support organizations in your state may offer workshops on transitioning into the public school system. Find out about them from your EI coordinator, and take advantage of whatever they offer.

Get to Know Your School District Personnel

As you will learn in the next half of this chapter, part of the educational planning process involves meetings with various members of the school's administration. In all likelihood, you will be working with these individuals for years to come. Your school principal and the special education director are two key players you will really need to get to know. Find out from your PAC and parents of other children with special needs in your district the answers to these questions, and take good notes on what you learn:

- How are the principal and SPED director perceived?
- How do they operate?
- Are they problem solvers?
- Are they open to creative solutions?
- Are they good listeners?
- What motivates them?
- To what length will they go to support the needs of a child?
- How much latitude do they have when it comes to making decisions?

Once you have completed this step, sit back, and take the time to digest it all. Experiences and expectations can vary from parent to parent, and some administrators may present themselves poorly with parents even though they are good administrators. Try not to make snap judgments.

IN A SENTENCE

Thorough preparation can place you in a strong position to advocate for your child.

Navigating the Public School System

GETTING A CHILD into a special education program in the public school system can be, even at its best, like entering a labyrinth. The path is full of intricate forms and complex procedures; there may be numerous blind alleys, hidden passages, sudden reversals, confusing signs, and perplexing arrangements. To accomplish this with a minimum of pain and a maximum of gain, there are some important steps to take.

Enrollment requires a formal process that you can begin by either:

1. Having your local Early Intervention Program do it on your behalf if you are enrolled in EI. It just requires that you fill out a form with EI requesting it.

or:

2. Doing it yourself by:
    a. Calling your school and getting the contact information for the special education coordinator.
    b. Contacting the special education coordinator and finding out about the district's eligibility process
    c. Following up your conversation with a letter.

Your School District Will Want to Get to Know Your Child

Once you have been referred by your local EI Program, you have officially begun the Individualized Education Program (IEP) process. Your school district will now take the necessary steps to get to know your child. This may include one or more home visits by a social worker or special educator. If your child is enrolled in a community-based play group, child care program, or preschool, they may want to visit your child in these settings. And they will want to review any evaluations and reports from your EI program and team members. Your EI program will provide them with their assessments, but you may want to supplement them with reports of your own from your other team members.

Help the school district personnel by providing whatever will give them a complete and accurate picture of your child.

Find Out What Your School District Has to Offer

If you haven't done so already, now it is time to find out as much as you can about your district's program and how appropriate it will be for your child. Ask your EI coordinator or another helpful member of your professional team to accompany you to informally survey the quality of what your school district has to offer.

You'll want to investigate what the different classroom settings and teachers are like so you can determine what is the right fit for your child. When you ask for permission to view classes, you will likely get one of three common responses from school personnel.

1. Yes, without any reservation.
2. You are initially told no, but you can talk them into it.
3. They refuse to permit you despite friendly persistence, meetings, and rational discussions.

If they will not allow you to view classes despite your most civil efforts, it is time to consult your special education attorney or advocate. Parents' rights and recourses on this matter differ from state to state; however, sometimes just a phone call from your attorney to the school's attorney will resolve the matter.

Only agree to put your child in a program or classroom that you have scrutinized carefully.

If you are able to examine the program, your reaction will fall into one of the following categories:

○ You love it.
○ You like it a lot but feel minor modifications will be needed.
○ You basically like it but feel that some major modifications will be needed if you are going to accept it for your child.
○ There is no way you would ever put your child in the program as it is.

Based upon this survey, the professional team member who accompanies you should write up a full report with recommendations for modifications. A copy of this report must be filed with your IEP team well before the formal IEP meeting is to occur.

Preparing for Your IEP Meeting

The IEP meeting is the next step in the formal process. This a place for the educational team (consisting of the parents, special education coordinator or director, special educator, regular educator, speech and language pathologist, physical and/or occupational therapist, social worker, school psychologist, and sometimes the school principal) to discuss:

○ the child's strengths and challenges
○ the parents' concerns related to enhancing the child's education
○ evaluations and reports
○ the needs of the child
○ how the child's disabilities might affect participation in the school, activities, and the curriculum
○ placement, services, supports, and accommodations for the coming year (including extended-year and after-school services)

There is much to do to get ready for this meeting, so you will need ample time to prepare. Open your copy of *The Complete IEP Guide* by Lawrence Siegel, turn to the chapter called "Preparing for the IEP Meeting," and start doing the steps it lays out.

IEP Meeting Preparation List

Things to do before the IEP meeting:

○ Find out the date, time, and location for the IEP meeting.
○ Get a copy of the school's agenda.
○ Make your own agenda.
○ Prepare your IEP material organizer.
○ Draft IEP plan.*
○ Find out who is attending on behalf of the school district.
○ Invite and prepare your own IEP participants.
○ Give the school a copy of the following one week prior to your IEP meeting:
   • independent evaluations
   • documents such as formal reports and work samples
   • names and titles of people attending the IEP meeting
   • notice of intent to audio record IEP meeting (if applicable)
○ Create a meeting reminder list of items you want to be sure to remember.[1]

*While IDEA requires that you and your school district draft the IEP document together, I always find it helpful to draft portions of the plan beforehand with my professional team, so that when I go into the meeting, I am fully prepared and know exactly what I want.

General Guidelines for Preparing for the IEP Meeting

ASSUME THE RIGHT ATTITUDE

You should always walk into your IEP meetings as a team player, assuming the school district will be cooperative in doing everything appropriate for your child's needs. Your outlook should be one of finding ways to establish a good working relationship with the school whenever possible.

Going in with an adversarial posture is sure to result in a deadlock and have negative long-term consequences for both you and your child. The school personnel may have to obey the letter of the law, but they are unlikely to be flexible or go beyond the minimum required if you go in with guns blazing. And remember, you may not be able to undo a bad first impression.

You should always assume that they will try their hardest to provide what is necessary and appropriate for your child. At the same time you should be fully prepared with an appropriate soft (but firm) response if they do not.

It is always best to go into your meetings more equipped and knowledgeable than anyone realizes. This means:

- knowing the laws
- knowing what other programs are available elsewhere (so you can compare them with what the school is offering you)
- having your team's recommendations with you and being fully familiar with them

At the same time, it is best to display your knowledge only as needed to accomplish your agenda. Be a bit of a poker player—learn to show the right card at the right moment, never too much and never too soon.

The general rules that govern business relationships work well here:

- Be factual and persuasive without getting overly emotional.
- Always do your preparatory research, and keep your notes handy in the meetings.
- Document everything, especially earlier conversations and agreements.
- Choose your battles carefully. Don't expend a lot of energy on unimportant points. Learn when to fight and when to relax and roll with the punches.
- Present yourself as cool and collected—even when you don't really feel that way.

This all takes practice and a lot of patience, so view it as an exercise you simply have to master.

TAKE CAREFUL NOTES ABOUT EVERYTHING

Whenever you work with the school district on your child's IEP, whether you have conversations by phone or in person with school representatives, taking excellent notes is necessary. Include in your notes the name of the person you spoke with, date, time, and details of the conversation. Be sure to include what was discussed and any conclusions or agreements that may have been reached. For official IEP meetings, ideally you would bring a second person with you to take notes so you can give more attention to what is being said and ask questions.

If you plan to audio record the meeting, you must notify the district at least twenty-four hours in advance. And keep in mind that if you do record it, people will be guarded in what they say. (Personally, I take a tape recorder only if things are becoming contentious and the SPED director and my educational consultant are present.)

If you don't feel comfortable taking notes during your IEP meetings and cannot arrange for another person to accompany you to take notes, be sure to debrief yourself in writing immediately afterwards.

You should also use your notes to follow up on action items that were agreed on during the meeting.

GET USED TO WRITING LETTERS

Use your conversation notes to send letters to school district personnel to confirm what was agreed on. Keep copies in your files. For particularly important matters, you might want to use registered mail to confirm receipt of your letters or documentation.

OBTAIN OUTSIDE EVALUATIONS OF YOUR CHILD

The school has the right to evaluate your child every three years. Do some research, and inquire into the qualifications of the professional(s) who will be evaluating your child. The evaluators are most likely employed by the school district, and their conclusions (or the wording of their conclusions) may be influenced by district policy and/or budget. In some cases, a school district may use evaluators who have limited experience with ASD.

After your research, if you have any doubts regarding the qualifications of the personnel the school will be using, you should seriously consider having well-qualified outside professionals perform this evaluation work first.

Also, depending upon which evaluations you already had done by outside professionals, district evaluators might just accept these as part of their battery. For example, certain neuropsychological tests may not be repeated within a specified period of time, so they may just accept those results from the outside evaluator. Thus, find out what tests your school district will want to do on your child and how often (usually every three years).

> By the time my daughter was ready for kindergarten, we had moved to a new school district. I arrived with a full set of evaluations in hand, and I was prepared with reports from our developmental pediatrician, neuropsychologist, neurologist, and other team members, because I knew they had the expertise and objectivity and would make recommendations based on my daughter's needs and not a school budget.

BE POSITIVE AND PERSISTENT

In most cases, schools are working with limited resources. If you remain clear, positive, and persistent, you may be able to work as a team with your local school district. A path of cooperation is always preferable to conflict, especially given the time and expense involved. However, if a program is proposed that does not meet the child's needs or is contrary to clinical opinion, you may need to pursue other means. In addition to hiring an advocate or lawyer, you may also contact the special education director for your district or state. In some states, the Department of Education has a special office dedicated to dispute resolution for parents and schools.

BECOME AN EXPERT ON THE IEP PROCESS

Until you know cold the ins and outs of the process, *The Complete IEP Guide* and Wrightslaw.com need to be your constant companions and advisors.

USE THE LANGUAGE OF
THE IEP PROCESS

Remember to speak of what is "appropriate" for your child, not what is "best" for him or her; object to placements that are "too restrictive an environment"; and so forth.

SEND IN ALL NEEDED
REPORTS ON TIME

Ensure that the school IEP team receives copies of needed reports at least one week prior to the meeting. If it is impossible for certain reports to be submitted in time, realize that additional IEP meetings will likely be necessary on those topics for which you do not have substantial professional evaluations to support your service requests.

OBTAIN THEIR EVALUATIONS
BEFORE THE MEETING

Send the special education director or coordinator a written request that you receive copies of the school's evaluations at least one week prior to the meeting so you can be prepared with your responses or any questions you may have. It is best to let each evaluator know as he or she is evaluating your child that you are going to make this request in writing. If it is not put in writing in advance, you may not receive this report until the day of the meeting or worse—after the meeting.

DECIDE IF YOU NEED TO
BRING IN ANY OUTSIDE TEAM
MEMBERS TO YOUR IEP MEETING

If it's too costly to have them attend in person, or if they are not available, do the next best thing: have them participate in the meeting via teleconference. Alternately, you can hold them "in reserve" if you are unhappy with the results of the first meeting and need to reinforce your position with one or more of your team members.

DO NOT SIGN OFF ON THE IEP DOCUMENT WITHOUT CAREFUL STUDY

Never sign the IEP document at the meeting. Always take the time to read it over carefully and compare the services, supports, and modifications offered to those on your list. Mistakes and omissions happen, and they can cost you dearly. *I have never, ever received an IEP document that was ready to sign the first time it was proposed.*

If you have any doubts or reservations, you should consult an advocate or special education attorney. He or she will suggest the best course of action depending upon the school's proposal. At this point, you might also want to bring in your other outside specialists to put a finer edge on your counterproposal.

If an agreement cannot be reached, be familiar with your options. This situation is discussed in Month 7 in the book and, of course, is covered in great depth in *The Complete IEP Guide.*

Attending the IEP Meeting

When at all possible, bring your spouse or partner, friend, grandparent, or other individual who will be there to support you, take notes, serve as a witness, and provide a reality check for you when it comes to your impressions and recollection. It is not wise to attend an IEP meeting alone unless you are a seasoned veteran, and even then, it is always better to have another set of eyes, ears, and voice. IEP meetings can be very intimidating—even when they are not contentious—so plan to bring someone who knows your child well and who can provide the support you need.

Writing the IEP document is the collaborative job of the team, and since the parents are an essential part of the team, they should be involved in all aspects of the planning process, including writing the IEP document. The school should not be presenting a completed IEP plan without first obtaining input from the parents in advance.

Another member of the team who is often left sitting on the sidelines is the regular education teacher. Even though she is required to attend the meetings, you may see her sitting passively at the meeting because she believes she has no say in the development of the IEP document. This is part of the reason the regular educator sometimes feels that the child is not her responsibility, but this could not be further from the truth. By insisting on her involvement, you are showing the school that despite the challenges, your child's academic goals and achievement are important and should be taken seriously.

Still, most schools will come to the meeting with a rough draft of the IEP document in hand and expect that the team, which includes the parents, will make any necessary changes to the document as agreed to by the team. Since you are just starting the process, you may not have all the reports you need (such as the neuropsychological evaluation) to get the services and supports required. Therefore, you may not get everything your child needs in the first go-round. You may have to reconvene the team at a later date as soon as you have the reports.

Some schools will come to the IEP meeting with a completed document in hand, expecting you to sign it on the spot. They may tell you, "This is the program we have for your child," and expect you to accept it as is. Remember, IDEA guarantees you a spot on the team as part of the planning and not just as the rubber stamp.

In any event, you should not sign the document at the conclusion of the meeting, no matter how happy you are with it. Like any contract, you should take a few days to make sure the document is complete and covers everything you need for your child. *Remember: You are not required to sign off on the entire IEP document to start your child on services. You can accept parts of the IEP and reject others.* In this way, your child can at least start on some services. At a later date when you have the needed reports in hand, you can schedule another IEP meeting to enlarge the scope of services.

Also remember: even if you have already signed off on an IEP document, you can always reconvene the IEP team to modify the plan or write a new one should problems arise or information become available (new reports, etc.).

One reason to completely reject an IEP document is if the current program is serving your child well and your school district suggests a change. For example, if your child is in an out-of-district placement that is meeting all his needs, but school personnel want to return him to the district in order to reduce expenses, they must first demonstrate that they have a comparable program of their own. Another reason to reject an IEP is when the program they recommend is at odds with the recommendations of your team—for example, a self-contained classroom as opposed to a typically developing class (or vice versa). Even then, perhaps you can reject the classroom but keep the occupational and speech-language therapies.

Timing

To make sure all matters about your child's program are resolved before the school year begins, ensure that the IEP meeting(s) occur in the spring (March or April) of the preceding year. In this way you should have enough time to sort through any disagreements before the new year starts.

Characteristics of Effective Interventions

In 2001, the results of a major national study on the education of children with autism were published. This study was sponsored by the National Research Council—which itself is sponsored by the National Academy of Sciences.

This study was undertaken at the request of the U.S. Department of Education's Office of Special Education Programs. Its mission was "to consider the state of the scientific evidence of the effects of early educational intervention on young children with autistic spectrum disorders."[2]

In the final chapter of the book that resulted from this study ("Conclusions and Recommendations"), the researchers summarized their findings on what made an intervention program an effective one. Because these findings are considered authoritative and carry a lot of legal weight, the information will be especially important should you have to resort to an appeal or legal process to obtain services through your public school system.

When you need to develop your IEP, I strongly recommend you read the section on "Characteristics of Effective Intervention," pages 218–229 in *Educating Children with Autism*. What follows is an extraction of the major points.

The researchers strongly agreed that the following features are critical:

- "entry into intervention programs as soon as an autism spectrum diagnosis is seriously considered;
- active engagement in intensive instructional programming for a minimum of the equivalent of a full school day, 5 days (at least 25 hours) a week, with full year programming varied according to the child's chronological age and developmental level;

- repeated, planned teaching opportunities generally organized around relatively brief periods of time for the youngest children (e.g., 15–20 minute intervals), including sufficient amounts of adult attention in one-to-one and very small group instruction to meet individualized goals;
- inclusion of a family component, including parent training;
- low student/teacher ratios (no more than two young children with autistic spectrum disorders per adult in the classroom);
- mechanisms for ongoing program evaluation and assessments of individual children's progress, with results translated into adjustments in programming."[3]

They also made the following substantive observations and recommendations:

"The key to any child's educational program lies in the objectives specified in the IEP and the ways they are addressed. Much more important than the name of the program attended is how the environment and educational strategies allow implementation of the goals for a child and family. Thus, effective services will and should vary considerably across individual children, depending on a child's age, cognitive and language levels, behavioral needs, and family priorities. . . .

It is well established that children with autism spend much less time in focused and socially directed activity when in unstructured situations than do other children. Therefore, it becomes crucial to specify time engaged in social and focused activity as part of a program for children with autistic spectrum disorders.

. . . Based on a set of individualized, specialized objectives and plans that are systematically implemented, educational services should begin as soon as a child is suspected of having an autistic spectrum disorder. Taking into account the needs and strengths of an individual child and family, the child's schedule and educational environment, in and out of the classroom, should be adapted as needed in order to implement the IEP. Educational services should include a minimum of 25 hours a week, 12 months a year, in which the child is engaged in systematically planned, developmentally appropriate educational activity aimed toward identified objectives. Where this activity takes place and the content of the activity should be determined on an individual basis, depending on characteristics of both the child and the family.

. . . A child must receive sufficient individualized attention on a daily basis so that individual objectives can be effectively implemented; individualized attention should include individual therapies, developmentally appropriate small group instruction, and direct one-to-one contact with teaching staff.

. . . Assessment of a child's progress in meeting objectives should be used on an ongoing basis to further refine the IEP. Lack of objectively documentable progress over a 3 month period should be taken to indicate a need to increase intensity by lowering student/teacher ratios, increasing programming time, reformulating curricula, or providing additional training and consultation.

. . . To the extent that it leads to the specified educational goals (e.g., peer interaction skills, independent participation in regular education), children should receive specialized instruction in settings in which ongoing interactions occur with typically developing children.

. . . Six kinds of interventions should have priority:

a. Functional, spontaneous communication should be the primary focus of early education. For very young children, programming should be based on the assumption that most children can learn to speak. Effective teaching techniques for both verbal language and alternative modes of functional communication, drawn from the empirical and theoretical literature, should be vigorously applied across settings.

b. Social instruction should be delivered throughout the day in various settings, using specific activities and interventions planned to meet age-appropriate, individualized social goals (e.g., with very young children, response to maternal imitation; with preschool children, cooperative activities with peers).

c. The teaching of play skills should focus on play with peers, with additional instruction in appropriate use of toys and other materials.

d. Other instruction aimed at goals for cognitive development should also be carried out in the context in which the skills are expected to be used, with generalization and maintenance in natural contexts as important as the acquisition of new skills. Because new skills have to be learned before they can be generalized, the documentation of rates of acquisition is an important first step. Methods of introduction of new skills may differ from teaching strategies to support generalization and maintenance.

e. Intervention strategies that address problem behaviors should incorporate information about the contexts in which the behaviors occur; positive, proactive approaches; and the range of techniques that have empirical support (e.g., functional assessment, functional communication training, reinforcement of alternative behaviors).

f. Functional academic skills should be taught when appropriate to the skills and needs of a child."[4]

A few other things you should consider:

❑ Insist that the special *and* regular educators, as well as paraprofessionals, schedule common planning time to develop the child's curriculum. If the regular educator is not involved in this planning process, the child may end up becoming the sole responsibility of the special educator. Both regular educators and special educators should be collaborating on establishing goals, setting high expectations, and helping the child achieve these goals. Often the paraprofessionals are left out, but in truth, they usually spend more time than anyone with your child, know much more than anyone might realize, and should be included in this planning process.

❑ Insist that recess is structured or facilitated and is part of your child's educational program. Depending upon the child's unique circumstances, recess time may be as important (or even more important) than academics, especially in the early grades. The understanding and relationships developed during casual social circumstances are pivotal to the child's feeling of self-confidence and often translates into interest (or lack of interest) in academics.

❑ There are only so many hours in a day and only so many resources to stretch. Always weigh the potential gains your child may get from one service available versus what else he could be doing. For example, at some point you might want to do what you can to bias his schedule so he gets as much structured socialization time as possible. Or perhaps the OT services don't seem to be yielding as much just now as more time spent in tutoring to spark his interest in reading. You should always be mindful of achieving the best balance for any particular period of his development.

IN A SENTENCE

> *As with any bureaucratic process, careful attention to detail in determining your child's IEP plan is key to success.*

HALF-YEAR MILESTONE

Hopefully by now you are feeling much more knowledgeable, a little better oriented, and ready to tackle the next six months. You have learned a lot about:

○ YOUR LEGAL RIGHTS AND INSURANCE PLAN
○ HOW TO PLAN FINANCIALLY
○ MANY OF THE TREATMENT OPTIONS AVAIL-
  ABLE
○ INTEGRATING TREATMENTS
○ YOUR CHILD'S EDUCATIONAL NEEDS AND
  HOW TO GO ABOUT LOOKING FOR A SCHOOL
  PROGRAM THAT MEETS HER NEEDS
○ HOW TO PREPARE FOR THE IEP PROCESS

Now give yourself a pat on the back for getting through the first six months!

When You're Not Getting What You Need from Your School District

LET'S SAY YOU have done your best to make clear what you and your team feel would be appropriate for your child's educational program: a small classroom of no more than twelve children with a mixture of special needs and typically developing children and a teacher to child ratio of 1:2. The school offers you a choice between a self-contained classroom with nine children (all on the spectrum, ranging from mild to severe, with a 1:3 ratio) and a full-inclusionary classroom with eighteen children (1:9 ratio). You and your team feel strongly that neither option will work for your child. What do you do?

Sometimes the IEP process gets bogged down when agreement cannot be reached. If this is the case for you, your first step would be to try to convince the school personnel by using persuasive logic and the reports they have in hand and by reminding them of the law. If the disagreement is over a big issue (like the example mentioned above), break it down into more manageable pieces, and use language from your reports (and, if appropriate, from the school's reports) to make your case. Stick to the facts and recommendations from your expert team members, and be sure you have documentation to back up everything you are asking for. Prepare yourself for this moment in advance, especially if you are going to request something important that the school might not want to give you, like a one-on-one paraprofessional, weekly home parent training, or an after-school program. When in doubt, ask your team members to help you position your case in the most appropriate way. And remember, ask for what is most appropriate for your child and not what is best.

If you find you are not making any progress, especially with the bigger issues, no matter what you say, it might be best to put it aside for now, and move on to some of the smaller concerns. *By establishing agreement on basic services or smaller matters to which the school may more readily agree, it might be possible to work toward resolving the more complex issues.* Just be sure to choose your battles carefully.

Try not to get emotional, as difficult as it may be. If you feel as if you are about to burst into tears or say something you may later regret, excuse yourself, and head to the bathroom if you need a moment to regroup. Whatever you do, try to keep the meeting calm and business-like no matter what happens.

Let the school personnel know at the end of the meeting that you disagree with their recommendations for X, but you will take it into consideration and get back to them. This will give you time to prioritize the list of items with which you disagree, think about next steps, and determine if the disagreement is worth getting your attorney or advocate involved.

At the extreme, the school may even deny that your child has autism. I have heard of some cases in which the parents presented district officials with the diagnosis and supporting documentation but the district's IEP team completely denied the child had autism. Should this happen to you, just keep in mind it is very unlikely there is anyone on the school's team who is qualified to diagnose autism. In this case, since they are essentially refusing to accept the diagnosis, you may have to consult your special education attorney or advocate as to how to proceed.

Partial or Complete Rejection of the IEP Document

In situations in which you disagree with some of the IEP document, you should check off the approval box for those items with which you do agree and list in detail your specific disagreements on the parent addendum sheet (or a separate piece of paper, which you should attach to the proposal).

Should you disagree with the entire proposal, indicate in the appropriate box that you did attend the meeting and that you disapprove of the proposal. As with a partial disagreement, you should indicate in explicit detail why you disagree. You could also indicate in general terms what would be acceptable.

The IEP Document Is a Contract

Once you and the school representatives sign the IEP document, it becomes the school's contract with you and therefore legally binding. School staff have a considerable job to do to get all the services implemented, often with limited resources, so a certain amount of fairness, understanding, and consideration is certainly due them. But after a reasonable period of time has passed, if the goals are not being met, it is imperative you find out why. A week would be too soon to expect full implementation; two months would certainly be too long.

At the beginning of the school year, I compile a checklist from the IEP document of all the supports, services, and classroom accommodations that the school is supposed to provide for the school year. I check them off as they are implemented. Next, I make a chart with goals for the year in one column and two blank columns for dates and notes about my thoughts related to the goals. This serves as a way to monitor my child's progress toward IEP goals periodically (or as often as needed). This also helps to keep track of dates for services that may or may not be delivered as agreed upon. If needed, this can lend an air of credibility when it comes time to discuss specific issues at a team meeting.

Sensing Something Is Wrong

If you sense that something is wrong with the school services your child is receiving (or not receiving), you must become vigilant without jumping to conclusions. Keep in mind, though, all students (particularly those with ASD and ADHD) need time to acclimate to change. It can take your child weeks or months to settle in. Don't impulsively make any changes without first allowing some time for the child to transition to the new environment, expectations, teachers, and peers.

If you feel in your gut something is *really* not right, trust your instinct. You know your child better than anyone. While your child may not be able to talk, he can tell you certain things with his behavior. Watch for inexplicable changes in behavior that may be indicators of some kind of problem.

Monitoring and Measuring Progress

You should keep a watchful eye to make sure that promised supports, services, and classroom accommodations are in fact being provided. You can do this in a variety of ways: through a daily communication book, monthly or quarterly reports, periodic onsite observations (this may need to be arranged in advance with your special education coordinator or principal), scheduled face-to-face meetings or telephone calls with your child's teacher and/or paraprofessional, and your child, if she is able to communicate using words, gestures, or pictures. It is your job to stay on top of this, and *you must document everything.*

When you first detect something is wrong, begin looking at your child's IEP document to determine if your school is meeting its obligations vis-à-vis the services, supports, accommodations, modifications, and goals to which it committed. Take the following steps:

1. If available, review any data provided by the school supporting your child's achievements with a member of your professional team. Is your child meeting the established IEP goals? The IEP requires goals that must be measurable, so there should be quantifiable, measurable benchmarks embedded in the IEP document that can be used to identify what may be wrong.

   For example: Your IEP document might state one of the annual goals for your child as, "Jason will improve his ability to demonstrate appropriate peer interactions during semi-structured activities with support from staff." The benchmarks might be:
   - Given prompting, Jason will seek out and initiate social interaction with a peer 50 percent of the time;
   - Jason will have a succession of ten back-and-forth interactions with the peer 60 percent of the time;
   - Given one cue, Jason will use appropriate eye contact with the peer 60 percent of the time; and

- Jason will play with a peer for ten minutes in three out of five opportunities.

   Now ask yourself, have you or any of your team members seen any
   progress over time in your child's social interactions outside of school? It
   is certainly possible that your child is able to meet these goals within the
   classroom but not yet able to generalize these skills in environments outside the classroom, so you will need to investigate more closely. A member
   of your professional team can help you sort this out. Move on to the next
   two steps.

2. Check the daily communication book and progress reports to see what
   you can learn from them. What do they say about your child's progress
   relative to this goal? Be certain to share this with your professional team
   member(s). The teacher or paraprofessional should be making entries in
   the communication book on a regular basis. This is vital input from the
   staff, and if it does not exist, you must ask for it. Just be sure to specify in
   your IEP document that you want a daily communication book and that
   you want it to include progress notes relative to the IEP goals. But remember, the communication should be two-way. It is equally important
   for the teacher and paraprofessional to know what is going on at home,
   where you are seeing progress, and where you are having difficulty. Just a
   word of caution: choose your words carefully, especially if you write it
   quickly. Notes and emails can be easily misconstrued and taken personally. If in doubt about how you may be coming across, opt for a phone
   call instead so that you can read each other's cues and explain something
   in greater detail.

3. Get permission from administration to go in and observe, preferably in
   such a way that your child never sees you. Some classrooms have observa-
   tional rooms or one-way mirrors, or if the child won't be too distracted,
   you can sit off to the side or in the back of the classroom. As an alternative, you might request that your educational consultant, psychologist, or
   other team member observe your child, the program, the staff, and the
   techniques they use, and provide feedback and recommended strategies to
   the school team. This should be followed by a written report. Be sure the
   observer addresses the following questions:
   - What are the observer's conclusions based upon observations?
   - Is your child engaged and interacting with staff members and peers?
   - Has your child made any progress toward meeting his goals?

- Are the services, supports, accommodations, and modifications in place as specified in the IEP document?
- Is your child getting the individualized attention he needs? Is the teacher, paraprofessional, or other skilled professional helping to facilitate social interactions between your child and his peers? Or is your child wandering aimlessly and being left alone? And are there too many missed opportunities where social interactions should have been facilitated but were not?
- Are staff members working diligently on specified goals using the benchmarks?
- Has your child adapted well to the classroom environment? Does the program meet his needs? If not, what is wrong with it? The report should be specific and factual, using language from the IEP document and prior written reports.

The educational consultant or psychologist who observed your child in his classroom may find the program to be working well for him and simply may need to suggest a few techniques or strategies to the teaching staff so your child can reach his goals. However, if there are more serious problems with the program, then it might be wise to reconvene the team and have the educational consultant or psychologist attend the meeting either in person or via telephone. Just be sure your special education director or coordinator receives the report one week in advance. This might be the perfect time to tape record the meeting, but make sure you let the school know in advance. Yes, having your educational consultant or psychologist attend may cost you up front, but in the long run, it will save you a lot of precious time, aggravation, and money.

If the school personnel are reluctant to let you observe because there is a risk of meltdown and loss of time for the child, ask them to brainstorm ways to make a visit work. If the school will not allow you to observe your child in class under any circumstance, you should treat this as a flagrant red flag and confer with the appropriate team members, including your attorney or advocate.

IN A SENTENCE

> *Keep careful track of your child's progress; handle any problems while they are still small.*

living

Learning How to Advocate for Your Child

PARENTS MUST KNOW and assert their rights. The IEP process can be intimidating, with one or two parents having to deal with a room full of ten or twelve school professionals. But it is important not to get intimidated. Here are some basic guidelines for you to follow:

- ○ Treat it like a business meeting: hide your emotions, and be tactful.
- ○ Have someone with you who can help if you have to play "good cop, bad cop."
- ○ Do not give anyone the upper hand. You know your child better than anybody. You probably know what is best, but you have to talk about what is most *appropriate*, and you have to stick to the facts. Always use the proper language of the law. This is very important.
- ○ You may be in a school with great teachers, many of whom do know what is best for your child, but the fact of the matter is that the funding available to the school is going to dictate the services that your child receives. Teachers and therapists may be pushing for certain services for your child,

but they may be prevented from offering these services because of the lack of funding. Focus on your child's needs, not on the cost of the services you are asking for. Try to stick to your child's goals—what it is the child needs and the appropriate options for meeting those goals.

○ Choose your battles; learn which to fight and which to yield on (because it may not be as important). Keep in mind your prioritized objectives.

○ Always ask for more than you are willing to settle for, so you have some negotiating power. Seek some items that you would be willing to dispense with if necessary. For example, you might request speech and language therapy four times per week in thirty-minute sessions, but perhaps you are willing to settle for three times per week. Or you might be asking for an out-of-district placement and a summer program (because the out-of-district school doesn't offer a summer program), but you might be willing to settle for getting the out-of-district placement and paying for the summer program yourself.

○ Ask lots of questions when you have doubts about the truth of something. Take the position that you are confused and are trying to clarify what is being said; this will be less threatening.

○ Be persuasive but not threatening. Tact is necessary. Stay with the facts and your reports.

○ Be sure to read and understand everything in the IEP document. It is a contract; you should never sign it quickly.

○ *Never sign an IEP document at the meeting, even if it is already prepared.* Take it home, and read it over carefully, checking it against your list. When in doubt, let members of your team review the IEP document.

○ Don't be pushed into making any kind of decision on the spot. If you sense something isn't right, say, *"I'm going to have to think about this and get back to you."*

○ On the other hand, if you are positive something is not going to work for your child, you need to state so up front after school personnel present their views.

○ You don't have to sign the IEP document in full. You can sign off on parts of it so you can get your child into a class and started on some services. Don't reject it all unless it is completely wrong.

○ If you feel the IEP document is entirely wrong—there is nothing in it to which you can agree—then you have no choice but to reject it. Just realize that you will not be able to get any services from the school district until the matter is resolved.

When Discussion and Informal Negotiations Fail

Informal negotiation is a much easier way to resolve disagreements; there is less formality, less stress, and ultimately less cost. Seeking informal negotiations before any other more precipitous actions can also preserve your image as someone who acts with a fair mind and a cool head.

But if it becomes clear that despite your best efforts, there are no good results to be had using simple, discussion-based remedies, it may be time to break out the heavier tools.

> Essential and complete advice on how to handle unresolving disagreements can be found in Lawrence Siegel's *The Complete IEP Guide.* In the fifth edition, the relevant material is in chapter 12, "Resolving IEP Disputes through Due Process," and chapter 13, "Filing a Complaint for a Legal Violation." I strongly advise you to use them as your major references on this topic.

In general, these tools may include:

1. Building or participating in a parent coalition
2. Filing a complaint
3. Due process, mediation
4. Due process, hearing

Each tool has an appropriate time and place for use, and it is important to know when to use each.

1. BUILDING OR PARTICIPATING IN A PARENT COALITION

There is strength in numbers, particularly if such a group is well organized. If you can find a group of parents who have had similar problems with a district, this kind of group action can be very effective in bringing about change. To keep costs low, it is necessary to have the parents do as much of the legwork as possible and have everyone in full agreement as to the exact outcome.

I organized such a coalition at one point when I was in a district with a poor summer program. I brought together a group of parents who were all on the same page insofar as what we felt was needed in such a program. I did the research to hire an attorney, we all shared in the costs, and I brought the attorney in to consult with us. It was a powerful process, and the results, if not a total win, ultimately satisfied each of the parents involved.

2. FILING A COMPLAINT

When a district is in obvious noncompliance with federal and state IDEA regulations, you can file a complaint with either the federal or the state education agency. Complaints are useful in cases in which the district, for example, fails to hold IEP meetings despite your requests, fails to do an evaluation of your child, fails to implement an agreed-to IEP plan, or fails to take any other legally mandated actions.

3. DUE PROCESS, MEDIATION

Due process actions are used when there is a dispute over matters of facts as opposed to what the law required the district to do. For example: the district determines your child is not eligible for special education services, will not agree to the goals you desire, and will not grant a placement request—insisting that the district can provide appropriate services—and you do not agree.

Mediation is the first step in due process. It is easier and less confrontational than a hearing but at the same time demonstrates to the district that you mean to be taken seriously.

4. DUE PROCESS, HEARING

A hearing is like a formal courtroom trial, except that it is not held in a courtroom. It requires the same planning and preparation that a trial would demand: thinking through and documenting the issues, preparing evidence and exhibits, calling for the sworn testimony of witnesses, cross-examination, etc. If you have been careful about documenting your IEP process to this point, you are well prepared. While the decision made by the hearing officer is legally binding, such decisions may also be appealed to state or federal courts.

Keep in mind that IDEA regulations do change, and you need to keep on top of them. You can check for updates on the websites of both the U.S. Department of Education and your state's Department of Education.

THE STAY-PUT RULE

IDEA specifies that while you are in any dispute with the school district about placement, your child has the right to remain where he or she is. However, *The Complete IEP Guide* also advises that the "stay put" provision is a complex legal right and that you should consult an attorney or nonprofit disability rights organization at once.[1]

The Liability of "Recovery"

It can happen that with a good, integrated treatment regime, your child may improve significantly, perhaps even beginning to emerge from the phenomena that qualify him for an ASD classification. That is to say, by the judgments of some clinicians, he may no longer meet the current diagnostic criteria (see Day 4, "Learning: Is Recovery Possible?"). At this juncture, a terrible irony can occur: because of the structure and budgetary conditions of public school systems, the present wording of DSM IV, and IDEA regulations, the hard work of you and your team may be cut short by the fact that your child no longer qualifies for some of the very services that have been responsible for his tremendous progress.

As their symptoms subside to subclinical levels, such children are still extremely vulnerable to relapse. They are usually neither truly off the spectrum nor recovered but in a wobbly state of improvement. The delicacy of these remissions can be completely missed or, in some cases, used to reduce a school district's special education costs.

What is actually needed at this point is to continue the successful program until stable recovery is achieved. As the parent you may find yourself in the problematic position of being penalized for success, and you will have to find an appropriate means to deal with this ambiguity. You may have to fight even harder to keep the supports and services that helped get your child into an improved situation in the first place.

Do You Need an Attorney?

If you do get into disputes with a school district, you will find your experience much more tolerable if you have a good special education attorney.

Depending upon the complexity of the situation, you may want to hire her initially just for consultation. Bringing her in to deal with the school district in your stead will immediately make the IEP process more expensive and more adversarial.

HOW TO HIRE AN ATTORNEY

When searching for an attorney, look for one who has handled many cases involving children on the autism spectrum within the last year. This is because within special education law, it is a specialty that has changed a lot recently. Not just any special education attorney will do.

- ○ Go to Wrightslaw.com, and print out the list of special education attorneys for your state.
- ○ Speak with parents who have already been down this road, including members of your PAC.

Usually a handful of special education attorneys in every state have a great deal of expertise in handling ASD cases. Often you can get a free evaluation or consultation to determine if the attorney is willing to take your case and if it will be a good match.

One practical determining factor is how communicative the attorney is. How clearly and directly does she answer questions? Can you reach her easily by phone or email? (Once on the case, most attorneys will charge for email, but it can be a very useful means of rapid communication.)

If you cannot afford an attorney, go to your local legal aid society, and try to find someone who has the experience in special education who will take your case on a pro bono (free) basis. It will be more likely to find this in larger law firms that specialize in special education law. Alternately, it might be more prudent to find yourself a skilled special education advocate (discussed below).

When you interview attorneys, get them to tell you how strong they believe your case to be. This should give you a sense of whether or not you should incur the expense of hiring an attorney at all.

If you do decide to hire one, ask the attorney up front what you can do to minimize your costs. I always offer to do as much of the legwork as possible. For instance, if the attorney needs to create a sequential list of what transpired, I create the list. If she needs to get copies of reports from a therapist or other team members, I send out requests via email or make telephone calls and then follow up. Simply have the attorney tell you what she needs so she doesn't have to put in the time herself.

RECOVERY OF LEGAL FEES

Many parents believe that if they win a legal battle with their school district, they will recover their legal fees. This is not necessarily the case, even if you win. The agreement that is reached at the end of a victory may not include recovery of legal fees.

Some schools have you sign an agreement upfront that forbids you to pay legal costs out of pocket while expecting to have the district held liable for reimbursement. Nevertheless, you do need to keep track of all your legal expenses in case fee recovery becomes a possibility.

Working with a Professional Special Education Advocate

A special education advocate (also called a "parent advocate") is a professional who can assist you by becoming your voice in situations in which you are not yet expert with the intricacies and nuances of the IEP process. This person is not an attorney, but because of his extensive knowledge and long experience in dealing with special education issues, he has become expert at "working" the system.

An experienced special education advocate will be of great value when:

○ your efforts at obtaining the appropriate services for your child have been stymied by the school system
○ you are feeling intimidated by school system "experts" who speak with high authority (but may be using poor judgment)
○ you don't know how to object to an inappropriate IEP
○ you don't know how to use the recourses available to you
○ you are confused about any aspect of how to proceed with the IEP process

The advocate can steer you through these rocks and shoals, and even speak for you at meetings when it all seems too overwhelming. He should be able to use all available remedies up to the point when due process is your only recourse. At that stage, a special education attorney should oversee the next steps.

HIRING A SPECIAL EDUCATION ADVOCATE

Your best bet in finding an experienced advocate is by referral from another parent or trusted team member. You should also follow all the steps given on the Wrightslaw.com web page entitled, "How Can I Find an Advocate?" (http://www.wrightslaw.com/info/advo.referrals.htm).

Another good resource is PKIDs Online (Parents of Kids with Infectious Diseases), which provides a listing of advocacy organizations for people with disabilities by state (http://www.pkids.org/pdf/phr/11-06disabilitydirectory .pdf).

Do not take for granted that a special education advocate is skilled in all of the appropriate areas. Indeed, you should take essentially the same steps given above for selecting a special education attorney.

As you would with any team member, research the candidates you are considering, and be sure to find out the answers to these questions:

1. How well trained is he in the specific kind of advocacy you require?
2. How well does he know and understand special education laws for your state?
3. How long has he been an advocate?
4. How well does he know the lay of the land in your specific school district?
5. How does he like to work? How does he approach solving problems like the ones you are facing?
6. Does he appear to have a professional manner about him? How do you feel he would come across to school representatives?
7. Does he clearly accept the fact that you are the final decision maker?
8. Does he seem to be objective in his thinking? Or does he appear to constantly relate your problems to those he has experienced?
9. Can he think in terms of "agreeable settlements" (i.e., resolving matters so both parties feel they have won something in the negotiations)?
10. What is his record of successes? Can you speak with clients he has helped?

11. How well does he want to get to know your child and understand his or her needs and specific situation?

12. Will he attend meetings with you?

13. Will he work with other team members? If so, how?

14. At what point might he recommend that you see an attorney? (Does he seem to know the limits of his knowledge and expertise?)

15. What is his fee structure?

Download and study the latest edition of *A Parent's Guide to Selecting a Special Education Advocate in Massachusetts* (even if you do not live in Massachusetts), published by the Federation for Children with Special Needs. The current web address for this brochure is: http://www.fcsn.org/pti/advocacy/advocacy_brochure.pdf.

Self-Advocacy

Even without an attorney or professional advocate, you can do quite a lot if you are willing to learn the ropes. Here are some examples of situations in which self-advocacy (also known as "parent advocacy") can be effective:

○ Community members in daily situations may give you frowns or looks of disgust when they see your child "misbehaving" in a store or on the street. They think it's due to bad parenting, and you want to either crawl under a rock or throw something at them. Instead, you arrange to conduct an interview with a local newspaper or radio station to share with the public what it's like to raise a child with autism. Because of this powerful interview, many more people within your community have a greater understanding of how this disorder affects not only your family's life but the lives of many other families within the community. And because of your interview, members of the community are now beginning to reach out to these families with understanding, empathy, and offers of assistance.

○ In Sunday school, your child is too much for the teacher to handle, and he is becoming disruptive in class. The church cannot afford an aide to be with your child. Instead of removing your child from Sunday school, you speak to the congregation, explain the situation, and arrange for weekly assistance from a local high school student, who will provide one-on-one support for your son and will receive community service credit for the hours she puts in.

❍ Your district has a summer program for children with special needs, but it is held in a high school building that is much too overwhelming for small children with sensory issues. The staff is not trained in working with children who have ASD, and there is a limited amount of services and supports for the children.

You organize a group of parents and collectively petition the school district. As a result, the program is moved to an elementary school, it is staffed with experienced professionals, and the services and supports are increased.

❍ Your insurance has inconsistent reimbursement practices. The amount of reimbursement appears to depend a lot upon which claims representative was handling the case. You question the representatives and their supervisors to find the company policy but achieve no results because the company's policies are kept confidential.

You implement a campaign to change the mindset of individuals within the company or perhaps the entire company. You appeal the denied claim; you get letters from MDs showing that the treatment is a medical necessity. If you get no favorable results, you appeal to your state insurance board and turn it into a public relations problem for the insurer by going to the press, if it continues to ignore you. You coordinate a group of parents in similar situations and start a petition, maybe even a class action suit if it seems feasible and warranted.

❍ You find you are not getting much emotional support or physical help from family members. They almost never call you to see how you are doing; they are not there for you when you need someone to babysit so you can go grocery shopping or get out of the house by yourself. They don't really understand about the disability or the limitations it places on you.

You decide to educate them about what your life is like and how even the smallest offer of help can make a big difference.

A BASIC SELF-ADVOCACY PROCESS

Here is the general sequence of actions you should take when advocating:

1. Specify what you need.
2. Assess what is being offered, and identify the specific unmet needs.
3. Consider what you are up against to get what you need.
4. Evaluate the degree of difficulty.

5. Assess your personal resources (financial, emotional, network of contacts, time, patience, skills).
6. Come up with a basic approach.
7. Develop a plan.
8. Implement the plan.

Let's now examine in more detail how this process might be used when dealing with a school district. The example used is from my personal experience—the one described above about a deficient school summer program.

1. SPECIFY WHAT YOU NEED

In my case, I was greatly in need of a summer program for my daughter. My goal was not just to make sure the program met her needs but also to keep her in the community so she could be with her friends.

2. ASSESS WHAT IS BEING OFFERED, AND IDENTIFY THE SPECIFIC UNMET NEEDS

They offered a "one size fits all" summer program that was very inadequate:

- The location was at the high school, which was physically too big and overwhelming for children in kindergarten through sixth grade.
- The program was staffed by a few teachers with assistance from inexperienced high school students.
- The classrooms contained too wide a mixture of children with different disabilities.
- The teachers had no experience with children on the autism spectrum.
- The program consisted of four half-days for only five weeks, which may have been fine for some children with disabilities. But the children with social and emotional disabilities, like ASD, required an eight-week program with full six-hour days to give their lives the needed structure and consistency.
- There were no opportunities for social interactions with typically developing peer models.
- Academically, the children were being taught at one level even though they functioned at different levels, either much lower or much higher.
- No occupational therapy was offered.

3. Consider What You Are Up Against to Get What You Need

During my investigation, I sought answers to these questions:

- Is this school district meeting the child's individual needs or offering "one size fits all"? *(Answer: No, it offers "one size fits all.")*
- Do school personnel seem open to sending a child out of district to a private summer placement? *(Answer: No.)*
- Are they willing to negotiate, or will they dig their heels in the ground? *(Answer: Not clear.)*
- Have they kept up with times and developed a summer program specifically tailored for children with ASD? *(Answer: No.)*
- Have they spent any resources to develop their summer program? *(Answer: Only minimally.)*
- Are they willing to hire an ASD consultant to help them develop their summer program? *(Answer: No.)*
- Have they ever offered a full-time summer program before? *(Answer: No.)*
- Is their philosophy "This is the way the program is, and we're not changing it"? *(Answer: Yes.)*
- What is the willingness of administration to work with you and with other parents who are having similar problems? *(Answer: Very low interest, unresponsive.)*
- Is the school district taking advantage of the available federal funds and grants? Usually program deficiencies come down to limited funds, so I looked into the financial constraints of the school district by attending school committee meetings and town meetings and then reviewing the school budgets. *(Answer: No, it was not.)*

4. Evaluate the Degree of Difficulty. (Is This Battle Worth Fighting?)

- Are school administrators open to the idea, or is it something that will clearly need to be fought for? *(Answer: When approached by me or by other parents in the same situation, they were not open to making any changes to the summer program. On several occasions, I tried speaking with higher-level school officials, but the response was always the same: "This is the program we have to offer.")*

○ What approach is best suited to get what you need? Personal petition? Parent coalition? Public relations campaign through the local press? Due process using an attorney? *(Answer: It was clear that without an experienced special education attorney, I would not get what my child needed.)*

○ Was it likely to be worth the cost of waging the battle versus letting it go? *(Answer: In my situation, it was an emphatic* yes! *I could not afford to pay for a summer program myself, and after making a few inquiries, I discovered that at least twelve other sets of parents in the district were as unhappy with the summer program as I was.)*

5. ASSESS YOUR PERSONAL RESOURCES (FINANCIAL, EMOTIONAL, NETWORK OF CONTACTS, TIME, PATIENCE, SKILLS)

I did not have the money to hire an attorney on my own, but I had good contacts and could coordinate a coalition.

6. COME UP WITH A BASIC APPROACH

I decided to pull together a group of parents of elementary school children who were diagnosed with ASD and who had the same basic concerns, to see if we could do as a group what we could not accomplish individually: to pool funds to hire an attorney and develop a program that would meet our needs.

7. DEVELOP A PLAN

Our plan was:

a. Establish common goals for the program so we were all asking for the same things.
b. Pool funds to hire an attorney.
c. Establish a single point of contact for the attorney with the group.
d. Support in all ways necessary the attorney's efforts to develop the issues not being met for each child.

e. Have the attorney approach the school district's attorney with the collective issues and seek an agreement before taking any more expensive (due process) steps.

8. IMPLEMENT THE PLAN

The goal of changing the district's summer program was only partially successful; however, we did get essentially what we needed, one way or another:

- ❍ The school district agreed to move the program to an elementary school.
- ❍ The length of the day was extended by an hour.
- ❍ They brought in typical peer models during lunchtime for at least minimal social interactions.
- ❍ One parent received additional tutoring for her child.
- ❍ A few parents got additional therapies.
- ❍ Two parents were offered out-of-district placements.

Particularly for those who sought (and received) out-of-district placements, the energy and money spent on the advocacy effort was definitely worth it financially. Once an out-of-district placement is granted, it tends to stay that way unless the school can offer something comparable. A good summer program could have cost $5,000 if I had to pay for it out of pocket. Each family contributed $1,100 in attorney fees. and my out-of-district summer placement lasted three years. Because of this, my $1,100 outlay saved me about $13,900.

In the world of advocacy and the school district in particular, you get out of it only what you put in it. If you're not willing to fight for something, you'll get very little in return, unless you are in a particularly progressive school district.

A lot of parents don't want to make waves or have the school "think ill" of them or their child. What they may not realize is that they can keep these battles away from the day-to-day school personnel by conducting this business only with the district's special education director—and not with the local school's special education coordinator, principal, or teachers, who have no power to change district policy. Often, these individuals are cheering you on quietly and hoping you will pave the way for other families.

The most comprehensive sources of information on parent advocacy can be found on Wrightslaw.com. Go to http://www.wrightslaw.com/info/advo.index.htm, or search on the website for "special education advocacy." I also recommend the book by Peter W. D. Wright and Pamela Darr Wright, *Wrightslaw: From Emotions to Advocacy: The Special Education Survival Guide*, 2nd edition (Hartfield, VA: Harbor House Law Press, 2008).

Other important advocacy organizations include:

○ Council of Parent Attorneys and Advocates, Inc. (COPAA): This is an "organization of attorneys, special education advocates and parents. COPAA's mission is to be a national voice for special education rights and to promote excellence in advocacy. Our primary goal is to secure high quality educational services for children with disabilities."[2] COPAA offers a searchable list of attorneys and advocates by state. See: http://www.copaa.org/index.html.

○ Council for Exceptional Children (CEC): This is "the largest international professional organization dedicated to improving the educational success of individuals with disabilities and/or gifts and talents. CEC advocates for appropriate governmental policies, sets professional standards, provides professional development, advocates for individuals with exceptionalities, and helps professionals obtain conditions and resources necessary for effective professional practice."[3] See: http://www.cec.sped.org.

○ Families and Advocates Partnership for Education (FAPE): The FAPE project "is a partnership that aims to improve the educational outcomes for children with disabilities. It links families, advocates, and self-advocates to information about the Individuals with Disabilities Education Act (IDEA). The project is designed to address the information needs of the 6 million families throughout the Country whose children with disabilities receive special education services."[4] See: http://www.fape.org.

○ Federation for Children with Special Needs (FCSN): FCSN provides "information, support, and assistance to parents of children with disabilities, their professional partners, and their communities. We are committed to listening to and learning from families, and encouraging full participation in community life by all people, especially those with disabilities."[5] See: http://fcsn.org/index.php.

IN A SENTENCE

Regardless of whom you hire, you will always be your child's first and best advocate.

MONTH **8**

learning

Identifying Coexisting Conditions

THE NUMBER OF children who have some form of autism and who also have one or more accompanying disorders is extraordinarily high. Though statistical studies are sorely lacking, this fact is painfully apparent to virtually all biomedical professionals who specialize in autism spectrum disorders and who work in clinical practices. As discussed in Week 2, "Learning: Diagnosis Is Not Enough," these simultaneous or accompanying conditions are called "comorbid disorders."

In fact, the biomedical practitioner is confronted with multiple medical disorders interwoven with one another that severely aggravate—and, indeed, contribute to—the collection of behaviors known as "autism."

Thus an autism diagnosis cannot be treated as an aggregate condition but must be peeled apart, layer by layer. Each layer can be diagnosed, and for each layer, causes and treatments can be identified. This is why it is so important to have a team of professionals who collectively span all the related disciplines that the overlapping disorders may cover.

For example, a large number of children with autism may have seizures at some point in their lives. For this reason, you will need a neurologist who specializes in seizure disorders to diagnose and help treat this condition.

Other possible overlapping disorders might include:

- allergies
- anxiety disorder
- asthma
- attention deficit/hyperactivity disorder (AD/HD)
- bipolar disorder
- depression
- gastrointestinal disorders
- immune dysfunction
- intellectual disabilities
- obsessive-compulsive disorder
- tics
- and more.

(Definitions for most of the above can be found in the glossary.)

Your biomedical specialist should be able to pinpoint which disorders are affecting your child. Nevertheless, because you have enlisted professionals from a variety of disciplines, remember that they may not share a common model of disease or treatment. Often there will be disagreement on diagnosing a particular comorbid disorder. For example, a child's mood dysregulation may be diagnosed by a pediatrician as part of the autism, a psychiatrist may diagnose it as ADHD or bipolar disorder, and a biomedical specialist may identify the problem as resulting from a yeast overgrowth, colitis, or a bacterial infection. Also, some practitioners may suggest a "Band-Aid" or quick patch approach instead of the more difficult, comprehensive treatment path toward true alleviation or cure.

This can be confusing until one realizes that the most correct diagnosis is one that points in the direction of treatments that reduce the actual condition—not just suppress its symptoms. (Naturally, there are often instances when a Band-Aid approach is all one can do until a better solution is found or developed.)

The preceding example of a child with mood dysregulation is an actual one. In this particular case, the following occurred:

○ The pediatrician was unable to pinpoint a specific diagnosis for the child's extreme hyperactivity, attentional problems, impulsivity, rages, obsessive-compulsive behaviors, tics, gastrointestinal problems, and allergies other than autism.

○ The psychiatrist diagnosed the child with early onset bipolar disorder and ADHD. This resulted in treatment consisting of different psychiatric meds, which helped to suppress some of the symptoms but did not address any of the causes.

○ The gastroenterologist conducted a **colonoscopy, endoscopy**, and allergy testing and diagnosed the child with severe colitis, which is inflammation of the colon. This led to a treatment of digestive enzymes and supplements, restrictive diet (gluten-free, casein-free, soy-free, dye- and additive-free), and antifungal medication. This treatment significantly reduced the hyperactivity and gastrointestinal problems, but it helped only as long as the child was on the diet, supplements, and medication. It addressed some important secondary causes but did not get at the root cause of the problem.

○ The biomedical specialist, an integrative medicine practitioner, conducted extensive testing, which included a complete blood count, basic urinalysis, basic blood chemistry, nutritional and metabolic tests, food allergy and sensitivity testing, immune testing, and testing for heavy metal overload. The specialist agreed with the treatment recommended by the psychiatrist and gastroenterologist, although he tweaked the supplements based on tests conducted and began a course of detoxification.

○ In addition, the biomedical practitioner diagnosed the child with pediatric autoimmune neuropsychiatric disorders associated with streptococcal infections (PANDAS), a condition in which a strep infection sets off an immune response that results in antibodies attacking the basal ganglia in the brain (the basal ganglia is responsible for movement and behavior). This can result in a sudden onset of symptoms, including motor or vocal tics, obsessions and/or compulsions, irritability, and mood disorder.

○ The biomedical specialist prescribed a daily antibiotic treatment for the PANDAS, and the child responded immediately. Her rages, once violent, were nearly eliminated, and her heightened anxiety, mood swings, tics, and obsessive-compulsive behaviors were significantly reduced. Four years later, the child continues on a daily treatment of penicillin, and although it greatly reduces the violent rages, continued use of antibiotics has further compromised the child's immune system.

The biomedical specialist, along with the child's immunologist and gastroen-terologist, recommended a three-month trial of **intravenous immune globu-lin** treatments, which has shown promising results in the treatment of PANDAS. Immune globulin (IG) is a type of protein found in the blood that can be injected to balance or modulate a patient's immune system. Since IG is administered in-travenously (IV), the treatment is commonly called "IVIG." The child has recently completed her third month of treatment, and the doctors are very optimistic about her progress. The tics, obsessions, mood swings, and anxiety—once very debilitating for this child—have nearly disappeared.

Clearly progress has been made in helping this child, and in getting to the root cause. It is encouraging to realize that as long as the scientific method is used to develop treatment programs, one can start with failures but end up with successes. (See the section entitled "A Basic Treatment Development Pro-cess" in Week 2.) Of course, the primary cause of failure would be neglecting to address comorbid disorders in the first place. In the words of Dr. Kenneth Bock:

"Two of the major factors that underlie and provide a link between the 4-A disor-ders (autism, ADHD, asthma, and allergies) are increased oxidative stress and chronic inflammation. Oxidative stress involves very reactive molecules that dam-age cell membranes and other cellular structures and functions. Inflammation can be seen in the gut, skin, lungs, immune system, and brain of these children.

Pursuing a biomedical approach to these disorders must always include the question "What is driving this increased oxidative stress and/or chronic in-flammation?" Considerations include toxins, such as chemicals and heavy metals, infections, and allergens. Addressing these factors, and working to-wards remediating them, coupled with appropriate clinical, behavioral, and educational interventions, can result in significant improvement and, in an in-creasing number of cases, even recovery."[1]

IN A SENTENCE

Whenever possible, choose the road that will actually improve conditions rather than just suppress the symptoms.

living

More about Peeling
Away the Layers

THE PROBLEM WITH coexisting conditions is that they can block your road toward finding ways to reduce symptoms of autism. For example, the child is hyperactive and has extreme obsessive tendencies. These characteristics may be due to food allergies or other dietary problems; their presence will make it difficult to treat the autism. Coexisting conditions need to be peeled away so the treatment for autism can be more effective.

In Week 2, "Learning: Diagnosis Is Not Enough," we laid out a basic treatment development process. This process is really just a straightforward application of the basic scientific method. In this section we are going to add a "front end" to the process. That is, we are going to introduce a few additional steps that will become the entrance into that process. These steps will act as a sort of focusing device, allowing you to aim the treatment toward resolving issues that you feel are most important at any given moment.

These additional steps are:

1. "Broad shoot," that is, cast your net over a wide list of issues that you have observed in your child and might want to target

for treatment. (The reason for doing this, rather than just focusing on what you observed in the original step 1 of the basic treatment development process, "analyzing a manifestation of the disorder," is that often what is first noticed is not necessarily the best place to begin treatment.) Be sure you get input from your medical, therapeutic, and educational team members, as they will be more objective than you. An example of such a comprehensive list might be:

- little or no eye contact
- does not respond to name or to questions asked (does not seem to comprehend what is being said)
- language delay
- no gestures
- does not share interest in an object or activity jointly with a preferred adult
- lacks social reciprocity
- displays rigidity and gets stuck on certain activities
- expresses insistence on sameness and resistance to change
- demonstrates inappropriate play or behavior
- tantrums easily
- has unusual motor behaviors and motor planning
- lines up toys and objects in obsessive manner
- makes repetitive movements with hands
- prefers to be alone; does not enjoy being with other children
- displays self-injurious behaviors
- is over-reactive to sensory input (touch, sound, taste, sight, hearing)
- gets over-aroused very easily
- has difficulty processing sensory information
- loses skills that were once gained
- has low muscle tone
- has difficulty sleeping
- has short attention span
- has frequent gastrointestinal problems (e.g., reflux, stomach pains, diarrhea, constipation, etc.)
- is extremely picky or has unusual eating habits
- experiences mild seizures

2. Now select the items you and your team feel are most important to focus on at this time, and prioritize them based upon parent or child awareness

and with the advice of your team. Highest priority should be given to issues that affect your child's health and medical necessities, ability to function in daily life, ability to communicate, and ability to socialize. A prioritized list might look like this example:

a. Eliminate seizures.

b. Eliminate gastrointestinal problems.

c. Eliminate self-injurious behaviors.

d. Improve ability to communicate needs and wants through gestures and words.

e. Improve ability to engage, relate, and interact with parents.

f. Increase eye contact.

g. Stabilize mood dysregulation.

h. Improve sleep patterns.

3. Have your team members verify that the proposed sequence is doable. Also ask them to give you insight into how realistic the sequence is in addressing the problem.

Example: Addressing issues involving the child's problems of attention would be difficult if not impossible to address while the child is experiencing wild swings of emotions. Thus mood dysregulation would have to be addressed before deficits in attention.

4. Review (or do, if not yet done) your child's unique profile (Week 2, "Living: Understanding Your Child's Individual Profile"), and update as needed. As your child progresses with treatment, her profile will change. It is important that you stay on top of this. Improving one skill (or eliminating one issue) may give you better access to improving three more skills (or eliminating three more problems).

Example #1: Minimizing a child's gastrointestinal problems may help toward eliminating the self-injurious behaviors and improve his sleep patterns. In turn, the child may now be able to sit long enough so you can begin focusing on his communication and social interactions.

Example #2: Improving a child's ability to express her needs and wants may help to lower her level of frustration and improve her moods. As a result, it may now be easier to focus on engaging, relating, and interacting with her through **social-imitative play**.

5. Share the updated profile with all team members.

6. Decide who is going to be your lead clinician for this effort. Choose someone who

- is a good investigator
- can think outside the box
- is a team player
- can look at the whole picture and pull theories together
- will look at your child individually and act solely in his best interests

7. Convene a team meeting (often impossible), or convene a teleconference (more likely but can be very difficult), or work with each team member separately (easiest to do in terms of accessing each team member but inconvenient for you).

   a. Have each team member suggest possible contributing factors and/or disorders from her professional perspective.

   b. Get as wide a selection of possible contributing factors or disorders as the team can manage.

   c. Narrow the list to likely targets (issues). This process consists of
      - Considering the experiences of the team clinicians
      - Looking for supporting evidence and challenging logical flaws
      - Using "gut instinct"
      - Proving or disproving theories by clinical tests and/or doing trial treatments (in cases in which the risks of doing so are judged to be acceptable)

8. Develop a treatment plan using the basic treatment development process described in Week 2. The narrowing down steps above should also reduce the number of team members and specialists essential to conducting this process. (See Appendix 2, "A Strawman Treatment Development Process," for a presentation of the full process.)

This process is repeated as needed until the "onion" is peeled to the point at which appropriate and effective treatments are now possible. As the child's condition changes in response to treatment and other environment variables, the process is continued, with constant updates to the treatment plan.

Sometimes Band-Aid approaches—or temporary fixes—may be necessary until you can get to the root of a problem.

Example: A child who is experiencing severe mood swings, tantrums, rages, tics, obsessive-compulsive disorder, or anxiety may benefit from appropriate nutraceuticals or pharmaceutical medication, at least until you can peel enough layers to get to the root cause.

When Specialists Disagree

INCOMPLETE COMMUNICATION

Disagreements occur when people can't or don't exchange ideas fully. Since it is usually extremely difficult (or expensive) to convene an in-person meeting of everyone on your team, disagreements are common in these situations. In the absence of live communication in an open forum, you as the team leader will have to facilitate full exchanges of communication through whatever means possible:

- O moderating teleconferences and email exchanges, and/or creating a blog.
- O obtaining reports and ensuring each appropriate team member receives a copy, reads it, and responds
- O continuing these back-and-forth exchanges until as full an understanding as possible is reached

INTRACTABILITY

Another cause of disagreement is intractability of viewpoint. This can manifest as an inability or outright refusal to look outside the box, to be open to the viewpoints of other disciplines, or to be able to think in an integrative rather than in an exclusive, traditional manner. This can be due to the professional's education, experience, and/or personal traits.

Often there will simply be difference in personal opinion or philosophy that cannot be resolved with any amount of communication. In this case, you as the team leader must recognize it as such and let them at least agree to disagree, leaving the final judgment (as always) up to you. At times it may also become clear that some intractable team member needs to be replaced for the group to continue to function properly.

Guidelines for "Peeling the Onion"

Many disorders can manifest in so many different ways (gastrointestinal overlapping with immune dysfunction overlapping with wild mood swings overlapping with allergies overlapping with social, emotional, and communication problems) and interact in so many complex ways that diagnosis can be quite difficult for practitioners with limited experience.

Nevertheless, after a few layers have been pulled off, the next layers may be easier as the case has "settled down" a bit (that is, the child is not so over-reactive).

In general, the top priorities for treatment are

○ seizures

○ mood dysregulation

○ functional criticality (conditions that affect the physiological function and health of the child's body; for example, the whir of an air conditioner or flush of a toilet may throw a child's regulatory and sensory systems into excessive overdrive and cause extreme agitation and self-injurious behaviors)

○ medical necessity (affecting health)

○ ability to communicate and socially interact

○ body burdens of toxins

○ antagonistic environmental factors

Other Factors Affecting the Treatment Plan

Technical feasibility	Is the technical expertise available to perform the treatment needed?
Invasiveness	How much pain and potential risk are involved?
Required duration of treatment	How long is the full course of treatment likely to run?
Cost, financial resources, insurance coverage	What are the costs and coverage for the treatment—not just for the initial treatment but for the full course of treatment that may be required plus any follow-ups.
Doctor's willingness to prescribe	Does the doctor support the treatment? Has he or she prescribed it before? Or is he or she uncomfortable prescribing it for some reason?
Availability of/accessibility to treatment	Is the treatment delivered at a practice, clinic, or hospital accessible to you?
Prospective gain	What are the realistic expectations?
Side effects / contraindications of treatment	What are the potential side effects and how could they affect the child's other existing disorders?

continues

continued

Team consensus	Are there dissenting opinions that should be considered?
Research supported	What is the quality of the evidence in support of the treatment's efficacy?
Interactions with concurrent treatments	How might other treatments the child is simultaneously receiving affect one another?
Sequences called for or advisable by the treatments themselves (treatment prerequisites)	Is it advisable or necessary for a treatment under consideration to be preceded by some other modality?

THE IMPORTANCE OF THE PARENT AS AN OBSERVER

The success of the investigation is dependent upon the completeness of data. This is why it is so important that parents discuss freely with the doctor what they observe because much valuable information will be known only to parents.

HIDDEN INFLUENCES

Matters concerning the child's environment and the support systems being used are commonly sources of change or influence out of view of the clinician and commonly not mentioned by the parents.

Example: A child is supposed to be on a restricted diet (gluten-free, casein-free), but he sneaks a wheat-based snack just before his speech and language therapy sessions. The child is agitated and distracted, and he loses the ability to focus. The speech and language pathologist is perplexed and cannot figure out why the therapy sessions are going awry.

IN A SENTENCE

Peeling away the layers requires talent, insight, methodical investigation, and the advice of a skilled team.

Feeling Isolated, Staying Positive

EVEN IF YOU are doing everything you can possibly be doing for your child, do you feel as though you are fighting one battle after another and quickly burning yourself out? Perhaps you are not even able to get out of the house because of your child's tantrums or other behavioral issues. On top of that, there may be friction between you and your partner or spouse. Needless to say, you're probably not getting any time for yourself to exercise or have any fun.

One of the most difficult parts of this journey is the overwhelming feeling of being isolated—from your community, society, your friends, even your family and your spouse. It can really get the best of you sometimes. Parents of children with autism have written a lot about this problem; indeed, I touched on this back in Day 2 and Day 3.

Still, there is one central, practical question that should rise above all personal reactions to your child's disorder: how do you deal with it on a day-to-day basis so that it doesn't impair your ability to be an effective team leader, an advocate for your child, and a loving, involved parent?

Self-Support: Taking Care of Yourself

First and foremost, *if for no other reason*, you have to take care of your own needs so you can continue to be an effective team leader, advocate, and parent for your child and the rest of your family.

There will be days you will feel so overwhelmed by all this that you just want to go back to bed and pull the covers over your head. Perhaps you are having a day when nothing seems to go right and your child is having one tantrum after another, your head is throbbing, and you are not accomplishing anything, except to upset those around you.

When I feel this way, I may lie down on the sofa for an hour and take a nap or watch a soap opera so I can become absorbed by someone else's problems, not my own. Or I may go for a walk, take a drive, work out at the gym, or get a massage—whatever I can do to make myself feel a little better about the situation and better about myself and what I'm doing.

There will be days when everything that could go wrong will go wrong—days when you feel totally inept, when you feel you are not contributing to your child or your family. Those are the days when you have to step back and take care of yourself—because if you don't, nobody will.

Since there are so many children diagnosed with autism today, there are many possibilities for finding support; some will make sense for you, and others will not. Here are a few for you to consider:

○ In general, it helps a great deal to connect with other parents and support organizations. There are parent-to-parent organizations, online chat rooms, Listservs, and many other forms of such support. If you are new to the world of autism (and still in crisis mode), a professionally organized group may be your best bet. This is discussed more in the next section.

○ You can try individual counseling with a therapist or counselor.[1]

○ Having a child with autism places an enormous stress on a marriage, often leading to divorce. Marriage counseling might be wise, especially early on, before matters can build to "irreconcilable differences."

○ Consider respite care, which is a service provided to parents and other primary caregivers of persons who require constant care, such as children with autism spectrum disorders. This care can be given in the family's home or the respite provider's home by a licensed nurse or, in the case of a child, a specially trained babysitter. The idea is to give the primary caregiver(s) needed breaks, whether it is for a few hours, overnight, or for a weekend. When parents have a firmly established, supportive network of neighbors and extended family, their need for the services of professional respite care workers is generally much less. In current American society, however, parents often do not have an adequate network of family members near them to whom they can turn. This kind of support can bring a great deal of relief and provide some badly needed stability for the family. Respite providers can sometimes also be sources of new experiences and activities for the child.

A great place to search for respite care near you is the National Respite Locator Service that can be found on the Chapel Hill Outreach Project website: http://chtop.org/ARCH/National-Respite-Locator.html.

Connecting with Your Child

At the end of the day, when I am drained and feel as if I have nothing left to give, my daughter and I partake in a nightly ritual of holding one another and connecting emotionally if we are too exhausted to talk. Other times, we end the day by snuggling and telling each other one thing that made us happy that day. Sometimes just being able to reconnect with my child and remember why I am doing all this makes me feel less lonely and overwhelmed—when I feel the energy and the love, I know that what I'm doing is worthwhile.

What Other People Think

Parents have to be careful not to become isolated from friends, neighbors, and relatives. This happens all too frequently because they may be exhausted and feel embarrassed about how their child behaves in public. And sometimes they sense their friends get tired of hearing about autism every time they see them.

As parents, we need to be surrounded by friends and relatives who care. So for all the friends and relatives who may read this book, reach out to those parents, get involved, and try to understand what it's like to live in our world. We need your understanding, compassion, and support. Instead of standing on the sidelines, please get involved.

And the next time you see a parent you don't know struggling at the supermarket with a child who is throwing food all over the floor and screaming at the top of his lungs, suppress that urge to glare or criticize; instead, offer a helping hand. After all, the chances are high that the child may have autism.

Sharing the Load

From the beginning, parents need to be careful about sharing the load and not letting everything fall to one parent, even if that parent is not bringing home any income. Perhaps the parent who is working outside the home all week can take over during the weekends so that the other parent can get a break and regroup.

I would take to task any spouse who tells me that because he is the sole breadwinner, he has the more difficult job. Not only is that simply not true, it is a blatant retreat from marital and familial responsibility. If you find that you and your spouse argue over whose job is tougher and one or the other "wins" the battle, realize that your marriage is in trouble. The situation has to be equally shared. Quite frankly, nothing else will work.

In some families, many of the responsibilities fall to an older sibling. This can be a good thing. He or she may develop a sense of responsibility and a compassion and understanding of others that far exceeds that of their peers. Some have gone on to successful careers caring for children with special needs. Nevertheless, the good can be turned upside down if they have responsibilities forced on them and are prevented from pursuing their own natural interests. Siblings do need to have their own time and space so they can develop their own lives. Don't allow them to get overwhelmed by having to take on too much, too soon.

Maintaining Other Family Activities

It is important for your family to seek out ways to maintain at least some of the activities you did before autism entered your world. Perhaps you cannot do all of them as you did before as a whole family, but you can find ways to do some of the activities with different combinations of family members.

Some activities that most families do together (such as meals, for example) may require modification because of behavioral issues. They simply might work better now in "shifts" because a child with autism might not do well in a group setting.

Here are two must-read books:

Robert A. Naseef, *Special Children, Challenged Parents: The Struggles and Rewards of Raising a Child with a Disability,* revised edition (Baltimore: Brookes Publishing, 2001)

Karen Siff Exkorn, *The Autism Sourcebook: Everything You Need to Know about Diagnosis, Treatment, Coping, and Healing* (New York: ReaganBooks, 2005)

IN A SENTENCE

Life in the autism world can be isolating and exhausting, and always a challenge, but it is essential that you stay positive.

living

Finding Resources and Building Your Support System

ONE OF THE most challenging tasks for any family who has a child with autism is finding the necessary resources to build a solid support system. This is particularly important now. You need to have a lifeline and others to lean on. You cannot isolate yourself, as ultimately this could draw you into a state of depression. Try to get as much emotional, professional, neighborhood, and community support as you can find.

In every state there are resources to help you build your support system. Here are a few ideas about how to get started:

❍ Your best resource is an experienced parent. Ask your local Early Intervention Program to recommend an experienced parent you can speak to and see if they offer a parent support group; strike up conversations with parents while sitting in waiting rooms for medical, clinical, or therapeutic appointments.

Come with a notebook in hand to any meetings or places you may encounter other parents of children with autism. They will always be your first line of valuable information about local resources.

Your Early Intervention coordinator and clinicians can be great resources. They can often be helpful in assisting you to find resources you may need:

- articles about treatments or other services that might be available
- information about community activity groups in which you can involve your child
- reviews on independent service providers or doctors
- other agencies to contact
- where to get funding
- how to meet other parents with a recently diagnosed child so you can create a play group or with experienced parents who can give you advice

Many of these professionals have been known to go far out of their way to help out parents who are newly dealing with the world of autism. EI providers are some of the most committed and hardest working (yet underpaid) professionals I have ever met.

○ Members of your professional team will be invaluable. Ask them who and what they think are the best resources (people, places, programs). They hear everything about what's working and what's not—from parents and from direct observation.

○ Get out with other parents and observe therapy sessions with their kids. Even the waiting rooms of these therapy sessions are natural support groups.

○ Go to autism workshops and conferences in your area.

○ Your local school district may have a listing of local resources.

○ Stay informed by subscribing to online newsletters.

○ Subscribe to the *Schafer Autism Report*. This is an excellent daily e-newsletter (first mentioned in Day 5). It also provides a quarterly calendar of events for every state. See the website http://www.sarnet.org.

○ Subscribe to *e-Speaks*, Autism Speaks' weekly email newsletter: http://www.autismspeaks.org.

○ Use "Google Alerts": email updates of the latest relevant Google results (web, news, etc.) based on your choice of query or topic. For more information see http://www.google.com/alerts.

○ Get referrals from Wrightslaw.com and its "Yellow Pages for Kids," particularly its listing of disability organizations and information groups. Go to http://www.yellowpagesforkids.com/help/dis.orgs.htm for a list of your state's organizations that offer resources or can direct you to them.

○ Find a chapter of The ARC in your state. Go to http://www.thearc.org/ NetCommunity/Page.aspx?&pid=207&srcid=1386 to find your local chapter of this organization.

○ Check out the website of the Autism Society of America: http://www .autism-society.org.

○ Go to the website of the Parent Advocacy Center for Educational Rights (PACER Center), a nonprofit organization staffed primarily by parents of children with disabilities: http://www.pacer.org. PACER works in coalition with eighteen disability organizations and provides assistance to individual families in Minnesota and nationwide. It also offers workshops, materials for parents and professionals, and leadership in securing a free and appropriate public education for all children.

○ Check out the website of Parent to Parent USA (P2PUSA), a national nonprofit organization committed to assuring access and quality in parent-to-parent support across the country: http://www.p2pusa.org. This site highlights statewide organizations that have parent-to-parent support as a core program and are committed to implementing evidence-based practices. Parent-to-parent programs provide emotional and informational support to families of children who have special needs most notably by matching parents seeking support with an experienced, trained "support parent."

○ Find babysitters. Good candidates are paraprofessionals or aides and college students studying special education.

Finding a Support Group

Look for a support group that serves the needs you have at any given time. For example, if your child has been newly diagnosed with autism, you might need a group focused on emotional support to help you deal with accepting the diagnosis and how to proceed. At another point in time, it may become more important for you to get solutions and resources for problems you encounter. So it is best to consider what type of support you need and look for a group that supports that need.

Another important aspect is to learn who is running the group, how it is run, and the types of people participating before you commit to it. As much as possible, it is best to make sure that the personalities of the participants generally match, complement, or at least don't heavily conflict with your own.

Emotional support groups, if not well run, can become quite draining if a few individuals are allowed to dominate the discussions with their problems.

Always attend at least one meeting of the group to see if it is for you before you commit to it.

There are support groups out there for every type of situation imaginable:

- parents of the newly diagnosed child
- general autism support
- individuals with autism
- dads of children with autism
- siblings of children with autism
- grandparents of children with autism
- families with children on the gluten-free, casein-free diet
- parents of children with Asperger syndrome

and more.

There are also spontaneously created support groups that occur when parents meet in waiting rooms. This can be the best way to meet other parents—where you can share stories, resources, and tips or tricks, and become friends. I used to look forward to taking my daughter for her twice-weekly occupational therapy, because I could hang out in the waiting room with the other parents and talk about anything we wanted. There was no topic we couldn't discuss. Some days we laughed until we cried, and other days we helped each other sort out problems or recommended resources. Some days we lingered much longer after our children finished their therapy. There was a real camaraderie.

The best way to find out what is available in your area is through the internet. I provide suggested websites on the following page, but if any web addresses have changed, your best bet is to do a search on the names given in the left-hand column to find the organization's current URL.

You can also do internet searches on, for example,

- "[name of your city or county] + autism support groups"
- "autism support groups newly diagnosed"

These types of searches should turn up a number of possibilities.

Local information is also available through your local Early Intervention Program office.

Autism Society of America	The organization provides a wide variety of support programs and local chapters around the world. http://www.autism-society.org/
Autism Speaks	The organization is dedicated to increasing awareness of autism spectrum disorders, funding research into the causes, prevention, treatments, and cure for autism, and advocating for the needs of affected families. Search the resource guide by state at http://www.autismspeaks.org/community/resources/index.php and then look for support groups.
Children's Disabilities Information	The website provides an annotated list of support groups and Listservs for parents of children with autism, Asperger syndrome and Pervasive Developmental Delay. Groups are listed by various categories, such as "Autism Diet Groups." http://www.childrensdisabilities.info/autism/groups-autism-asperger.html
The Arc of the United States	Among many other services, the Arc operates support groups for parents of newly diagnosed children. There are local chapters in every state (some have autism support centers). http://www.thearc.org/

Listservs

If you can't get out of the house and you want to communicate with other parents, you can subscribe to an autism Listserv. Listservs are programs hosted on websites that permit subscribers to email entire lists of members. There are many, many such groups out there. For example, at this writing Yahoo! hosts 3,352 Listservs on the topic of autism. See: http://groups.yahoo.com.

Staying Informed

Every month, every week, every day there is something new in the world of autism. Staying informed will pay off in learning about

- new research results
- new studies your child might benefit from being involved with

❍ approvals for new treatments (which is relevant to your insurance coverage)

❍ changes in insurance laws

By far the best way to stay informed is the *Schafer Autism Report* (http://www.sarnet.org). The cost is minimal (two hundred issues for $35, or free with a scholarship subscription), but the service provided is unbelievably comprehensive.

Attend conferences when they come to your area. This information is available through the *Schafer Autism Report*.

IN A SENTENCE

There are many resources available, but remember: your best supports will always be other parents who know exactly what you are going through.

MONTH **10**

learning

Refining Your
Child's Treatments

YOU HAVE BEEN through a very busy and critical nine months, establishing your team, identifying your child's needs, getting to know your child better, and trying to identify which treatments might be most effective. By now you should have a fairly comprehensive program in place. This is a good point to reassess the steps that have been taken and determine what refocusing and corrections are needed to make the program even more effective than it is.

It is easy to become complacent and trust that everything is going the way it should be, but you have to remember, your team members are not there 24/7 with your child, and they may not see the nuances you are seeing. Further, they have many patients or clients and cannot possibly know what is best for your child the way you can. You must be vigilant, watch for signals from your child, and always listen to your instincts.

Perhaps you have reached a plateau and don't know why. Perhaps one of your therapists has not been able to connect with your child. And perhaps you are using a treatment that is just not working. Now is the time to find out and make some modifications to refine your course.

Reassessing

When reassessing the treatments and program you have in place, the following questions should be answered:

1. Is the treatment program set forth by your team an appropriate one? Do you believe this to be true? Are all of your team members in agreement? If not, what needs to be changed?
2. Is your child adapting to treatments? Is he happy during therapies and in his school or home-based program?
3. Are his treatments focusing on what is really important?
4. Are the treatments chosen correctly for the results desired?
5. Are they being applied correctly, methodically, consistently, and completely? Is there follow-through on treatments at home? On weekends? During the summers?
6. Are treatments being layered appropriately?
7. Are treatments being modified according to the child's indicators and your own best instincts?
8. Are you getting feedback from teachers, therapists, and doctors to your satisfaction?
9. Are your team members an asset to your child's progress? Are they supporting you the way you would like?
10. Are you keeping data (tracking results, side effects, developments, changes?)

The charts on pages 278–281 may help you in assessing where you are now.

IN A SENTENCE

Refining your course will make the path smoother, more effective, and less costly.

About the Child	Questions to Pose
Educational Program	Is the program using methodologies that benefit your child, and are they consistent with the IFSP/IEP? Are supports in place, and are they being used properly? Are goals appropriate and attainable for your child? Are they too easy? Is your child reaching his goals? Is he making progress? Regressing? Staying the same? Why? Is there a formal assessment in place that helps to measure progress?
General Environment	What is your child's reaction to the environment? Is the environment safe, calm, organized, and conducive to your child's needs? Or is the environment visually cluttered, busy, or noisy? What are the positive and negative influences?
Classmates or Peers	Is your child getting along with classmates or peers? Is she making connections and friends? Are peers appropriately matched? Is someone facilitating social interactions? What are the positive and negative influences? Any concerns?
Teacher(s), Paraprofessional(s)/ Aide(s)	Does this seem to be a good fit? Is your child connected to him? Does she get enough one-on-one attention? Is he complying with your child's IFSP/IEP document? Does he have the expertise, knowledge, understanding of your child, and compatible style to match your child's needs? Is your child being challenged sufficiently? What are the positive and negative influences? Will he accept input from you? Do you have a good relationship with him, and are you getting the necessary daily feedback on your child? Any concerns?

About the Child	Questions to Pose
Therapeutics	
Speech and language pathology (SLP), occupational therapy (OT), physical therapy (PT), other therapies	Does this seem to be a good fit?
	Is your child connected to the therapist?
	How does your child react to the environment?
	Is the therapist complying with your child's IFSP/IEP document?
	Does she have the expertise, knowledge, understanding of your child, and compatible style to match your child's needs?
	Are the treatments helping?
	Has your child made progress?
	Has there been any regression? Has he stayed the same? If so, why?
	Is your child being challenged sufficiently?
	Will the therapist accept input from you?
	Do you have a good relationship with the therapist, and are you getting the necessary feedback on your child?
	Any concerns?
Medical/Biological	
Gastrointestinal, immune, nutritional/dietary, metabolic, neurological, and other systems	Are you happy with your clinician?
	Is he helping your child?
	Is he working with other team members?
	Supporting and listening to you?
	Contributing solutions?
	Thinking outside the box?
	What changes have you seen in treatment regimes?
	Were they implemented correctly, methodically, consistently, and completely?
	What was your child's reaction to the treatment?
	What were the outcomes?
Social	
Play dates and other social interactions	What are the quantity and quality of your child's social interactions in a day or week?
	What are they with adults?
	What are they with peers (siblings, friends, etc.)?
	What is your child's level of social gains?

About the Parents	Questions to Pose
Social Issues	Are you feeling isolated? How much *real* social contact do you have with the rest of your family and the outside community? Are you maintaining friendships?
Emotional Issues	How is your stress level? (on a scale of 1 to 10) How well are you dealing with the stress? How do you deal with it? Are you getting the help you need? Are you calm with your child(ren)? Do you watch the tone of your own voice? Do you have a way to alleviate your stress? How is your energy level? Are you getting the support you need from your spouse? Other family members? Friends? Are you seeking counseling?
Physical Health/ Medical	How is your health? Do you exercise? Are you eating a healthy diet? Are you getting regular checkups?
Marriage/ Relationship	How is your marriage/relationship? Is it on the backburner? Are you sharing the load with one another in an equitable way? Do you feel supported by your partner? Are you supportive of your partner? Are you communicating with one another in a healthy way? Are you seeking outside counseling or support?
Educational Issues	Are you up to speed on latest research? Are you continuing your education and knowledge of your child's condition and its treatments? How are you getting your knowledge? Team members? Books, articles, research studies? Workshops, conferences?

About the Family	Questions to Pose
Social Issues	Are you in good communication and up to date with the rest of your family?
	Are you doing things together as a family?
	How are family relationships? Are you supportive of one another?
	Are you able to give your family members the love and attention they need?
	Are you getting love and support from other family members?
	Is there any resentment? How are you dealing with this?
	Are you able to talk about anything other than autism?
	Are you able to laugh together?
	Do other family members have social lives?
	Are they feeling isolated?
	Are the kids getting out with friends?
	Do they have their own time with each parent?
Emotional Issues	Are family members understanding of, accepting of, and compassionate toward one another?
	Do they pitch in and help?
	Do they participate in support groups or counseling (if needed)?
Physical health/ Medical	How is their health?
	Do they exercise?
	Are they eating a healthy diet?
	Are they getting regular checkups?
Educational Issues	Does the rest of the family (including extended family and friends) understand the child's disabilities and issues?
	Do they understand why certain measures are needed in the home and community to maintain an appropriate environment for the child with autism?
	Do they partake in the educational process?
Financial Issues	Is there sensible financial planning?
	Is the situation manageable? Or are you struggling or out of control?
	Are you taking advantage of all available support and financing?
	Are you thinking outside the box to come up with ways to make ends meet?
	Are the necessary lifestyle modifications being made to maintain solvency within the family unit?
	What are the levels of financial stresses? How is it being handled?
	Are you seeking outside counseling?

living

Assessing Your Professional Team and Using It Wisely

Establishing an excellent team can take years. It is vital that you evaluate and make changes to your team on a continuing basis. Understand who is bringing what to the table. Ask yourself:

○ Is my child making the best possible progress?
○ Can anyone else do (the team member's function) better?
○ Can anyone else bring a fresh perspective?
○ Am I leaving any stones unturned?

Certain team members may be taking a backseat to the others, but that doesn't necessarily mean you don't need them. (A team member may "lie dormant" for a couple of years and suddenly become necessary again.)

When your professional team members disagree with one another, remember that doctors' recommendations are just that—"recommendations." As the team leader, you have to decide what to do. Personally, I appreciate it when there are different perspectives and different opinions.

Team Member Assessment Form

Use this sample form, and tailor it to your specific situation. You will need to both pose the questions and answer them. Be brutally honest in this process.

About the Team Members (including you as the team leader)	For each team member, determine the answers to the following questions:
Knowledge of Your Child	Does he know your child well enough (through observation and test results) to prescribe the best possible treatments?
Contributions, Effectiveness, Results	How has she contributed to your child's recovery?
	Does she recommend treatments that you think are important for your child?
	Is she listening to you? Taking your input?
	Do you see results occurring, or are you just going along with her program without analyzing it?
Advocacy / Legal Issues	Does he fully understand the problems, barriers, and direction in which you need to go?
	How has he contributed to your child's advocacy or legal needs?
	Is he listening to you? Taking your input?
Knowledge / Expertise	Does she have the knowledge and technical expertise to do her job well?
	Does she tell you if she doesn't know the answer?
Reports	Does he prepare the reports you need?
	Are they comprehensive and cover everything you want?
	Do you review them before they are finalized and make suggestions for modification?
Flexibility	Is she flexible in how she works with you or your child? Is she open to new ideas?
Financial Aspects	How often do you need to see him?
	What does he charge?
	Does he take insurance?
	Does insurance reimburse you for services?
	Is he able to provide you with a creative way to pay for it? (sliding scale, etc.)
	Is he worth what you have to pay out of pocket?

continues

continued

About the Team Members (including you as the team leader)	For each team member, determine the answers to the following questions:
Logistics	How far do you have to travel to see her?
	How difficult and expensive is the travel?
	Is it worth it?
	Do you need someone to come with you to help? Is it manageable?
Coordination / Collaboration	Is he able to collaborate with other team members as needed?
	Is he open to input from other team members?
Communication	Does she communicate with you and other team members as you would like?
	Does she follow through as promised?

Are you using your team members wisely?

1. For any team member's lack of performance, check to see if you (as team leader) bear any responsibility for this.
2. Are you using your team members sufficiently for:
   - Increasing your own knowledge of research, techniques, or treatments?
   - Referrals?
   - Suggestions of additional avenues to pursue?
   - Tapping into all the resources they may know about in your community or in your state?

Using the Team Assessment Results

1. Make a list of things that have worked well.
2. Make a list of things to fix about the team and your child's program.
3. Prioritize list #1 in terms of what can be further supported if doing so might bring more positive results.
4. Prioritize list #2 in terms of what needs to be fixed first, second, etc.
5. Now combine the priorities from steps 3 and 4, making one master list of priorities.
6. Plan how you can resolve this list.

For nonperforming members of the team, if it is indeed they who are not contributing (not your oversight in using them fully, etc.), then seek a replacement. Start your search by getting referrals from high-performing team members. (Unless the situation is extreme, it is usually best to have a replacement lined up before letting go of the current team member.)

Beware of becoming "frozen at the controls." Are you fearful of stopping a series of therapy appointments even though you know this treatment is not producing benefits, yet you dutifully keep on bringing your child back to the therapist's office?

IN A SENTENCE

Continually assess how team members are contributing to your child's care; be an indomitable force with velvet gloves.

MONTH **11**

learning

Defining and Measuring Success: Assessing Your Mission and Goals

FOR SOME PARENTS, your goal might be for your child to be able to communicate with the world around him. Or it might be for her to be fully integrated into an inclusionary classroom with minimal supports. Perhaps your goal is for your child to look as indistinguishable from his peers as possible. It might even be for your child to graduate from college someday and live an independent and meaningful life.

No matter what goals you have chosen for your child, how will you know if you're "getting there"?

In Day 5, "Living: Managing the Business of Recovery," you were asked to describe your mission, which we defined as the overall mountain you wanted to climb. The goals were then defined as milestones along the way that theoretically would measure your progress toward accomplishing the mission.

But as in the rest of life, things happen, and you must begin to readjust your plans as you encounter the realities that are so vastly different from what you thought possible. This is simply the way life turns out: things change, and we must learn to roll with the change as best we can.

Success is a personal matter. Your definition may be different from that of other parents, whether or not they have children with disabilities. Only you can define what success means to you. It does not imply precision, finality, perfection, or magnitude. Success is merely an abstract concept that can be complex, fluid, and often unpredictable. No one—not even top professionals—can predict what the future will hold for your child. There are too many variables, too many unknowns. You may be thinking for months that you have failed, and suddenly you realize that your goals (or your mission) were wrong.

Success to you may mean your child

- ❍ has a really great month (or at least has made progress)
- ❍ is safe, secure, and happy
- ❍ learns to communicate (any way possible)
- ❍ tolerates a hug
- ❍ has a warm, loving relationship with you
- ❍ interacts with other family members
- ❍ can go out in public without having a meltdown
- ❍ is sleeping through the night
- ❍ has full inclusion by kindergarten
- ❍ is making and sustaining friends
- ❍ learns to read and write
- ❍ graduates from high school or college
- ❍ learns how to tell a joke
- ❍ can hold a job or have a career
- ❍ has the daily living skills to live independently
- ❍ may someday get married

These may all be attainable goals. But what does success mean to *you* right *now*? Your goals and definition of success will certainly change over time as your child gets older and moves through different stages of development. As she gets older, your child's own personal goals will help shape them for you in a more meaningful way.

And then there is the "little" matter of finding out something that all parents do sooner or later: what your child really wants might be different from

When my child was in second grade and was starting to understand what autism is and what we were trying to accomplish, she told me that she wanted to come to the next IEP meeting. She wanted to tell the school team what she wanted. And so she did. At the beginning of the meeting, she came in and told everyone what was important to her in her school program, what was working, what was not working, and what needed to be fixed.

Nowadays, at the age of thirteen, my daughter plays a more active role. Before every IEP meeting I sit down and discuss with her any changes to the program, supports, or services I am considering; I get her input about what is working or not working; and if I am thinking about a new therapist, I'll bring her to meet the therapist ahead of time before we commit to anything. Or she may initiate a request to have something in her program changed (as an example, last year she requested that her speech/language group be changed to once a week so she could take a drama class). I make sure she buys into whatever I am suggesting to the team.

This translates to all aspects of my daughter's life: activities, vacations, meals, clothing, redecorating her room, etc. One thing is certain: my daughter is opinionated and has something to say about everything! If you ask her, she will tell you about her dreams of owning a horse, attending a university where she can ride every day and compete internationally, and someday owning a ranch where she can help children with disabilities feel as though they are no different from anyone else. These are the moments that can take your breath away and feel that it is all worth it.

what you want for her or what she is really capable of achieving. To ensure you are all on the same page, consider having periodic family meetings.

Regardless of what your mission is or what you consider to be your goals, it is always important to acknowledge the little wins along the way. If you are always waiting for "that one big victory" and are discounting anything else, you are almost certainly never going to get there. Why? Because the simple fact of the matter is that the big accomplishment is composed exclusively of all the little ones added together. If those smaller gains are not properly acknowledged as being important, the larger steps are virtually impossible.

Short-Term versus Long-Term Goals

When your child is younger, your short-term goals might be weekly or monthly goals; long-term goals might be annual. However, when your child is older, your short-term goals might be monthly and more often than not will be annual, whereas long-term goals may become more like five years away.

Especially in the first few years, your goals should be reevaluated much more frequently. After a while, this process will become second nature to you, and you will know when it is time to readjust the goals or set them aside for the time being.

Upon review, you may find that some goals you expected to take years were attained in months and the bar can be set higher. Others, you may realize, are simply unobtainable or not important at this point. As you will probably be emotionally attached to some of these "unobtainable" goals, it may help to articulate them to someone else to begin the process of converting them into something more attainable. This is *not* to say you give up hope on some goal; just don't lock it into a time frame that ends up making it a big loss because it wasn't attained by the date you wished for. After all, hope is what keeps you going.

IN A SENTENCE

> *Do not fear redefining your goals or even your mission.*

living

More about Goals:
Is There a Difference Between
Your Stated Goals and
Your "Real" Goals?

WHEN I FIRST wrote out goals for my daughter's program, I was guided by my Early Intervention coordinator. She did a really good job of helping me as far as she could without my knowing what I could expect. As time went on, I became more familiar with what was possible. In the process of working with clinicians, therapists, and other Early Intervention professionals, I developed more goals. By the time my daughter's first IEP document was being written, there were many more still.

At some point I began to ask myself: Are these really my personal goals? Or are they just quick, convenient ways to make real to other people some corner of the wishes I keep deep in my heart? What were these goals I didn't communicate to anybody? How closely have I inspected them? How honest am I being about them? How much have I resigned myself to other people's ideas about what they think I should want—about what they think is possible?

When I finally looked this over, I realized my IEP goals were quite generic and much less personally relevant to her—more tied to academics and skills. My real goals for my daughter's education had to do with her being able to explore the world and her interests, to feel happy, safe, and confident—goals my IEP plan didn't even begin to deal with.

Do you have two sets of goals? And if so, just how far apart are they?

If you were to pursue the goals you feel are important, how would you measure them? What would be your yardstick of success? And exactly how could you measure incremental success?

It may sound difficult, but it's actually simpler than you might imagine. If you want to "measure" if someone is feeling safe, happy, and confident, take notice of whether or not she tends to walk around with a smile on her face or what kind of mood she is often in. Is she protesting or crying a lot? Does she spend more time expressing frustration or enthusiasm about engaging in some activity? When people come to visit, whether a therapist, relatives, or friends, does she seem happy to see them, and is she interested in engaging with them?

Perhaps one major goal I still hold for my daughter is to graduate from college someday. What is that really a symbol of? If I were honest, doesn't that represent to me her achievement of independence and self-sufficiency?

So what is truly important here? *What* she achieves? Or *how* she achieves it? Shouldn't it be perfectly acceptable for her to realize her potential by whatever alternate means she may choose?

These are difficult questions, but sometimes they need to be asked.

IN A SENTENCE

Be clear, at least to yourself, about your actual goals.

MONTH **12**

learning

Finding Balance, Knowing You Have Made a Difference

AT THE END of the first year it's the perfect time to take stock of where you are and what you have accomplished. It may be the time to make some changes. If you are anything like me, your plate is always filled to the brim, and you're exhausted all the time. When you're not on the floor playing with your child or trying to extinguish the third rage of the day, you're on the internet researching, on the phone scheduling appointments, arranging play dates, battling with your insurance company, trying to get dinner ready on time, bathing your kids, preparing for your IEP meeting, and any of the other ten thousand things that must get done that day. It may be impossible to find time to go to the bathroom, let alone take quality time for yourself or your spouse.

If you find yourself in this predicament too often, then it may be time to make a change. But before you can do this, you must arrive at an important realization: going on and on and on with no time to re-center yourself and recharge your batteries will lead to a personal train wreck.

Once you arrive at this understanding, let me then offer you these steps:

1. Simplify your life as much as you can

To do this, ask yourself these questions:

- ○ Are you taking on too much? Be honest with yourself about this. Are you really comfortable with the load you have?
- ○ Do all these tasks you have accepted really have to be done? Do they have to be done today? If so, can anyone help with the chauffeuring, cooking, cleaning, scheduling, and/or researching? Can you combine two or more tasks? Perhaps condense ten activities into four days instead of seven?

Part of simplifying your life may be leaving yourself one day to do "nothing"—a day with no obligations, a day of rest.

If you're going to work harder at something, permit yourself to let go of something else that may not be as vital at the moment.

Learn how to say no to people. Do not take on projects you might like to do but for which you do not really have the time or emotional resources to accomplish without overworking yourself.

Use some of the time your child is in therapy to get other things done or to take a walk.

2. Get a good night's sleep

Yes, I know, we all have good reasons why sleep must be sacrificed. But sacrificing it too often is part of the formula for an inevitable personal train wreck. Learn to give yourself a cut-off point.

If you don't do these first two, it is unlikely you will get around to the next three.

3. Exercise

I have tried everything, but over the years exercise always seemed to fall lowest on my list of priorities. I bought exercise equipment to work out at home, but, sadly, it rarely got used. I always had an excuse as to why I couldn't work out.

Finally this year—after a jolt from my doctor who told me I better start exercising if I want to be around for my daughter—I joined a health club and hired a trainer twice a week. I knew the only way I would stick with this routine would be if I had a set appointment. The externally imposed discipline really helped! At the very least, schedule a walk with a friend three times a week. If you do this, try to find a scenic place to do it, so it also nurtures you.

4. Have some fun

I am no great example of this, but I do take myself to a movie now and again—a movie that makes me *laugh*. Sometimes I go alone, but I prefer to go with one special friend who is easy to be with and has a great sense of humor. Sometimes I just sit on the pier in the harbor and watch the boats go by. Or I may get a pedicure, massage, or some other service where I am the one being taken care of for a change.

5. Feed your soul

Everyone has his or her own version of this. I find my inspiration comes from the beauty of nature. Whenever I am overwhelmed and feeling the need to recharge my batteries, I try to set aside an afternoon when my daughter is in school so I can head to the harbor or beach by myself and let the natural beauty around me feed my soul and help to reintegrate my physical, emotional, and mental well-being. Sometimes it takes only a few minutes, and other times, when I am feeling very overwhelmed, I may need a few hours or more. It certainly makes coming back to the tasks and decisions still waiting so much easier to complete without feeling so depleted.[1]

Knowing You Have Made a Difference

Yes, certainly you realize you have a long way to go, but now that you have reached the end of the first year, there is no better time to acknowledge how far you have come. Try to take joy in the changes in your child and in having attained at least some of your goals and perhaps even more than you thought possible.

Maybe you were not able to accomplish everything you set out to, but that is okay. Most of us never do. Realize it was through your hard work that your child can now say a word or be able to gesture or have a play date.

Perhaps you are considering reaching out to others in the same position as you—giving back some of the support others have given you. A lot of parents want to do that. My advice is before you start branching out, be sure you have enough time and emotional energy to do this while still having plenty for your own child and family. It is easy to get sucked up into other causes.

But if you do reach out, you will find there is great value in contributing your time and creativity to a local advocacy group, volunteering at your child's school, or even starting a special education community recreation center.

Not only have you already made a difference, but you are going to make an even bigger difference.

Clearly the journey doesn't end here; it's just beginning. You've made it through the first year, and you should definitely give yourself a pat on the back for making it through a difficult period. If your child has not yet entered the public school system, the hardest part of the journey might still lie ahead, but certainly you are much better prepared now and will be able to deal with it more easily.

One characteristic of autism spectrum disorders is the constant ups and downs, so do not be surprised when they happen. And too, there will be battles (perhaps with the school system, perhaps within your own family) that you will lose; this must be expected. But losing a battle now and again does not ever mean you will lose the war. It is your persistence in the face of these losses that will be the truest test of your character.

Within the first year, you likely have achieved an intellectual acceptance of your child's condition. What you should now seek to attain is a feeling of acceptance in your heart—and when it lives there, nothing will sway you from your course.

When this finally happens, you may lose an occasional battle or even many battles, but these losses will not become justifications to abandon your own internal vision of what you are trying to accomplish.

IN A SENTENCE

> *Part of maintaining your balance is knowing that, regardless of any distractions, you are on the right path.*

living

Feeling Empowered, Finding Joy and Humor in Your Life

WHETHER YOU ACCOMPLISHED 75 percent or 25 percent of everything suggested in this book, what's important is that you commend yourself for having accomplished something for your child. Take the time to ask yourself these questions:

- How has the first year gone; for you, your child, and your family?
- How has it gone for you as a parent? As the team leader? As an advocate?
- Do you feel you have been sucked up by the vortex of overwhelming events? Or have you truly embraced it, truly owned it?
- Have you become the driver, or are you sitting in the back seat?
- Have you been able to break down barriers that seem to be thrown in front of you every step of the way? Or are you stumbling over them?

○ Are you feeling charged and empowered by what you are able to accomplish for your child? Are you able to bounce back quickly from those moments or days of feeling frustrated (and perhaps defeated)?

○ How skilled have you become at *disagreeing*?

Disagreement may sound like an odd skill to master, but it is as valuable as any skill can be in this world. One needs to become comfortable disagreeing with unacceptable courses of action, with what other people believe is possible or impossible, with what others assert to be an inevitable outcome.

And by disagreeing you will naturally be making waves.

How secure have you become in the face of disagreements with team members, school district personnel, other professionals who "know more" than you do, and even family members?

Granted, it may take some time to master the ability to disagree politely and constructively, but it is well worth your energy. As you become more and more comfortable with disagreement, see how skilled you can become at not just asserting your point of view, but also—if gradually—converting others to a new perspective on what is possible.

By the same token, it is equally important that you become a good listener and absorb what your team is telling you. It does not mean you need to agree. Just listen, and then weigh both sides, before giving your point of view or decision.

Drawing Power

As part of reviewing your team members and what they bring to the table, consider these questions:

○ Have you developed a team from which you can draw power?

○ Do you feel strengthened and more informed by their presence, participation, and imparting knowledge?

○ Are there team members who overtly or covertly make your job more difficult? Perhaps they disagree with your methods, discourage you from trying something new, and never support you. It is one thing to challenge you or another team member; this is an entirely necessary function of any team member. However, discounting or criticizing everything you suggest without giving it any thought or consideration is not acceptable. If you find any team member doing the latter, regardless of his status or credentials, recognize that he is draining your strength away instead of adding to it. After all, the entire purpose of the team is to *add* strength to you and your team, certainly not weaken it. Thus you must be brave enough to be able to cut out any team member who is weakening your team.

You can also draw power from your child, from your family, and (of course) from deep down inside yourself. You will be amazed to see what you can do that you never thought possible. When put to the test, parents can do Herculean things for their children. This can be the most gratifying experience in your life. No matter how tough it can get, somehow you find the inner strength to keep on going. You can also become more aware and appreciative of the little things in every day life: when you see the smile on your child's face or when she speaks her first word or throws her arms around you and tells you she loves you. This is what makes it all worth it.

The Son-Rise Program at the Autism Treatment Center of America

Son-Rise is the first book I read about autism back in the mid-1970s, when it was first published, and I have never forgotten this profoundly moving story.[2]

According to the Autism Treatment Center website, "the Kaufmans' unique program, which marked a complete departure from existing methods of treatment, transformed Raun from a mute, withdrawn child with an IQ of less than 30 into a highly verbal, socially interactive youngster with a near-genius IQ."[3]

Raun graduated from Brown University with a degree in biomedical ethics, and he is now a successful international speaker, writer, and teacher for the Son-Rise Program and CEO of the Autism Treatment Center of America. I have met Raun, and he is warm and engaging, funny, bright, and a dynamic speaker. I could see no trace of autism whatsoever.

What is so exceptional about the Son-Rise Program is that it teaches parents how to feel empowered, enjoy their child, and see that child as a true gift. It gives parents the hope and vision to see that all things are possible. This is what all parents need to succeed in their journey, no matter what the outcome may be!

Finding Joy

Speaking for myself and many other parents I have come to know well, I found that what we find joy in has undergone a profound change. I used to look forward to holidays in the sun and elegant dinners out—these things somehow don't mean as much to me. Profoundly simpler things have taken their place: watching a sunset, listening to the ocean lapping at the shore, seeing a smile on my child's face and the twinkle in her eyes, feeling her embrace me, and hearing her say, "I love you. Thank you, Mommy, for doing this for me." Hearing words from her I thought I'd never hear—that brings me power and peace of mind. It prevents me from feeling isolated or lonely—though I probably have every right to feel so.

Finding Humor

I've found I now look for more humor in situations the worse they are—that has become my way of dealing with them. Even if my daughter has been raging for hours, breaking doors and pulling fixtures out of walls, there is some way to find humor in it.

I remember one time when Sarah had been vomiting all over the bathroom—the floors, the walls, even the air vents—I just sat down on the floor in the middle of all the puke and started laughing until tears were streaming down my face. My daughter didn't know what to make of it at first. She asked, "Mommy, are you all right?" When she understood, she started laughing too—the two of us there, surrounded by puke, doubled over with laughter, and feeling connected to one another. It's things like this that just keep you going.

Putting It All Together

As you begin to enter the second year of your journey, you will notice that your perspective and outlook will change over time. As you become more informed, feel more empowered, and start seeing positive changes in your child, you will begin to understand how your child thinks and feels. Along the way, as you celebrate every little accomplishment and get to know your child as no one else can, you will dream again.

As Robert Naseef says so eloquently in the book he edited with Cindy Ariel, *Voices from the Spectrum*:

"You cannot accept yourself or any experience without seeing it clearly and with compassion in a tender sympathetic way. . . . Accepting our pain and ourselves leads to accepting and enjoying our child and our family life. That awareness is the gateway to love and wholeness. . . .

That deep connection that a parent feels with a newborn, or a child's first steps, or first words, can be felt at any moment when we are truly aware and attuned to our child.

This awareness keeps the heart open and the mind as clear as possible. Yearning for what we don't have blocks knowing and loving the child we do have. Seeing our child for who she is and giving what she needs from us to whatever extent that is possible. That is the path of acceptance for families."[4]

Courage

Just know that what you are doing for your child is truly heroic and so very admirable. Don't doubt it for a moment.

In her beautiful book, *Autism Heroes: Portraits of Families Meeting the Challenge*, Barbara Firestone writes, "The parents I have met are remarkable people—heroic in their efforts on behalf of their children—it is the heroism that is born of love and sustained by love. They have stayed the course—their love is unconditional and long lasting. Their insights are inspiring and speak to the very essence of what it means to truly love."[5]

But let's not forget that our children are heroes too. Remember what they go through day in and day out, the struggles before them in the years to come, and the teasing they inevitably will endure. It's not an easy life, but it is certainly one worth living and, hopefully, even more beautiful because of what they had to endure.

My daughter will always be my number one hero. If it weren't for her dreams, her perseverance, and her commitment, she would not be where she is today. She keeps me strong and keeps me going on days I never thought I could.

The road ahead may be long and winding and filled with many bumps and uncertainties, but if you take the time to draw inspiration from your child and appreciate what you have, tomorrow won't seem so daunting.

Books to Read

○ Barbara Firestone, *Autism Heroes: Portrait of Families Meeting the Challenge* (Philadelphia: Jessica Kingsley Publishers, 2007)

○ Cindy N. Ariel and Robert A. Naseef, eds., *Voices from the Spectrum: Parents, Grandparents, Siblings, People with Autism, and Professionals Share Their Wisdom* (Philadelphia: Jessica Kingsley Publishers, 2006)

IN A SENTENCE

Find your sources of strength and a deep connection to your child.

The Early Indicators
of Autism

Social Interaction

1. NONVERBAL BEHAVIORS

Nonverbal behaviors are those things people do to convey or exchange information or express emotions without the use of words. These include eye gaze (looking at the face of others to see what they are looking at and to signal interest in interacting), facial expressions (movements of the face used to express emotion and to communicate with others nonverbally), body postures (movements and positioning of the body in relation to others), and gestures (hand and head movements to signal, such as giving, reaching, waving, pointing, or head shaking). In the first year of life, children learn to coordinate nonverbal behaviors to regulate social interaction so that they can use their eyes, face, body, and hands together to interact. At the same time, children learn to read or understand the nonverbal behaviors of others. For example, they learn to follow gaze and look where someone else is looking; understand when others show with their face or tone of their voice that they are happy, sad, or angry; or look at what someone is pointing at. Before learning to talk, children can take turns with nonverbal behaviors in back-and-forth interactions. A child with ASD will not use gestures or facial expressions to draw attention to something for the sake of sharing attention. He may become upset or frustrated, but he will not use eye gaze or gestures to convey his emotions.

2. ENGAGING IN INTERACTION

Engaging in interaction with adults and peers refers to a child's interest in being with and interacting with adults or other children by looking at them, smiling, and communicating in verbal and nonverbal ways. A typical six-month-old will relate to her parent with joy, smiling often while playing with her caregiver. A typical twelve-month-old will show more interest in the parent or caregiver than in objects and toys. With experience in child care settings, a typical child will show an interest in other children, and respond to and initiate offers for interaction with peers. A child with ASD may show more interest in objects and toys than engaging in interaction with people.

3. SHARING ATTENTION

Children seek to share attention with others spontaneously during the first year of life. Shared or joint attention is first accomplished by the caregiver looking at what the infant is looking at. Infants learn early to seek joint attention spontaneously by shifting gaze between an object of interest and another person and back to the object (also called "three-point gaze"), following the gaze or point of others, and using gestures to draw others' attention to objects (e.g. holding out and showing an object or pointing to an object), either by pointing to it or by eye gaze. This desire to share attention to objects builds to sharing enjoyment by looking at others while smiling when enjoying an activity, drawing others' attention to things that are interesting, and checking to see if others notice an achievement (e.g., after building a tower of blocks, looking up and clapping and smiling to share the achievement). Ultimately, children learn to talk and use language to share enjoyment, interests, and achievements and later to share ideas and experiences. Impairment in joint attention is a core deficit of ASD.

4. SOCIAL RECIPROCITY

Social reciprocity is the back-and-forth flow of social interaction. The term "reciprocity" refers to how the behavior of one person influences and is influenced by the behavior of another person and vice versa. Social reciprocity is the dance of social interaction and involves partners working together on a common goal of successful interaction. Adjustments are made by both partners until success is achieved. The skills involved in social reciprocity in very young children begin with showing interest in interacting with others and exchanging smiles. This builds to being able to share conventional meanings with words, and later topics, in conversation. Impairment in social reciprocity may be seen in not taking an active role in social games, preferring solitary activities, or using a person or a person's hand as a tool—as if it is a mechanical object. This may lead to not noticing another person's distress or lack of interest in the focus or topic of conversation.

Communication

5. EXPRESSIVE AND RECEPTIVE LANGUAGE

Expressive and receptive language (also referred to as spoken language) is the use of verbal behavior, or speech, to communicate thoughts, ideas, and feelings with others. Language involves learning many levels of rules—combining sounds to make words, using ordinary meanings of words, combining words into sentences, and using words and sentences in following the rules of conversation. Expressive language is the ability to produce or say words and sentences. Receptive language is the ability to understand or comprehend words and sentences that others use. Children with ASD can range from having no functional language (do not use words conventionally for communication) to having very proficient vocabulary and sentence structure. Usually, those who talk have odd intonation (flat, monotonous, stiff, or "sing songy" without emphasis on the important words), and those who do not yet talk make unusual sounds. The common feature of spoken language difficulties in children with ASD is pragmatics, which are the social rules for using verbal and nonverbal communication in a meaningful and functional context. Some children with ASD have no understanding of words and do not respond to speech, so that they appear as if they are deaf. Other children are able to understand speech and follow instructions, but have difficulty understanding humor or nonliteral meanings, such as "It is raining cats and dogs."

6. CONVERSATION

Once children learn to use functional spoken words and form sentences, they learn to initiate and sustain conversation about a shared topic. The ability to initiate and maintain a conversation begins with joint attention on objects and events and social reciprocity. Infants first learn to take turns and coordinate attention during social games, such as peek-a-boo, looking at books, or playing with toys. During these early social activities children learn to follow the attentional focus of others as well as draw others' attention to things that are interesting. This back and forth sharing is foundational for conversation. Because of the core deficits in joint attention and social reciprocity, children with ASD who learn to speak usually have difficulty following the topics of others and initiating topics that are interesting to others.

7. REPETITIVE LANGUAGE

Children with ASD who learn to talk usually have repetitive use of language. Repetitive language is seen in the use of echolalia, which is the repetition of words, phrases, intonation, or sounds of the speech of others. Children with ASD often display echolalia in the process of learning to talk. Immediate echolalia is the exact repetition of someone else's speech, immediately or soon after the child hears it. Delayed echolalia may occur several minutes, hours, days, or even weeks or years after the original speech was heard. Echolalia is sometimes referred to as "movie talk" because the child can remember and repeat chunks of speech like repeating a movie script. Echolalia was once thought to be nonfunctional but is now understood to have a communicative or regulatory function for the child.

8. SOCIAL-IMITATIVE PLAY

Social-imitative play is pretending to act out the actions of daily routines (e.g., stirring food or brushing hair) or the actions of others (e.g., a parent talking on the telephone) in the context of play. In typical development, by about eighteen to twenty-four months a child should be engaging in simple pretend play, like feeding a doll or putting it to bed. The lack of this spontaneous social-imitative or make-believe play appropriate to a child's age or developmental level is one of the criteria for a diagnosis of ASD. Children with ASD may become preoccupied with the toy itself or parts of a toy or object (like spinning the wheels on a car over and over) rather than engaging in pretend play or social imitation.

Repetitive Behaviors and Restricted Interests

9. RESTRICTED PATTERNS OF INTEREST

The term "restricted patterns of interest" refers to a limited range of interests that are intense in focus. These may also be referred to as stereotyped or circumscribed patterns of interests because of the rigidity and narrowness of these interests. This may be particularly apparent in verbally fluent children with autism or Asperger syndrome who often become obsessed with a single topic for months or even years.

Restricted interests, obsessions, and compulsions can interfere with a child's normal activity or social interaction and can be related to anxiety. In young children with ASD, similar restricted patterns may be evident in repetitive movements with objects. Rather than playing with toys in simple pretend play, or using objects in appropriate ways, children with ASD line up or stack toys or objects in the same way over and over again, persistently knocking down and rolling objects, or wobbling or spinning objects, and/or may show an intense focus and interest in how these actions or objects look.

10. INSISTENCE ON SAMENESS

Insistence on sameness refers to a rigid adherence to a routine or activity carried out in a specific way, which then becomes a ritual or nonfunctional routine. Children with ASD may insist on sameness and may react with distress or tantrums to even small changes or disruptions in routines. Sometimes such reactions are so extreme that they are described as catastrophic.

A child's response of insistence on sameness may reflect difficulty with change in activities or routines or being able to predict what happens next, and therefore may be a coping mechanism. Young children with ASD may also show some repetitive movements with objects, such as lining things up, collecting objects, or clutching similar small toys.

11. REPETITIVE MANNERISMS

Repetitive motor mannerisms are stereotyped or repetitive movements or posturing of the body. They include mannerisms of the hands (such as hand flapping, finger twisting or flicking, rubbing, or wringing hands), body (such as rocking, swaying, or pacing), and odd posturing (such as posturing of the fingers, hands, or arms). These mannerisms may appear not to have any meaning or function, although they may have significance for the child, such as providing sensory stimulation (also referred to as self-stimulating behavior), communicating to avoid demands, or requesting a desired object or attention, or soothing when wary or anxious. These repetitive mannerisms are common in children with ASD.

12. PREOCCUPATION WITH PARTS OF OBJECTS

A preoccupation with a part of an object is a persistent unusual interest or fixation in one aspect of something that is usually to the exclusion of interest in people, or in using the object in social interactions or in a functional way. Young children with ASD may manipulate parts of an object, such as spinning the wheel of a toy car, flicking a handle, or opening and closing a door, rather than use the whole object functionally or in pretend play. Like preoccupations with restricted interests, preoccupations with parts of objects can interfere with a child's normal activity or social interaction and can be related to anxiety.

Regulatory and Sensory Systems

13. OVER-REACTIVITY

Over-reactivity or hyper-responsiveness is abnormal sensitivity to sensory input. This is the state of feeling overwhelmed by what most people would consider common or ordinary stimuli of sound, sight, taste, touch, or smell. Many children with ASD are over-reactive to ordinary sensory input and may exhibit sensory defensiveness, which involves a strong negative response to their overload, such as screaming at the sound of a telephone. Tactile defensiveness is a specific sensory defensiveness that is a strong negative response to touch.

14. UNDER-REACTIVITY

Under-reactivity to sensory input is one aspect of abnormal insensitivity to sensory input, or hypo-responsiveness, in which a child does not respond to sensory stimulation. A child who appears deaf, but whose hearing has tested as normal, is under-reactive. A child who is under-reactive to sensory input may have a high tolerance to pain, may be clumsy and sensation-seeking, and may act aggressively.

15. UNUSUAL SENSORY INTERESTS

Children with ASD often have unusual sensory interests in ways that may not always be socially acceptable. They may seek sensation(s) involving one or more of the senses (touch, taste, smell, sight, sound). A child may seek certain odd physical activities (e.g., crashing into objects or being attracted to dangerous situations), touch certain textures (e.g., licking toys or patting everyone's clothing), taste specific foods (e.g., favoring bitter or spicy flavors), smell certain objects (e.g., toys or clothing), fixate on specific items (e.g., fans or reflections of the sun), or listen to certain sounds (e.g., sirens or bugs).

16. EMOTIONAL REGULATION

Emotional regulation is a child's ability to notice and respond to internal and external sensory input, and then adjust his emotions and behavior to the demands of his surroundings. Emotional regulation includes the body's involuntary reactions (heart rate, respiratory rate, etc.) to events or perceptions, as well as voluntary responses. Voluntary responses may be behaviors that the child does to soothe or excite herself, such as spinning the wheel of a toy car, rubbing a smooth surface, rocking, or hand flapping. This may also include the use of communication to get help modulating emotion, such as reaching to request comfort when afraid.

Many children with ASD have difficulties with emotional regulation and often have abnormal or inappropriate responses to the ordinary demands of their surroundings. They may also have problems adjusting to change and transitioning from one activity to another, responding with strong negative emotions, tantrums, or stereotyped or even self-injurious behaviors.

Note: Definitions have been adapted from Amy M. Wetherby and Nancy D. Wiseman, "ASD Video Glossary," 2007, Autism Speaks, http://www.autismspeaks.org/video/glossary.php.

A Strawman Treatment
Development Process

IN THE LANGUAGE of the current business world, a "strawman" is a trial proposal that is put forward for the sake of beginning a discussion. The idea is that it can be criticized, picked apart, added to, improved, and finally turned into something that might just work. The person offering the trial proposal realizes that what results may look nothing like the original. Nevertheless, if offering a first version begins a process that leads to a valuable end result, the strawman has achieved its intended purpose.

In Week 2, "Learning: Diagnosis Is Not Enough," a basic treatment development process was first proposed. Later, in Month 8, "Living: More about Peeling Away the Layers," it was enlarged by expanding step 1 ("Analyze a manifestation of the disorder") to provide a more complete method for deciding what specific aspects of the disorder to target for treatment.

By combining these two processes, we now have this version of the "strawman":

1. Observe an unexpected, existing condition.
   Example: Child is having severe tantrums daily and sometimes multiple times a day.
2. "Broad shoot," that is, cast your net over the widest list of issues possible to determine if any are possibly related. Get input from your team members. For example:

- occasionally hits himself on the head
- has frequent ear infections and lingering cough
- has disrupted sleep
- is a picky eater
- is frustrated by not being able to communicate needs and wants
- prefers to play alone
- never seems to be upset when he walks into doors and walls or trips
- flaps hands and walks on tippy toes when excited
- has occasional constipation and diarrhea
- has dark circles under his eyes

3. Prioritize issues that require further investigation based on parent or child awareness and with the advice of your team. Highest priority should be given to issues that affect your child's health and medical necessities, ability to function in daily life, ability to communicate, and ability to socialize.

   Here is an example of prioritization:
   a. is frustrated by not being able to communicate needs and wants
   b. has disrupted sleep
   c. has frequent ear infections and lingering cough
   d. has occasional constipation and diarrhea
   e. has dark circles under his eyes
   f. occasionally hits himself on the head
   g. is a picky eater
   h. prefers to play alone
   i. never seems to be upset when he walks into doors and walls or trips
   j. flaps hands and walks on tippy toes when excited

4. Look for the likely trigger(s) of that manifestation and any discoverable antecedent or preceding factors.

   Example for 3a (above): Determine if the child is trying to ask for something prior to becoming frustrated.

   Example for 3g (above): Examine his diet closely. What foods does he favor?

5. Keeping in mind the results of the preceding steps, select tests or treatments that might lead to finding the underlying cause(s). Consider selecting a treatment that would benefit the child, have no adverse effects, and possibly help you to "rule out" or "rule in" any possible causes. For example:
   a. Begin speech and language therapy immediately to help the child learn how to communicate his wants and needs. See if this helps to reduce tantrums.
   b. Eliminate possible cause(s) for disrupted sleep (e.g., loud noises or activity in the house, eating or drinking before bedtime, inconsistent bedtime routine).
   c. through g. Conduct allergy and gastrointestinal testing.

    h. Begin play therapy to encourage interest and foster social reciprocity with others.

    i. and j. Begin sensory integration therapy.

6. Based on investigation and tests done so far, create a theory for the cause of the manifestation(s).

    Example: As a consequence of testing and exploratory therapies, it seems likely that the child may have gastrointestinal and immune-related problems possibly as a result of food allergies.

7. Choose treatment(s) or devise ways to manage the suspected causes, keeping in mind the following:

- In general, the top priorities for treatment often are:
  - objective (environmental) factors hostile or antagonistic toward the child
  - seizures
  - mood dysregulation
  - functional criticality
  - medical necessity (affecting health)
  - ability to communicate
  - body burdens of toxins
- Other factors affecting the treatment plan may be:
  - technical feasibility
  - invasiveness
  - cost / financial resources / insurance coverage
  - doctor's willingness to prescribe
  - availability/accessibility to treatment
  - required duration of treatment
  - prospective gain
  - side effects / contraindications of treatment
  - team consensus
  - research support
  - possible interactions with concurrent treatments (requires team coordination)
  - sequences called for or advisable by the treatments themselves (treatment prerequisites)

8. Implement the treatment(s).

9. Evaluate the outcomes from the treatment(s).

10. Begin again at #4, reanalyzing the manifestation in light of what is now known; go on to #5, digging deeper toward a more basic cause; and continue with the process. For each iteration of this process, revisit steps 1–3, and redo them if it seems needed.

Glossary

ALLERGY—A disorder of the immune system resulting in hypersensitivities and reactions to environmental substances (known as "allergens").

ANECDOTAL EVIDENCE—Anecdotal evidence is informal evidence that tends to support some particular theory. Often anecdotal evidence is obtained under noncontrolled conditions or without rigorous application of the scientific method.

ANGELMAN SYNDROME—"Angelman syndrome is a genetic disorder that causes developmental delay and neurological problems. . . . Infants with Angelman syndrome appear normal at birth, but often have feeding problems in the first months of life and exhibit noticeable developmental delays by 6 to 12 months."[1]

ANXIETY DISORDER—Any of several different forms of abnormal, pathological anxiety, fear, and phobia that are considered irrational or illogical worries because they are not justifiably based upon any objective, environmentally evident fact. See also: Generalized anxiety disorder.

ASTHMA—A chronic respiratory disorder marked by inflammation and constriction of the airways accompanied by excessive mucous and usually great difficulty breathing.

ATTENTION DEFICIT/HYPERACTIVITY DISORDER (ADHD)—A persistent pattern of inattention and/or hyperactivity, as well as forgetfulness, poor impulse control or impulsivity, and distractibility.

BIOMEDICAL SPECIALIST—A biomedical specialist is a health care professional who employs biological and physiological healing methods in the treatment of symptoms and diseases.

BIPOLAR DISORDER—A classification of mood disorders normally involving episodes of extremely elevated mood, energy, or compulsive thought patterns followed by a state of depression, extreme pessimism, despondency, etc. See also: Early-onset childhood bipolar disorder.

CHROMOSOMAL DISORDERS—Disorders caused by genetics.

COLONOSCOPY—An examination of the large colon and the lower end of the small bowel using a fiber optic camera on a flexible tube passed through the anus.

COMORBID DISORDER—A medical condition a patient may have coincidentally with some other, primary disease or disorder.

DEFEAT AUTISM NOW!—Physicians, researchers, and scientists committed to finding effective treatments for autism. Defeat Autism Now! is a project of Autism Research Institute (ARI).

DEMENTIA—Loss of cognitive function that may affect language, attention, memory, personality, and abstract reasoning.

DEVELOPMENTAL LANGUAGE DISORDERS—A child's disorder characterized by the failure to develop language skills expected by certain ages.

DIAGNOSIS—The word diagnosis has two basic meanings:
1. The identification of a disease or condition by its outward signs and symptoms
2. The analysis of the underlying causes for a disease or condition

At the present time, when the word "diagnosis" is used in connection with autism, we are using definition 1 above. The etiology or causes of the disorder are suspected but not confirmed. For this reason, when a child is diagnosed with the disorder, you cannot directly treat that condition since "autism" is merely a label for a collection of symptoms of unknown causes.

EARLY INTERVENTION (EI)—Federally mandated services for infants and toddlers from birth to age three (and in some states through age five) with disabilities, as well as support to their families. The goal of Early Intervention is to provide quality, early support services to enhance the capacity of families to meet the developmental and health-related needs of children within the specified ages that have delays and disabilities.

EARLY-ONSET CHILDHOOD BIPOLAR DISORDER—Once known as manic-depression, this condition includes frequent, drastic changes in mood, energy, thinking, and behavior. Rages are common. Children can experience rapid alternation of moods between mania and depression, and sometimes there are only short periods of clarity between episodes.

ENDOSCOPY—A medical procedure that involves looking inside the body using an instrument called an endoscope, which is essentially a camera with a lens at the end of a flexible fiber optic tube inserted through the mouth.

ETIOLOGY—The study of the causes of a disorder or condition.

FLOORTIME—"A treatment method as well as a philosophy for interacting with children (and adults as well) that involves meeting a child at his current developmental level, and building upon his particular set of strengths."[2]

FRAGILE X SYNDROME—A genetically determined neurological disorder with childhood onset, being the commonest cause of inherited intellectual disabilities.

FREE APPROPRIATE PUBLIC EDUCATION (FAPE)—The Individuals with Disabilities Education Act requires your state's schools to provide a free educational program that is "appropriate" for your child. (See Month 2, "Learning: Know Your Rights.")

GASTROINTESTINAL DISORDERS—Any continuing disturbance to the normal functioning of some part of the digestive tract, from the mouth to the anus.

GENERALIZED ANXIETY DISORDER—May be diagnosed in children who display excessive worrying, restlessness, and fears.

HEARING IMPAIRMENT—A loss in hearing that may range from mild loss to complete deafness.

IMMUNE DYSFUNCTION—Any failure of the body's mechanisms that protects it against disease and infection.

INCLUSION—The practice of delivering to a child the special services required by his or her IEP in the regular classroom setting. This means integrating them into the context of the normal classroom in a natural manner that does not call attention to the child's special needs in any embarrassing or obvious manner.

INDIVIDUALIZED EDUCATION PROGRAM (IEP)—The IEP is a central component of the Individuals with Disabilities Education Act (IDEA), allowing each child with a disability to have a "free appropriate public education" (FAPE) in the "least restrictive environment" (LRE). Each IEP has a written plan and legal document developed jointly in a meeting of parents and school officials that states a child's present level of functioning, specific areas that need special services, annual goals, short-term objectives, services to be provided, and the method of evaluation to be implemented for the child. See also: Free appropriate public education (FAPE); Individuals with Disabilities Education Act (IDEA); Least restrictive environment (LRE).

INDIVIDUALIZED FAMILY SERVICE PLAN (IFSP)—Refers to a process and the document developed from this process that address the status of the child, present levels of development, goals/outcomes, Early Intervention services, other services (if needed), the dates of duration of services, the name of the service coordinator, and transition information.

INDIVIDUALS WITH DISABILITIES EDUCATION ACT (IDEA)—In 1975 the U.S. Congress passed the Education for All Handicapped Children Act, renamed the Individuals with Disabilities Education Act (IDEA) in 1990, which established federal standards for the provision of special educational services to children with disabilities. Until that time, public schools either excluded these children or segregated them into separate facilities with little or no appropriate instruction or assistance. See also: Free Appropriate Public Education (FAPE).

INTELLECTUAL DISABILITIES—Formerly called "mental retardation," a condition in which a person has an IQ that is below average and that affects an individual's learning, behavior, and development. It is usually accompanied by limitations in adaptive functioning in various areas of life.

INTRAVENOUS IMMUNE GLOBULIN (IVIG)—Immune globulin (IG) is a type of protein found in the blood that can be injected to balance or modulate a patient's immune system. Since IG is administered intravenously (IV), the treatment is commonly called "IVIG."

LANDAU-KLEFFNER SYNDROME (LKS)—A childhood disorder whose major feature is the gradual or sudden loss of the ability to understand and use spoken language. Approximately 80 percent of children with LKS have one or more epileptic seizures, which usually occur at night.

LEAST RESTRICTIVE ENVIRONMENT (LRE)—Refers to the setting where a child with a disability can receive an appropriate education designed to meet his or her educational needs, alongside peers without disabilities to the maximum extent appropriate. LRE is related to access to and participation in the general education curriculum.

MAINSTREAMING—The practice of educating children with disabilities in regular education classrooms during specific times based on their skills and ability to keep up with the work assigned by the regular education classroom. Any special education services they may receive are delivered outside the regular education classroom in smaller instructional or therapeutic settings.

METABOLIC DISORDERS—Disorders related to the biochemical changes that take place within the body to produce energy and the body's basic building blocks.

MULTIPLE-HIT HYPOTHESIS—This is one theory about the causes of autism; as explained by Bryan Jepson: "The most likely scenario for the development of [autism] involves a series of negative responses to the environment in a baby who is at risk genetically."[3]

NEUROBIOLOGICAL DISORDER—An illness of the nervous system caused by genetic, metabolic, or other biological factors.

OBSESSIVE-COMPULSIVE DISORDER (OCD)—An anxiety disorder characterized by recurrent, unwanted thoughts (obsessions) and/or repetitive behaviors (compulsions). Repetitive behaviors such as hand washing, counting, checking, and cleaning are often performed with the hope of preventing obsessive thoughts or making them go away.

OPPOSITIONAL DEFIANT DISORDER (ODD)—Marked by uncooperative, defiant, and hostile behavior toward parents and other authority figures.

PARTIAL INCLUSION—Delivery of some special education services to a child required by his or her IEP in the regular classroom setting with other services being delivered in a separate classroom or setting.

PEDIATRIC AUTOIMMUNE NEUROPSYCHIATRIC DISORDERS ASSOCIATED WITH STREPTOCOCCAL INFECTIONS (PANDAS)—This term describes

"a subset of children who have Obsessive Compulsive Disorder (OCD) and/or tic disorders such as Tourette's Syndrome, and in whom symptoms worsen following Strep. infections such as "Strep throat" and Scarlet Fever.

The children usually have dramatic, "overnight" onset of symptoms, including motor or vocal tics, obsessions, and/or compulsions. In addition to these symptoms, children may also become moody, irritable or show concerns about separating from parents or loved ones. This abrupt onset is generally preceded by a Strep. throat infection."[4]

In PANDAS, the antibodies produced by the body in response to the strep infection appear to be responsible for attacking both the immune system and the basal ganglia in the brain. The basal ganglia are biologically associated with movement and behavior. It is believed that the strep antibodies interact with the basal ganglia, causing tics, obsessive-compulsive disorder, and other behaviors.

PHENYLKETONURIA (PKU)—A metabolic disorder that can be detected at birth, marked by intellectual disabilities and organ damage unless controlled with a special diet early in life.

PRADER-WILLI SYNDROME—"A complex genetic disorder that typically causes low muscle tone, short stature, incomplete sexual development, cognitive disabilities, problem behaviors, and a chronic feeling of hunger that can lead to excessive eating and life-threatening obesity."[5]

First signs are developmental delays and feeding problems in infancy. After age one, the child begins a pattern of compulsive eating, food obsessions, and extreme weight gain.

REACTIVE ATTACHMENT DISORDER—Often diagnosed in children who have been neglected or abused; characterized by lack of appropriate social behavior.

RESPITE CARE—Services provided to parents and other primary caregivers of persons who require constant care, such as children with autism spectrum disorders. This care can be given in the home by a licensed nurse or, in the case of a child, a specially trained babysitter. The idea is to give the primary caregiver(s) needed breaks.

SCHIZOID PERSONALITY DISORDERS—Lack of interest in social relationships, a tendency toward a solitary lifestyle, secretiveness, and emotional coldness.

SCHIZOPHRENIA—Characterized by hallucinations and delusions; rarely arising before the age of seven.

SELECTIVE MUTISM—Children who speak normally in some settings but are silent in others—often school or other socially demanding settings—may be diagnosed with this anxiety disorder.

SOCIAL-IMITATIVE PLAY—Play that involves pretending to act out daily routines (e.g., stirring food or brushing hair) or the actions of others (e.g., a parent talking on the telephone) in the context of play. In typical development, by about eighteen to twenty-four months a child should be engaging in simple pretend play, like feeding a doll or putting it to bed. This forms the foundation for make-believe play. The lack of spontaneous social-imitative or make-believe play appropriate to a child's age or developmental level is one of the criteria for a diagnosis of ASD. Children with ASD may become preoccupied with the toy itself or parts of a toy or object (like spinning the wheels on a car over and over) rather than engaging in pretend play or social imitation.[6]

SPECIAL EDUCATOR—A person trained to assess and address the needs of children with special needs.

SPED PAC—Special Education Parent Advisory Council. A committee or council of individuals interested in improving special education services in their district. Its contact information should be available from your school district's special education office. From a SpEd PAC you can get the "lay of the land."

STAY-PUT RULE—IDEA specifies that while you are in any dispute with the school district about placement, your child has the right to remain where he or she is. However, *The Complete IEP Guide* also advises that the "stay put" provision is a complex legal right and that you should consult an attorney or nonprofit disability rights organization at once. See Lawrence M. Siegel, "Your Child's Status during Due Process," in *The Complete IEP Guide*, 5th ed. (Berkeley: Nolo Press, 2007), 155.

TIC—A type of movement disorder involving an irresistible urge to make and repeat some movement, often in response to stresses and the urge to relieve those stresses. "Simple motor tics" can be brief movements such as eye blinking, shoulder shrugging, neck stretching, mouth movements, facial grimaces, etc. Simple phonic tics can be the making of nearly any kind of noise or sound such as grunting, coughing, sniffing, etc.

TUBEROUS SCLEROSIS (TSC)—TSC is a rare genetic disease that causes benign tumors to grow in the brain and on other vital organs such as the kidneys, heart, eyes, lungs, and skin. It commonly affects the central nervous system. In addition to the benign tumors that frequently occur in TSC, other common symptoms include seizures, intellectual impairment, behavior problems, and skin abnormalities. TSC may be present at birth, but signs of the disorder can be subtle, and full symptoms may take some time to develop. Three types of brain tumors are associated with TSC: cortical tubers, which generally form on the surface of the brain; subependymal nodules, which form in the walls of the ventricles (the fluid-filled cavities of the brain); and giant-cell astrocytomas, a type of tumor that can block the flow of fluids within the brain.[7]

VISUAL SPATIAL MEMORY—Refers to the ability to remember the placement of objects in space.

WILLIAMS SYNDROME—Williams syndrome is a rare genetic condition (estimated to occur in 1 in 7,500 births) characterized by medical and developmental problems, including heart and blood vessel problems, low birth weight, feeding problems, dental abnormalities, and others. Children with this syndrome usually are quite talkative and eager for social interaction but can also be inattentive, anxious, and prone to socially inappropriate behaviors. For more information, see the Williams Syndrome Association website: http://www.williams-syndrome.org/forparents/whatiswilliams.html.

Notes

Day 1

1. Martha Herbert, "Autism: A Brain Disorder, or a Disorder that Affects the Brain?" *Clinical Neuropsychiatry* 2, no. 6 (2005): 354–379; http://www.autismone.org/uploads/2006/Herbert%20Martha%20-%20handout.pdf.

2. Material drawn from Amy M. Wetherby and Nancy D. Wiseman, "ASD Video Glossary," 2007, Autism Speaks, http://www.autismspeaks.org/video/glossary.php; American Psychiatric Association, *Diagnostic and Statistical Manual of Mental Disorders*, 4th edition, Text Revision (DSM IV-TR) (Washington, DC: American Psychiatric Publishing, 2000).

3. Fred R. Volkmar et al., eds., *Handbook of Autism and Pervasive Developmental Disorders: Assessment, Interventions, and Policy* (Hoboken, NJ: John Wiley & Sons, 2005).

4. Ibid.

5. Material drawn from Wetherby and Wiseman, "ASD Video Glossary"; American Psychiatric Association, DSM IV-TR.

6. A. Cashin and D. A. Sci, "Two Terms—One Meaning: The Conundrum of Contemporary Nomenclature in Autism," *Journal of Child and Adolescent Psychiatric Nursing* 19, no. 3 (2006): 137–144.

7. Herbert, "Autism."

8. DSM IV-TR, xxix.

9. University of Pittsburgh Medical Center, "Health A-Z: Diseases and Conditions: Rett Syndrome," http://www.upmc.com/healthAtoZ/Pages/HealthLibrary.aspx?chunkiid=22489.

10. Mayo Clinic Staff, "Children's Health: Childhood Disintegrative Disorder," Mayo Clinic, http://www.mayoclinic.com/health/childhood-disintegrative-disorder/DS00801.

11. Stanley I. Greenspan with Nancy Breslau Lewis, *Building Healthy Minds: The Six Experiences that Create Intelligence and Emotional Growth in Babies and Young Children* (Cambridge, MA: Da Capo Press, 1999).

12. Copyright © 2001–2008 by First Signs, Inc.; http://firstsigns.org. The key social, emotional, and communication milestones were compiled from the following sources: Greenspan and Lewis, *Building Healthy Minds*; B. M. Prizant, A. M. Wetherby, and J. E. Roberts, "Communication Disorders in Infants and Toddlers" in *Handbook of Infant Mental Health*, ed. C. Zeanah, 2nd ed. (New York: Guilford Press, 2000); A. M. Wetherby, "Babies Learn to Talk at an Amazing Rate," *First Words Project*, Florida State University, 1999.

13. Material drawn from Wetherby and Wiseman, "ASD Video Glossary." For more information about screening and diagnosis, see Chris Plauché Johnson, Scott M. Myers, and the Council on Children with Disabilities, "Clinical Report: Identification and Evaluation of Children with Autism Spectrum Disorders," *Pediatrics* 120, no. 5 (November 2007): 1183–1215, http://www.aap.org/pressroom/AutismID.pdf.

14. M. Dawson et al., "The Level and Nature of Autistic Intelligence," *Psychological Science* 18, no. 8 (2007): 657–662.

15. "What Is the Prevalence of Autism?" in Frequently Asked Questions: Prevalence, Autism Information Center, Department of Health and Human Services, Centers for Disease Control and Prevention, http://www.cdc.gov/ncbddd/autism/faq_prevalence.htm.

16. Based on the autism prevalence rate of 2 to 6 per 1,000 (Centers for Disease Control and Prevention, 2001) and 2000 U.S. Census figure of 280 million Americans.

17. "Prevalence of the Autism Spectrum Disorders in Multiple Areas of the United States, Surveillance Years 2000 and 2002," Department of Health and Human Services, Centers for Disease Control and Prevention, http://www.cdc.gov/ncbddd/dd/addm prevalence.htm.

18. "What Is the Prevalence of Autism?" note 7, http://www.cdc.gov/ncbddd/autism/faq_prevalence.htm#ftnref7.

19. J. S. Palfrey et al., "Early Identification of Children's Special Needs: A Study in Five Metropolitan Communities," *Journal of Pediatrics*, 111 (1994): 651–655.

Day 2

1. Interview with Stanley I. Greenspan in *On the Spectrum: Children and Autism*, video, produced by First Signs, Inc., 2001.

2. A. M. Wetherby et al., "Early Indicators of Autism Spectrum Disorders in the Second Year of Life," *Journal of Autism and Developmental Disorders*, 34 (2004): 473–493, based on research by First Words Project, Florida State University.

3. Martha Herbert, "Autism: A Brain Disorder, or a Disorder that Affects the Brain?" *Clinical Neuropsychiatry* 2, no. 6 (2005): 354–379; http://www.autismone.org/uploads/2006/Herbert%20Martha%20-%20handout.pdf.

4. Kenneth Bock and Cameron Stauth, *Healing the New Childhood Epidemics: Autism, ADHD, Asthma, and Allergies: The Groundbreaking Program for the 4-A Disorders* (New York: Ballantine Books, 2007), 15.

5. Defeat Autism Now! http://www.defeatautismnow.com/mission.html.

Day 3

1. Yale Developmental Disabilities Clinic, "Frequently Asked Questions about Pervasive Developmental Disorders (PDD)," Yale Child Study Center, http://www.info.med .yale.edu/chldstdy/autism/pdd.html.

Day 4

1. About ASAN, The Autistic Self-Advocacy Network, http://www.autisticadvocacy.org.

Day 6

1. See Chris Plauché Johnson, Scott M. Myers, and the Council on Children with Disabilities, "Clinical Report: Identification and Evaluation of Children with Autism Spectrum Disorders," *Pediatrics* 120, no. 5 (November 2007): 1183–1215, http://www .aap.org/pressroom/AutismID.pdf.

2. "Diseases & Conditions—Living Well: Integrative Medicine," Duke Medicine and *U.S. News & World Report*, January 11, 2008, http://health.usnews.com/articles/health/ living-well/2008/01/11/integrative-medicine-overview.html.

Day 7

1. Interview with Dr. Karen Levine in *On the Spectrum: Children and Autism*, video, produced by First Signs, Inc., 2001.

2. Personal conversation with anonymous parent, September 2, 2008.

3. Ibid.

4. Stanley I. Greenspan and Serena Wieder, *Engaging Autism: Using the Floortime Approach to Help Children Relate, Communicate, and Think* (Cambridge, MA: Da Capo Lifelong Books, 2006).

5. Karen Levine and Naomi Chedd, *Replays: Using Play to Enhance Emotional and Behavioral Development for Children with Autism Spectrum Disorders* (Philadelphia: Jessica Kingsley Publishers, 2007).

Week 2

1. See Kenneth Bock and Cameron Stauth, *Healing the New Childhood Epidemics: Autism, ADHD, Asthma, and Allergies: The Groundbreaking Program for the 4-A Disorders* (New York: Ballantine Books, 2007), especially chapter 21.

2. Martha R. Herbert, "Autism: A Brain Disorder, or a Disorder that Affects the Brain?" *Clinical Neuropsychiatry* 2, 6 (2005): 354–379; http://www.autismone.org/uploads/2006/Herbert%20Martha%20-%20handout.pdf.

3. This is drawn substantially from Stanley I. Greenspan and Serena Wieder with Robin Simons, *The Child with Special Needs: Encouraging Intellectual and Emotional Growth* (Reading, MA: Addison-Wesley, 1998), with supporting material from Nancy D. Wiseman with Kim Painter Koffsky, *Could It Be Autism? A Parent's Guide to the First Signs and Next Steps* (New York: Broadway Books, 2006).

Week 3

1. R. S. Byrd et al., "Report to the Legislature on the Principal Findings of the Epidemiology of Autism in California: A Comprehensive Pilot Study," M.I.N.D. Institute, 2002, http://www.ucdmc.ucdavis.edu/mindinstitute/newsroom/study_final.pdf.

2. National Center of Medical Home Initiatives for Children with Special Needs, "Developmental Disabilities," American Academy of Pediatrics, http://www.medical homeinfo.org/health/dev_dis.html.

3. Bryan Jepson with Jane Johnson, "Autism Is a Disease, Not a Disability," in *Changing the Course of Autism: A Scientific Approach for Parents and Physicians* (Boulder, CO: Sentient Publications, 2007), 45–46, citing P. Ashwood, S. Willis, J. Van de Water, "The Immune Response in Autism: A New Frontier for Autism Research," *Journal of Leukocyte Biology* 80 (July 2006): 1–15.

4. Jepson and Johnson, "Does Mercury Cause Autism?" in *Changing the Course of Autism*, 112–139.

5. This material is covered in great detail throughout Dr. Bryan Jepson's book, referenced above. Also visit the Autism Research Institute website page on "Triggers of Autism," http://autism.com/triggers/index.htm.

6. Jepson and Johnson, "Autism Is a Disease, Not a Disability," in *Changing the Course of Autism*, 45–46.

7. Frequently Asked Questions, Autism Research Institute, http://autism.com/ari/faq.htm.

8. James B. Adams, "Summary of Biomedical Treatments for Autism," April 7, 2007, http://autism.asu.edu/Additional/Summarybiomed07.pdf. Future updates will be found at http://autism.asu.edu or http://www.autism.com.

9. Adapted from Stephen M. Edelson, PhD, and Bernard Rimland, PhD, "Application for ARI's New Clinician Registry," Autism Research Institute, http://www.autism website.com/practitioners/Defeat_Autism_Now!_Application.pdf.

Week 4

1. Pascal L. Trohanis, "Progress in Providing Services to Young Children with Special Needs and Their Families: An Overview to and Update on the Implementation of the Individuals with Disabilities Education Act (IDEA)," *NECTAC Notes* 12 (2002): 3, http://www.nectac.org/~pdfs/pubs/nnotes12.pdf.

2. Evelyn F. Shaw, Technical Assistance Specialist, National Early Childhood Technical Assistance Center (NECTAC) National Professional Development Center on Autism Spectrum Disorders, e-mail message to author, September 5, 2008.

3. "A Pediatric Practitioner's Guide: Referring a Child to Early Intervention in the U.S." [brochure], First Signs, Inc., 2001.

4. Lucas, Hurth, and Shaw, "The Early Intervention/IFSP Process," NECTAC, 2006, http://www.nectac.org/%7Epdfs/topics/families/ifsp_process_chart.pdf.

5. S. Goode, A. Lazara, and J. Danaher, eds., Part C Updates, 10th ed. (Chapel Hill: University of North Carolina, FPG Child Development Institute, National Early Childhood Technical Assistance Center, forthcoming). For more information on EIP, see Trohanis, "Progress," and the NICHCY website: http://www.nichcy.org.

Month 2

1. For more information see J. L. Hurth and P. E. Goff, "Assuring the Family's Role on the Early Intervention Team: Explaining Rights and Safeguards," NECTAC, 2002, http://www.nectac.org/~pdfs/pubs/assuring.pdf.

2. Lawrence M. Siegel, *The Complete IEP Guide: How to Advocate for Your Special Ed Child,* 5th ed. (Berkeley: Nolo Press, 2007), 11.

3. Ibid.

4. Peter W. D. Wright and Pamela Darr Wright, *Wrightslaw: Special Education Law,* 2nd ed. (Hartfield, VA: Harbor House Law Press, 2007), 103.

5. This list includes material drawn from and expanded upon from: Nancy D. Wiseman with Kim Painter Koffsky, *Could It Be Autism? A Parent's Guide to the First Signs and Next Steps* (New York: Broadway Books, 2006), 101–103.

6. "What You Should Know Before You Apply for SSI Disability Benefits for a Child," Social Security Administration, http://www.ssa.gov/disability/Child_StarterKit_Factsheet.pdf.

7. "Fact Sheet for States Interested in Using the TEFRA Option for Children with Serious Mental Disorders," Bazelon Center for Mental Health Law, http://www.bazelon.org/issues/children/publications/TEFRA/fact3.htm.

8. "HCBS Waivers—Section 1915 (c)," Centers for Medicare and Medicaid Services, http://www.cms.hhs.gov/MedicaidStWaivProgDemoPGI/05_HCBSWaivers-Section 1915(c).asp.

9. Mitzi Waltz, Autistic Spectrum Disorders: Understanding the Diagnosis and Getting Help, *Patient-Centered Guides,* 2nd ed. (Sebastopol, CA: O'Reilly, 2002).

10. Harvard School of Public Health, "Autism Has High Cost to U.S. Society," press release, http://www.hsph.harvard.edu/news/press-releases/2006-releases/press04252006.html.

11. Michael A O'Connor, Esq., "Year 2006 Tax Benefits for Parents of Children with Disabilities," Wrightslaw, http://www.wrightslaw.com/info/tax.2006.benefits.oconnor.htm.

12. International Co-operative Alliance, "What Is a Co-operative?" http://www.ica.coop/coop/index.html.

Month 3

1. A. M. Knivsberg, K. L. Reichelt, T. Hoien, "Effect of a Dietary Intervention on Autistic Behavior," *Focus on Autism and Other Developmental Disabilities* 18, no. 444 (2003): 248–257; A. M. Knivsberg et al., "A Randomized, Controlled Study of Dietary Intervention in Autistic Syndromes," *Nutritional Neuroscience* 5, no. 4 (September 2002): CD003498.

2. Remember that these are just examples to illustrate and not by any means a comprehensive list of possibilities. It would take a skilled evaluation to determine what is needed for your child. Details can be found on Bock's website: http://www.4ahealing.com/nutritionaltherapy.html.

3. J. B. Adams and C. Holloway, "Pilot Study of a Moderate Dose Multivitamin / Mineral Supplement for Children with Autism Spectrum Disorder," *Journal of Alternative and Complementary Medicine* 10, no. 6 (December 2004): 1033–1039; Autism Research Institute, "Parent Ratings of Behavioral Effects of Biomedical Interventions," *ARI Publications* 34 (March 2005), http://www.autismwebsite.com/ARI/treatment/form34q.htm#biomedical.

4. For further details on Kenneth Bock's suggested nutritional supplement programs, see http://www.4ahealing.com/elementtwo_supplementation.html.

5. W. Slikker Jr., "Developmental Neurotoxicity of Therapeutics: Survey of Novel Recent Findings," *Neurotoxicology* 1, no. 2 (February–April 2000): 250; S. J. James et al., "Metabolic Biomarkers of Increased Oxidative Stress and Impaired Methylation Capacity in Children with Autism," *American Journal of Clinical Nutrition* 80 (December 2004): 1611–1617.

6. Kenneth Bock and Cameron Stauth, "4-A Healing: Element Number Three: Detoxification," 4-A Healing, http://www.4ahealing.com/detoxification.html.

7. Kenneth Bock and Cameron Stauth, *Healing the New Childhood Epidemics: Autism, ADHD, Asthma, and Allergies: The Groundbreaking Program for the 4-A Disorders* (New York: Ballantine Books, 2007), 349.

8. Ibid., 350.

9. Ibid., 351.

10. Suggested reading on this subject: Timothy E. Wilens, *Straight Talk about Psychiatric Medications for Kids* (New York: Guildford Press, 2004).

11. Stanley I. Greenspan and Serena Wieder, "Developmental Patterns and Outcomes in Infants and Children with Disorders in Relating and Communicating: A Chart Review of 200 Cases of Children with Autism Spectrum Diagnoses," *Journal of Developmental and Learning Disorders* 1, no. 1 (1997): 87–141.

12. See http://www.icdl.com/dirFloortime/overview/index.shtml. Further description of the DIR/Floortime Model, with many illustrations as carried out in a variety of settings can be found in Stanley I. Greenspan and Serena Wieder, *Engaging Autism: Helping Children Relate, Communicate and Think with the DIR Floortime Approach* (Cambridge, MA: Da Capo Lifelong Books, 2007), and Stanley I. Greenspan and Serena Wieder with Robin Simons, *The Child with Special Needs: Encouraging Intellectual and Emotional Growth* (Reading, MA: Addison-Wesley, 1998). See also Stanley I. Greenspan and Stuart G. Shanker, *The First Idea: How Symbols, Language, and Intelligence Evolved from Our Early Primate Ancestors to Modern*

Humans (Cambridge, MA: Da Capo Press, 2004). See also this website: http://www.icdl .com, http://www.stanleygreenspan.com.

13. Robert Schramm, MA, BCBA, "What Is RDI and How Does It Compare to Applied Behavior Analysis and Verbal Behavior? http://www.lulu.com/content/800597.

14. "About the RDI Program," Peer Bridges, LLC, http://www.peerbridges.com/ id84.html. See also https://www.rdiconnect.com/RDI/default.asp, or go to the RDI home page, and click on "What is RDI Program?"

15. See the SCERTS Model website: http://www.scerts.com.

16. "What is the Son-Rise Program?," Autism Treatment Center of America http://www .autismtreatmentcenter.org/contents/about_son-rise/what_is_the_son-rise_program.php.

17. "Overview," More than Words The Hanen Centre, http://www.hanen.org/web/ Home/HanenPrograms/MoreThanWords/tabid/78/Default.aspx.

18. "Program Information," More than Words, The Hanen Centre, http://www.hanen .org/web/Home/HanenPrograms/MoreThanWords/Program/tabid/117/Default.aspx.

19. "Who Is It Most Suitable For?" Lovaas Institute, http://www.lovaas.com/approach -suitable.php.

20. "Why Discrete Trials Work," Lovaas Institute, http://www.lovaas.com/meeting point-2007-09-article-04.php.

21. "The Difference between Lovaas and Verbal Behavior (VB)," Autism Intervention Information, http://www.autismusaba.de/lovaasvsvb.html; see also "2008 Treatments for Autism: Verbal Behavior Intervention," Autism Speaks, http://www.autismspeaks.org/ whattodo/index.php#vbi.

22. UCSD Autism Research Program, "Pivotal Response Training," University of California Santa Barbara, http://psy.ucsd.edu/autism/prttraining.html.

23. Robert L. Koegel et al., *How to Teach Pivotal Behaviors to Children with Autism: A Training Manual,* available from the UCSB Koegel Autism Center website: http://kady .education.ucsb.edu/autism/behaviormanuals.html. See also http://psy3.ucsd.edu/ ~autism/prttraining.html and http://www.mcesa.k12.mi.us/Documents/AI%20Tip %20sheets/Pivotal%20Response%20Training.pdf.

24. "What is PECS?," Pyramid Educational Consultants, http://www.pecs.com/ WhatsPECS.htm.

25. Administration for Children and Families, "Positive Behavior Support: An Individualized Approach for Addressing Challenging Behavior," U.S. Department of Health and Human Services, http://eclkc.ohs.acf.hhs.gov/hslc/ecdh/Disabilities/Individualization/ Developmental%20Domains/disabl_art_00002_061605.html#positive, and "Positive Behavioral Interventions and Supports," National Technical Assistance Center on Positive Behavior and Intervention Supports, http://www.pbis.org/main.htm.

26. John T. Neisworth and Pamela S. Wolfe, eds., *The Autism Encyclopedia* (Baltimore: Brookes Publishing, 2005), 107, 133.

27. James K. Luiselli et al., eds., *Effective Practices for Children with Autism: Educational and Behavior Support Interventions that Work* (New York: Oxford University Press, 2008), 98.

28. Gary Mesibov, PhD., "What Is TEACCH?" Autism Independent UK, http:// www.autismuk.com/index4.htm.

29. "What Are Social Stories?" The Gray Center for Social Learning and Understanding, http://www.thegraycenter.org/store/index.cfm?fuseaction=page.display&page_id=30.

30. "Speech and Language Therapy for Children with Autism," Healing Thresholds, http://autism.healingthresholds.com/therapy/speech-therapy.

31. "Sensory Integration Therapy for Children with Autism," Healing Thresholds, http://autism.healingthresholds.com/therapy/sensory-integration.

32. Find further information on the website of the American Physical Therapy Association, http://www.apta.org, and Bright Tots, http://brighttots.com/physical_therapy.html.

33. For further information, see Q3 ("What is social skills training and why is it a priority? . . . ") in "Frequently Asked Questions," Social Skill Builder: Quality Learning Tools, http://www.socialskillbuilder.com/faq.htm#q3.

34. "What Is Auditory Integration Training or AIT?" Auditory Integration Training Services, http://www.aithelps.com.

35. "Vision Help for Children Who Struggle," Children's Vision Information Network, http://www.childrensvision.com/therapy.htm.

36. "Frequently Asked Questions about Music Therapy," American Music Therapy Association (AMTA), http://www.musictherapy.org/faqs.html.

37. Donna J. Betts, PhD, ATR-BC, "Art Therapy: Definition of the Profession (AATA, 2002)," http://www.art-therapy.us/art_therapy.htm. See also the American Art Therapy Association website: http://www.arttherapy.org.

38. For more information about hippotherapy, visit the website of the American Hippotherapy Association: http://www.americanhippotherapyassociation.org. See also Merope Pavlides, *Animal-Assisted Interventions for Individuals with Autism* (Philadelphia: Jessica Kingsley Publishers, 2008).

Month 4

1. This example is actually a composite of cases supervised by Stanley I. Greenspan, MD, and Mark Freilich, MD. Dr. Greenspan is a clinical professor of psychiatry at George Washington University Medical School, a practicing child psychiatrist, chairman of the Interdisciplinary Council on Learning and Developmental Disorders, and author or editor of thirty-eight books. Dr. Freilich is a developmental pediatrician with TOTAL Kids Developmental Pediatric Resources in New York City.

Month 5

1. Catherine Lord and James P. McGee, eds., *Educating Children with Autism* (Washington, DC: National Academies Press, 2001), 138.

2. "Special Education Inclusion," Wisconsin Education Association Council, http://www.weac.org/resource/june96/speced.htm.

3. Ibid.

4. Lord and McGee, *Educating Children with Autism*, 159.

5. Ibid., 183–184.

6. Catherine Lord, email message to author, June 5, 2005.

7. Ibid.

8. Individuals with Disabilities Education Act, 20 U.S.C. § 1401(9) and (29); the full text of IDEA can be found here: http://idea.ed.gov/download/statute.html.

Month 6

1. Lawrence M. Siegel, *The Complete IEP Guide: How to Advocate for Your Special Ed Child,* 5th ed. (Berkeley: Nolo Press, 2007), 125.

2. Catherine Lord and James P. McGee, eds., *Educating Children with Autism* (Washington, DC: National Academies Press, 2001), vii. The study is available online at http://www.nap.edu.

3. Ibid., 219.

4. Ibid., 219–222.

Month 7

1. Lawrence M. Siegel, "Your Child's Status During Due Process," in *The Complete IEP Guide: How to Advocate for Your Special Ed Child,* 5th ed. (Berkeley: Nolo Press, 2007).

2. "About COPAA: Mission," Council of Parent Attorneys and Advocates, http://www.copaa.org/about/index.html.

3. "About CEC: Overview," Council for Exceptional Children, http://www.cec.sped.org/AM/Template.cfm?Section=About_CEC.

4. "FAPE," Families and Advocates Partnership for Education, http://www.fape.org.

5. "Our Mission," Federation for Children with Special Needs, http://fcsn.org/aboutus/mission.php.

Month 8

1. Personal communication with Dr. Kenneth A. Bock, November 7, 2008.

Month 9

1. For more information see Lisa Jo Rudy, "Coping with the Stress of Autism: When to Find Professional Help," About.com, http://autism.about.com/od/supportforparents/p/pyschhelp.htm.

Month 12

1. This list is based loosely upon the section "Six Top Tips to Keep in Balance," in *Finding Balance: The Human Givens Approach to Balance, Balancing Our Inner and Outer Selves,* Speak Up Somerset, http://artofrecovery.com/magazine/issue30.pdf.

2. Barry Neil Kaufman, *Son-Rise* (New York: Harper & Row, 1976).

3. "History of the Son-Rise Program," Autism Treatment Center of America, http://www.autismtreatment.org/contents/about_son-rise/history_of_the_son-rise_program.php, and "Program Principles," Autism Treatment Center of America, http://www.autismtreatment.org/contents/about_son-rise.

4. Cindy N. Ariel and Robert A. Naseef, eds., *Voices from the Spectrum: Parents, Grandparents, Siblings, People with Autism, and Professionals Share Their Wisdom* (Philadelphia: Jessica Kingsley Publishers, 2006), 252.

5. Barbara Firestone, *Autism Heroes: Portrait of Families Meeting the Challenge* (Philadelphia: Jessica Kingsley Publishers, 2007), 160.

Glossary

1. Angelman Syndrome Information Page, National Institute of Neurological Disorders and Stroke, http://ninds.nih.gov/disorders/angelman/angelman.htm.

2. "Frequently Asked Questions: What Is Floortime?" The Floortime Foundation, http://www.floortime.org/faqs.php?faqid=4.

3. Bryan Jepson with Jane Johnson, *Changing the Course of Autism: A Scientific Approach for Parents and Physicians* (Boulder, CO: Sentient Publications, 2007), 45.

4. "PANDAS: General Information," Pediatrics and Developmental Neuropsychiatry Branch, National Institute of Mental Health, http://intramural.nimh.nih.gov/pdn/web.htm.

5. "Questions and Answers on Prader-Willi Syndrome," Prader-Willi Syndrome Association, http://www.pwsausa.org/faq.htm.

6. Adapted from Amy M. Wetherby and Nancy D. Wiseman, "ASD Video Glossary," 2007, Autism Speaks, http://www.autismspeaks.org/video/glossary.php.

7. Tuberous Sclerosis Information Page, National Institute of Neurological Disorders and Stroke, http://www.ninds.nih.gov.

Acknowledgments

THIS BOOK IS the result of my personal journey with my daughter, Sarah. She is the true inspiration for not only this book but also my work with First Signs. To her I owe my heartfelt gratitude for allowing me the time to write this book and for showing me that anything is possible.

I am so grateful to the thousands of parents and grandparents who reached out for help over the years and shared their stories; many of their questions and concerns are now part of this book.

My deep gratitude to Dr. Stanley Greenspan, whose brilliant work has influenced my two books, the organization I created, and my work with my daughter. He has been a wonderful mentor for nearly ten years.

It is a privilege to be able to thank my friend, mentor, and colleague, Amy Wetherby, PhD, whose research I so admire. No matter how busy, she always responds to my emails and phone calls quickly and helps to guide me. I am grateful for her invaluable time, wisdom, and contribution to this book.

My sincere gratitude to the professionals and parents who contributed their time, suggestions, and wonderful feedback: Kenneth Bock, MD; Mark Freilich, MD; Ira Glovinsky, PhD; Frances Glascoe, PhD; Richard Howard; Yvonne Domings; Stephanie Ross; Susan Sanford; Jean Rossettie; Deborah Flaschen; and Shelly Stravitz.

I am so grateful to my agent, Lisa DiMona of Lark Productions, for her wonderful advice and guidance over the past few years and for bringing me to Da Capo Press and Katie McHugh, my wonderful editor who really helped to strengthen this book. I would like to thank Howard Grossman for his cover design; Pauline Neuwirth, who designed the interior pages; Renee Caputo, the project editor who managed the book through editorial production; and Beth Wright, my copy editor, whose meticulous attention to detail was greatly appreciated.

My heartfelt thanks to our incredibly talented team of physicians, clinicians, and educators who have given us hope and a genuine commitment of their time over the years: Kenneth Bock, MD, and his staff at the Rhinebeck Health Center; Karen Levine, PhD; Rafael Castro, PhD; Stanley Greenspan, MD; Serena Wieder, PhD; Ira Glovinsky, PhD; Timothy Buie, MD; Elizabeth TePas, MD; Robert Fuhlbrigge, MD, and the clinicians at Children's Hospital Boston Infusion Center Waltham; Margaret Bauman, MD; Kelly Dorfman, MS; Ann Densmore, PhD; Janet Wozniak, MD; Lars Lundgren, MD; Robert Wharton, MD (who, sadly, passed away in 2002); Wendy Osgood, LMHC; Carol Taylor, PhD; Brenda Braunmiller MacKay and the clinicians at Pentucket Early Intervention; the clinicians at Building Blocks; Beth Doerr; the educators and clinicians at the Northshore Education Consortium and Pentucket Regional School District; Tara Savoie and the clinicians at OTA-Wakefield; and Ryan Plosker, Hollie Jacobs, and the educators and clinicians at New England Academy. I thank them for the amazing work they do. Sarah would not be where she is today if it weren't for their expertise and dedication.

To my attorneys, Richard Howard and Neila Straub, who helped me with the big battles. And my dear friend and colleague Andrée Cordella, who is always there to listen, cheer me on, and lend a hand when I need one.

To Nikki Roberts, Ellen Caruso, Kendra Bornstein, and Joan Dolan at the Merrimack Valley Skating Club (MVSC), I thank them for helping Sarah to reach her dream of becoming a competitive figure skater. And to Kathy Sullivan, Debbie Powers, and all my friends at MVSC, I thank them for keeping me smiling during breaks from writing this book and for their funny stories, camaraderie, and walks around the track while we waited for our kids to get off the ice. And to Sara Hoomis and Tom Friedrich at Verden Stables/ Advantage Riding Academy, my greatest admiration and thanks for nurturing Sarah's deep love of horses and for helping her to achieve her dream of owning a horse and becoming an accomplished equestrian.

To Joan Shepard, who helped prepare me for this journey so many years ago, I will always be grateful.

My deepest love and gratitude to my mom and stepdad, Beverly and Peter Eagleson, for always being there for me to lean on, to laugh and cry with, to get advice from, to love, and to share the tranquility of their home.

And to my brother, Bob Rich, who literally threw himself into helping me write this book. Without him, I never would have met my deadline. Although he knew nothing about autism before he started, his insight, objectivity, and understanding of processes were invaluable.

Index

CPSIA information can be obtained
at www.ICGtesting.com
Printed in the USA
LVHW04s2019270718
585150LV00001B/181/P